PRAISE FOR *MARKET A*
USER RESEARCH OPERATIONS

'Stephanie Marsh has written the Swiss Army Knife of ResearchOps books. *Market and User Research Operations* is packed with ready-to-use templates and guides that turn ResearchOps theory into practice. Essential reading whether you're taking your first steps or you've been in ResearchOps for years.'
Kate Towsey, author of *Research That Scales: The Research Operations Handbook*

'Strikes the right tone between theory and practice – heavy on the practice, which means there are things that you'll be able to do the moment you finish the book. It's accessible, with easy-to-understand language (that won't put you to sleep) and practical tips that you can lift wholesale to present to your manager/key stakeholders. Stephanie Marsh providers detailed guidance to give anyone interested in ResearchOps a thorough grounding in necessary processes and procedures. It's required reading, whether you're doing the generic ops busywork (templates, recruitment) all the way through to building a scalable ReOps practice within your organization.'
Natasha den Dekker, lead UX researcher

'I wish I had access to this when starting out in ResearchOps! Stephanie Marsh's book efficiently outlines the different approaches that can be taken for every aspect of ResearchOps, stipulating clearly what needs to be considered for each approach, and offering handy examples and templates along the way.'
Saskia Liebenberg, Research Operations Lead, Monzo

'Having worked closely with Stephanie Marsh, I know first-hand how deeply they understand the real-world challenges of ResearchOps. This book captures that knowledge and turns it into an indispensable guide for teams at every stage. A must-read for anyone building or scaling ResearchOps.'
Noémie Lozé, Research Operations Lead, Bumble

'Are you a Research Leader or a ResearchOps professional? This book is essential reading for you! Stephanie Marsh has created a hugely valuable resource for all levels of organisational maturity and scale. Whether you are new to Research Operations or an experienced professional, working in a small immature research team or a more advanced function, you will find plenty of practical takeaways, tips and templates you can put into practice straight away.'
Emma Boulton, research leader

'Whether you're setting up ResearchOps for the first time or the fifth time, this practical guide will feel like the friend you can turn to – for reminders that yes, it is a lot, and for the best practice templates, tools, and guides that are up to date and trustworthy. Get yourself the best ReOps friend you never knew you could have and get started!'
Brigette Metzler, Research Operations Lead, Bupa APAC, and former Co-chair of the global ResearchOps Community

'Stephanie Marsh has written an excellent, practical, no-nonsense field manual for setting up and running Research Operations from scratch, no matter the size of your team. This book is sure to be a go-to reference for anyone involved in the operations of a research team.'
Katie Taylor, UX research manager

Market and User Research Operations

Operationalize customer research for scale and impact

Stephanie Marsh

KoganPage

First published in Great Britain and the United States in 2025 by Kogan Page Limited

Kogan Page

Kogan Page Ltd, 2nd Floor, 45 Gee Street, London EC1V 3RS, United Kingdom
Kogan Page Inc, 8 W 38th Street, Suite 902, New York, NY 10018, USA
www.koganpage.com

EU Representative (GPSR)

Authorised Rep Compliance Ltd, Ground Floor, 71 Baggot Street Lower, Dublin D02 P593, Ireland
www.arccompliance.com

Kogan Page books are printed on paper from sustainable forests.

ISBNs

Hardback   978 1 3986 2052 0
Paperback   978 1 3986 2050 6
Ebook   978 1 3986 2051 3

British Library Cataloguing-in-Publication Data

A CIP record for this book is available from the British Library.

Library of Congress Control Number

2025020194

Typeset by Integra Software Services, Pondicherry
Printed and bound by CPI Group (UK) Ltd, Croydon CR0 4YY

To my chosen family; thank you for also choosing me.

CONTENTS

PART THREE
Advanced operations 231

10 How to use AI as part of the research process 233

11 Metrics for research and research operations 256

12 How to adapt to changing needs and requirements 271

Concluding thoughts 284

LIST OF FIGURES AND TABLES

ABOUT THE AUTHOR

Stephanie Marsh (she/they) is a leading customer research professional, working in and around human-focused research since 2003. She has been UX Research Operations Lead at Springer Nature based in London since 2019. They are the former Head of User Research and Analysis for the UK Government Digital Service and former Head of Digital for the UK Ministry of Defence. She was previously a consultant at Bunnyfoot, a leading UX consultancy in the UK. They have contributed chapters to a range of peer-reviewed texts in related fields and has delivered talks on UX research, research operations and UX strategies at a range of conferences and industry events.

PREFACE

This book is written for anyone doing the additional work to make any kind of customer research happen – whether you are doing it as part of being a person who does research, as a person with a side-hustle or if it's your full-time job. The work required to make robust, impactful customer research has always been there. As have full-time jobs dedicated to the managing of research. However, it was only in 2018 that it started being recognized as its own separate thing, thanks to Kate Towsey. I consider customer research operations to be an emerging field of practice. Those who practise the discipline of research operations are still learning at a rapid rate, as the practice matures and our knowledge grows and deepens. There is some notable documentation out there about the field, but as an emerging field the selection is still small.

ACKNOWLEDGEMENTS

Thank you to all those who I have had the honour to learn from and learn with over the years. I acknowledge that it is a very privileged position to share the knowledge and experience I have gained. Thank you to Kogan Page and the amazing editors I continue to work with. I am grateful to give back to communities of hard-working people who care deeply about the work they do. I am grateful for the opportunity to write this book. I am grateful to you for reading this, and I hope you find it useful.

LIST OF CONTRIBUTORS

Claire Alexopoulou

Emma Boulton

Angela Collins Rees

Rita Duarte

Lisa Koeman

Tiago Pinto

Tania Ramos

Antarika Sen

Rita Silva

Amy Stoks

Raina Thompson-Bridy

Stephen Tracy

Ola Trytek

Susana Vilaça

PART ONE

Managing infrastructure and the research process

This book begins with definitions and how to get started in doing research operations. I decided to start here as there are far more organizations that don't have established research operations compared to those who do (as of the time of writing October 2024), so we really do need to start at the beginning, with the foundations. My intention is that these six chapters can be used as a solid foundation on which to build a research operations function, in whatever context that may be. Whatever the circumstances, we can use a user-centric, data-driven approach to building and running our research operations and customer research practices, so first we need to understand what is needed for the context, before deciding what work needs to be done. But there are fundamental things that need to be done, regardless of the number of researchers, or the size of the organization. These will determine how we do things and at what scale, but they will need to be done regardless. These are the topics we cover in Part One. All the topics covered are critical to effective customer research and research operations and they are all interlinked:

- Whatever the context research is being done in, research needs to adhere to laws and regulations, and this is what we focus on in Chapter 3.
- Chapter 4 focuses on participant recruitment as we cannot do high-quality, robust and impactful research without recruiting the right people to

participate in the research. A lot of the laws and regulations we need to comply with will be related to these people (everything is connected!).

- Chapter 5 dives into data and knowledge management. The data has been generated through the research with our participants (everything is connected!) and transformed into knowledge through the research process. We can't have effective use of research without this.

- Chapter 6 looks at managing the research process overall (the things that need to be done beyond recruitment, data and knowledge management, which are done effectively and lawfully, everything is connected!).

Part One lays out the systems and processes needed to do customer research, and it's a lot, which in summary is why research operations are essential when we undertake customer research.

1

Defining research operations

Defining what we mean by research operations

Fundamentally, research operations (ReOps) refers to the people, infrastructure (processes, tools) and strategies that support researchers to plan, conduct, analyse and share their research.

Going deeper, research operations enable high-quality and impactful research at scale. It looks at the establishing, running and optimizing research operations practices within an organization.[1]

Research operations can happen at scale with a team of operations professionals supporting the team(s) of researchers. Research operations is equally relevant if you are a (research) team of one. We will cover the different ways of doing research operations depending on the structure of your organization and the people and resources available in depth in subsequent chapters.

For most researchers, including most of the time that I was a researcher myself, you have to deal with all the operations and admin as well as doing the planning, execution, synthesis and communication of the research. This is a heavy workload and cognitive load for any one person. The 'doing' of research comes with a lot of activities that aren't the research itself. Administrative tasks, for example, are necessary for a research project to be successful, because any type of project needs to be well planned and managed, which is what administration is.

Research operations has always been a part of the research process. But within the field of user research, research operations was started as a discipline in itself in 2018 by Kate Towsey and it has grown extremely quickly since then into a global community.[2]

There are other operations disciplines that came before ReOps that we can learn from, such as design operations (DesignOps), which was established within agile software development around 2014. With agile project management focusing on working at speed, it made sense to systematize and standardize parts of the design process to make it more efficient – this includes infrastructure, governance, budgets and education.[3] As with research operations tasks, people have been doing design operations long before the term was coined, when it would have been more commonly referred to as design management.[4] And a lot of inspiration has been taken from DesignOps in establishing user experience (UX) research operations.

Operationalizing research is still a young field of practice, that was only conceived in 2018 as a separate practice and set of skills outside the practice and skills of a researcher. Before 2018 researchers themselves would do most of the operational tasks as well as the research tasks, with perhaps the exception of participant recruitment.

People often describe research operations as taking away the administrative burden of research, but the admin doesn't magically or mysteriously disappear. ReOps can be someone else taking on some of the administration, for example the most common and long-established task would be outsourcing recruitment to an agency or another internal person. It could be someone taking on almost all of the research administration. Scaling up to its most mature state, ReOps could be a team of people, composed of specialists in different sub-disciplines within ReOps and not only taking on most of the tasks but also creating, maintaining and optimizing the infrastructure of research. This includes guidance, templates, repeatable, reusable things that increase the efficiency and effectiveness of research and can also be used for researchers self-serving, to give them a certain amount of autonomy when they need it. A great example of supporting researcher self-service comes from my current job, where my ReOps team (across three European countries) supports people doing research across six countries globally. So a colleague in China is sometimes doing research while the ReOps team is asleep, so they need to be able to access written guidance because we are not available. Timeliness is particularly important, for example in making sure we run a moderated research session in a legally compliant way.

The fields of market research and UX research use different terminology for the mechanisms of supporting the practice of customer research. For UX research it is research operations, and market research its playbooks. The terms are different, but the intention is the same, improving the efficiency and effectiveness of doing customer research.

There is less of an established community around 'market research operations', but there are lots of articles focused on playbooks for market research and what they could include,[5] which are synonymous with research operations. Operations for market research have been happening in some capacity ever since the practice of market research first started in the 1920s.[6]

My first full-time job after completing my doctoral research was as a user experience manager in the marketing department of a high street bank, but it was another 11 years before I discovered the notion of research operations. In fact, it has taken writing this introduction for me to realize that my first full-time job was in fact a research and design operations role! I was managing a combination of agency and internal UX research and design work. But I have been doing some sort of operations-type work related to customer research since 2003 when I started working on my doctoral research.

Why is research operations important?

If there is more than one researcher in the organization and all of them are doing their own admin and operations, not only is it inefficient but working in this way can lead to inconsistencies and duplication, as well as siloed data and insights (meaning that data and insight aren't accessible to everyone they should be). This siloed way of working also increases the risks associated with data privacy and protection.

Operations are there to support anyone who is doing the research; it may not be a researcher, so whoever is doing the ReOps needs to enable experienced people to get on with the work and those with less experience to be supported so they can deliver high-quality research in the necessary timescale with as little stress as possible. The challenge is to support and enable across the spectrum of experience and knowledge in customer research. Consistency of research becomes even more important when we're thinking in terms of the spectrum of experience in doing research.

Investing in operationalizing customer research will:

- save the business time, effort and money
- improve productivity and job satisfaction for the practitioners[7]
- reduce waste, by reusing past research and minimizing the potential for doing unnecessary research (repeating research is a very common issue)
- enable researchers to produce consistent, high-quality research insights in a lean and agile way, which is critical for meeting stakeholders' needs and building trust in the research
- enable new members of the team to embed themselves into ways of working, culture, etc., helping them to become effective team members that much quicker[8]

What will we learn?

We'll be looking at a multitude of ways to operationalize customer research practices. This will enable the scaling of consistent and robust research practices, contributing to high-quality impactful research outcomes that are trusted by stakeholders. Practitioners will not have to reinvent the wheel for each new research project.

There is a huge amount of overlap between operational needs and tasks whether you are doing user research or market research. I will talk about both together for clarity, using the term customer research. I will call out any difference between the two, as necessary.

As ReOps can span the whole of the research process and the building and running of a research team, we will dive into it all in the following chapters. Later in this chapter we look at what is included in each of the three sections of the book.

I would say the eight pillars of user research, created by Emma Boulton in 2019, are universally applicable to all customer research (see Figure 1.1). And we can see just how much is involved in doing customer research. Eight pillars is already a lot and each pillar itself has an average of seven elements; and each element in itself can be broken down further. Figure 1.1 demonstrates with visual clarity just how much is involved in supporting customer research to happen and systematizing the support and the research itself.[9] Tactical and strategic work are combined within the pillars, including what is needed to make a single research project happen, for example:

- access to a research library for previous research review
- scheduling
- participant coordination
- consent
- General Data Protection Regulation (GDPR) and risk management
- tools to conduct research
- incentives
- access to a research library for storing new research data
- sharing insights

More long-term strategic work includes:

- securing of budget to fund research and ReOps
- procurement of specialist tools

FIGURE 1.1 The eight pillars of user research

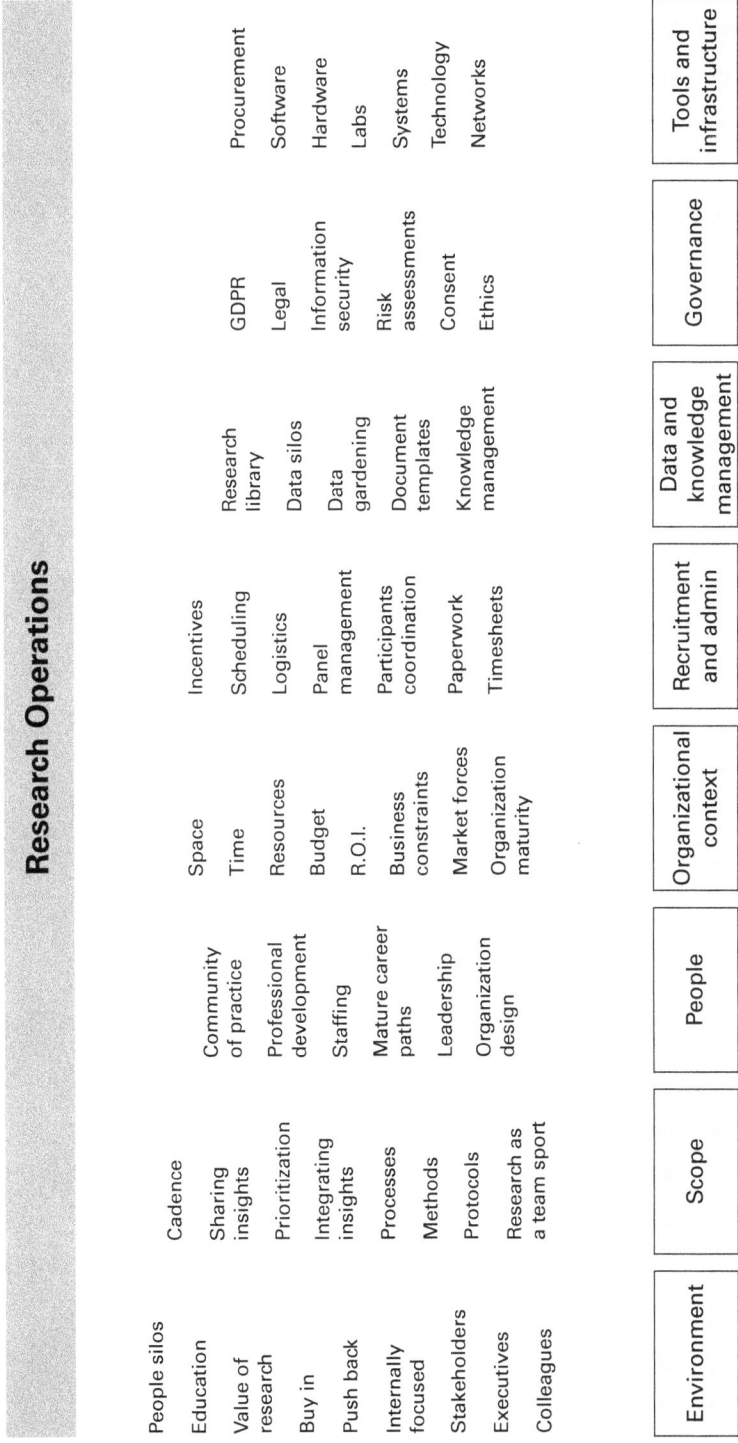

Research Operations

Environment	Scope	People	Organizational context	Recruitment and admin	Data and knowledge management	Governance	Tools and infrastructure
People silos	Cadence	Community of practice	Space	Incentives	Research library	GDPR	Procurement
Education	Sharing insights	Professional development	Time	Scheduling	Data silos	Legal	Software
Value of research	Prioritization	Staffing	Resources	Logistics	Data gardening	Information security	Hardware
Buy in	Integrating insights	Mature career paths	Budget	Panel management	Document templates	Risk assessments	Labs
Push back	Processes	Leadership	R.O.I.	Participants coordination	Knowledge management	Consent	Systems
Internally focused	Methods	Organization design	Business constraints	Paperwork		Ethics	Technology
Stakeholders	Protocols		Market forces	Timesheets			Networks
Executives	Research as a team sport		Organization maturity				
Colleagues							

SOURCE E Boulton. The eight pillars of user research, Global ResearchOps Community Medium Blog, 11 July 2019. medium.com/researchops-community/the-eight-pillars-of-user-research-1bcd28820d75a . Reproduced with kind permission of Emma Boulton

FIGURE 1.2 Holistic market research playbook

Prepare	Define	Gather	Analyse	Report	Team and resources
Framework: Methodology comparison table Prioritization tool Proposal selection scorecard **Templates:** Research proposal request Research work statement agreement Research plan Research proposal Participant profiles	**Tools:** Sample size calculator **Templates:** Standard survey Interview guide Focus group guide Participant screener form	**Tools:** Survey tool Recording tool (remote and in-person) **Templates:** Participant schedule	**Tools:** Statistical package **Templates:** Thematic analysis Social media sentiment analysis Website usage analysis	**Templates:** Secondary research report Focus group report Survey report Interview report Mixed method report	Skills frame works Job descriptions Market research strategy Tool list Policies Procedures Case studies Brand and tone of voice guide

SOURCE E James. What is a market research playbook? FlexMR article, 2021. blog.flexmr.net/market-research-playbook; E James. What is a market research playbook? LinkedIn Pulse Article, 14 April 2021. www.linkedin.com/pulse/what-market-research-playbook-emily-james; Demand Metric. Market research playbook, Slideshare, 2017. www.slideshare.net/demandmetric/market-research-playbook; Demand Metric. Market research playbook, American Marketing Association, 12 October, 2024. www.ama.org/toolkits/market-research-playbook/

- recruitment of researchers and ReOps people
- career paths to support retention
- professional development frameworks to improve maturing the research practice and also supports retention
- getting buy-in for the practice and its value from stakeholders

Market research playbooks can either focus on how to do a specific research project or can cover the overall research process, no matter the type of research that needs to be done. Figure 1.2 shows what is often included in a market research playbook.

We will cover all of the research operations pillars and the market research playbooks. However, what will be applicable to us, in our team, depends on a number of factors, such as organizational structure, how many people are doing research and whether there is a budget for operations specialists or not, and therefore the ratio of researchers to operations professionals.

Depending on what budget is available for operations there are several ways it can happen:

- side hustle while doing research or administration
- a dedicated person
- partly outsourced
- dedicated team

It's worth thinking about operations even as a team of one, so we don't have to think about how to do a particular thing each time we have a new project. It sets us up for a time when the team grows or others are doing research through a process of democratizing the research. The most important reason to think of operations as a solo researcher is data protection, and making sure everything we do complies with regulations, which is critical to all organizations, no matter their size.

Depending on the structure and make-up of the ReOps team, we may take a different approach to what operational responsibilities we take on, including factors such as team numbers, what time they can dedicate to Ops and what their skillsets are.

Assuming we'll be doing (some aspect of) the Ops or running the team that does the Ops, we can pick and choose the sections and chapters relevant to our role. If starting from scratch, and there are no defined roles, I recommend starting with the chapters here in Part One.

Part One: Managing infrastructure and the research process

- Chapter 2: Laying the foundations for successful research processes and practices
- Chapter 3: Data compliance in research operations
- Chapter 4: How to recruit participants: Models for best practice
- Chapter 5: How to manage data, information and knowledge
- Chapter 6: Supporting and managing the research process

WHAT WILL PART ONE PROVIDE?

When building a ReOps function from scratch or almost from scratch we can work on all the different aspects of research operations at once. Chapter 2 gives us the tools we need to work with the researchers to figure out the key areas to work on first. Next, we need to ensure that data protection and other regulations are being adhered to (Chapter 3). We will then focus on the point(s) in the research process where the researchers are experiencing the most issues. Spoiler alert – it's probably going to be participant recruitment (covered in Chapter 4), but maybe not! Let's not make too many assumptions.

Next to consider is knowledge management (Chapter 5). Knowledge management is one of the most sophisticated parts of research and research operations. It is also an essential part of an effective and efficient research practice. It is tempting to start with 'We need to have a tool to store our research and research insights in'. But there is so much more to knowledge management – it is a practice in itself, and we have to build towards having a well-managed tool that the researchers and the stakeholders can access easily. For example, research is not accessible unless we have established naming conventions that are consistently used and research artefacts are stored consistently. We can't make the assumption that it will happen without significant work, especially if there is a practice of siloed working within the organization.

Chapter 6 will provide templates and guidance that are relevant at each stage of the research process:

- planning
- set-up and execution
- analysis and synthesis
- sharing

To think about why these are useful, let's take the example of a research plan template:

- We don't have to think about what to include each time we need to create a research plan (decreasing cognitive load).
- Each research plan will include the same types of information each time (increasing consistency), e.g. objectives, sample criteria, sample size, etc., and this will help with the overall quality of research done.
- Less effort is required to create a plan that meets the expectations of other researchers and stakeholders.
- The researcher can focus on what rather than how.

Part Two: People

This section covers establishing recruitment processes for research and ReOps roles, who to recruit, and support the team's learning and development. And it also covers recruiting researchers:

- Chapter 7: Recruiting researchers
- Chapter 8: Recruiting the research operations team
- Chapter 9: Supporting research and operations learning and development to deliver effectively

WHAT WILL PART TWO PROVIDE?

Some of you may be wondering why I have included the recruitment of research practitioners (Chapter 7) but not how to support researchers' learning and development, whereas I have included both for ReOps practitioners (Chapters 8 and 9). There is a very good reason for that. Customer research practices, whether user or market research, are well-established practices and there is a lot of content out there for supporting learning and development in a research career. There is also documentation on the recruitment of researchers, for that matter. I have included recruitment content because if you are in an organization that is starting a research team (even if it is a team of one) for the first time it is important to have a comprehensive guide in one place of how to shape job descriptions depending on what skills are needed in a realistic way and then structure your interview in order to recruit the right people. The same is true of ReOps, and it is much more common to be recruiting ReOps people for the first time.

As ReOps is still an emerging field, a lot less has been written on supporting the learning and development and career progression of ReOps practitioners. I wanted to provide a starting place to create the frameworks to support the maturing of ReOps practices in a systematic way, that others can take and develop, creating a virtuous circle we can all benefit from. For most, career progression is important and it can mean different things for different people at different points of their career journey. A sense of progression is important for retention. For some, this can be a process of getting really good at the post they are in and expanding skills. Others will want to climb the ladder, becoming more senior within their chosen field of practice. Others may choose to transition their careers, for example from researcher to ReOps professional. Whatever each team member chooses in terms of their career, they will need to know what is expected; the responsibilities of each role and the skills required. This needs to be laid out in an understandable way that will support the team member and their line manager to map out their learning and development plan.

Part Three: Advanced operations

Advanced Ops are elements of research practice we need to consider once the groundwork of the fundamentals and the research process are established or are more sophisticated in the work required to develop and run them. This includes:

- Chapter 10: How to use AI as part of the research process
- Chapter 11: Metrics for research and research operations
- Chapter 12: How to adapt to changing needs and requirements

WHAT WILL PART THREE PROVIDE?

Using artificial intelligence (AI) in customer research and ReOps is a hot topic at the time of writing, as it is across many industries and fields. When and where to implement AI tools or AI functions within the research process requires careful consideration. The three key elements that make or break our use of AI are: 1) data protection; 2) potential for bias and exclusion; and 3) quality of output. With the current state of AI and its potential advancements in the next couple of years, there are still tasks within research where we should not utilize AI and there are other tasks where it can be an extremely useful buddy to a researcher, but it does require a solid understanding of the research practice and knowledge of how AI works and how we need to work with it to produce robust, high-quality outputs. Comprehensive datasets are a backbone of this, so we need to be aware of potential gaps in data and potential bias of algorithms to understand our AI augmented research results.

Now let's look at metrics. Measuring the impact of our work is extremely useful in terms of proving our value. This can be something that customer research and ReOps can struggle with. Practices that involve a lot of 'soft skills' such as 'talking to people' and that struggle to demonstrate value are often impacted with global and local economic changes. Over the last few years UX design and research has been impacted by redundancies within the tech industry, although revenue generated by user experience work is also still increasing year-on-year.[10] It is also true of market research – the first thing organizations cut from their marketing budgets is market research.[11] Yet for market research, revenue generated continues to grow year-on-year, with the US and UK leading the way.[12] Therefore, it is important to devote time to understand how to measure our work in an impactful way.

ReOps, whether it is being introduced to an organization or has been maturing within an organization for several years, is all about effective change management. The needs of the business, the needs of the people doing research and the technological landscape (and other landscapes) are ever evolving and ReOps needs to evolve with them to continue delivering the right thing at the right time to support customer research. This means as much as we are supporters, we are also disruptors. Whether we are iterating a process, migrating to a new tool or implementing new legal requirements, we need to ensure that research is still happening and being delivered as smoothly as possible while we embed the changes; this takes a lot of skill and thus deserves its own chapter.

Concluding thoughts

It is important to be aware when starting on a ReOps journey that everyone loves us when we're seamlessly enabling research to happen, taking some of the burden from the researcher. If we tell them that they can't do something because it's not GDPR compliant, or recruitment will take longer because we don't have consent to contact the sales database, or the overworked researcher decides they'll do the knowledge management side of things later as it's not as important as delivering answers to the product owner, but we're saying it's essential to do knowledge management at every step of the research process, then they don't love us so much. Resilience is key and this is an important element when building a community of practice, for example, which we will look at in Part Two.

Key takeaways

Research operations is about people, infrastructure and strategies to support those doing research to plan, conduct, analyse and share their research. It enables high-quality and impactful research to be done at scale.

Whether the size of the research teams is large or small, the demand for customer research is high and increasing. Operationalizing our research practices is important, whether we have a small or large number of people doing the research.

ReOps promotes consistency, reduces duplication and prevents important insights being siloed while mitigating risks. It saves time, effort and money, and improves productivity and job satisfaction.

Notes

1   K Kaplan. ResearchOps 101, Nielsen Norman Group, 16 August 2020. www.nngroup.com/articles/research-ops-101/ (archived at https://perma.cc/X26P-JGUF); ResearchOps Community. About ResearchOps, ResearchOps Community, 2024. researchops.community/about/ (archived at https://perma.cc/CF3T-E5R2); L Burnam. Research operations: The practice, the role, and its impact, User Interviews, 25 August 2022. www.userinterviews.com/blog/research-ops-what-it-is-and-why-its-so-important (archived at https://perma.cc/2V5R-BHDK)

2   K Towsey. ResearchOps community: A series of global workshops, Global ResearchOps Community Medium Blog, 5 April 2018. medium.com/researchops-community/researchops-community-a-series-of-global-workshops-d48058ece814 (archived at https://perma.cc/D9QL-8KYM)

3   M Espinoza Gotuzzo. DesignOps: When designing goes beyond product development, Bentley University, 2024. www.bentley.edu/centers/user-experience-center/designops-when-designing-goes-beyond-product-development (archived at https://perma.cc/C9H2-2TBD); K Kaplan. DesignOps 101,Nielsen Norman Group, 21 July 2019. www.nngroup.com/articles/design-operations-101/ (archived at https://perma.cc/VT2M-G6QU)

4   K Marchant. A short history of design operations, Sainsbury's Customer Experience Design, 5 July 2019. medium.com/sainsburys-customer-experience/a-short-history-of-design-operations-bf5ffe36d007 (archived at https://perma.cc/ZN7Q-8E5U)

5   E James. What is a market research playbook? FlexMR article, 2021. blog.flexmr.net/market-research-playbook (archived at https://perma.cc/8FMS-DG65)

6   B Booker. The 100-year history of market research – 1920 to 2020, Attest Technologies Limited Blog, 7 January 2020. www.askattest.com/blog/articles/history-of-market-research (archived at https://perma.cc/92SC-NUJZ)

7 L Burnam. Research operations: The practice, the role, and its impact, User Interviews, 25 August 2022. www.userinterviews.com/blog/research-ops-what-it-is-and-why-its-so-important (archived at https://perma.cc/B7W8-PKNS)

8 E James. What is a market research playbook? LinkedIn Pulse Article, 14 April 2021. www.linkedin.com/pulse/what-market-research-playbook-emily-jame (archived at https://perma.cc/V24D-W6WK)

9 E Boulton. Getting started with ResearchOps, Global ResearchOps Community Medium Blog, 8 October 2019. medium.com/researchops-community/getting-started-with-researchops-f77cd6779554 (archived at https://perma.cc/8B85-ZBGK)

10 Fortune Business Insight. UX services market size and share, by service type (UX research, UX design, UX audit, UX training, and UX strategy and consulting), by enterprise type (large enterprises and SMEs), and regional forecast, 2023–2030, Fortune Business Insight, 21 October 2024. www.fortunebusinessinsights.com/ux-services-market-108780 (archived at https://perma.cc/3NQ5-ATUX)

11 S Moore. The 5-step marketing research process, SmartBug Media, 14 March 2023. www.smartbugmedia.com/blog/the-5-step-marketing-research-process (archived at https://perma.cc/DC7P-W4MB)

12 Statista Research Department. Revenue of the market research industry worldwide from 2008 to 2023 with a forecast for 2024, Statista, February 2024. www.statista.com/statistics/242477/global-revenue-of-market-research-companies/ (archived at https://perma.cc/YC7P-RA68)

2

Laying the foundations for successful research processes and practices

Chapter 2 covers the key steps for establishing effective ReOps in an organization. It emphasizes the importance of prioritizing legal compliance, conducting thorough audits, understanding the research process and pain points, managing budgets, implementing structured onboarding and offboarding processes, and selecting appropriate tools.

The main steps include:

1 Ensuring compliance with relevant laws and regulations to prevent legal issues.

2 Auditing existing research artefacts, tools and infrastructure using spreadsheets to leverage available resources.

3 Engaging researchers to map out the research process, identify pain points and inform improvements through internal research.

4 Understanding and managing budget structures, expenditures, approval processes and stakeholder involvement.

5 Implementing structured onboarding and offboarding processes for smooth transitions and data security.

6 Regularly auditing and selecting tools that align with organizational needs, methodologies and compliance requirements.

By following these steps, organizations can establish a strong foundation for ReOps, enabling efficient research practices, strategic decision-making and high-quality research outputs.

If we're starting from scratch or close to it and assuming that the Ops to researcher ratio isn't one to one then we will need to figure out how to prioritize the things we need to work on. The most important things to do at the very beginning are to:

- understand what laws and regulations are relevant to our organization's research practice
- ensure that researchers are complying with all laws and regulations relevant to doing customer research for our organization
- know what budget we are working with
- audit everything to know what we are working with

If laws and regulations are being broken (even unintentionally), these are the issues to fix first. We will go into depth in terms of data protection in Chapter 3, but depending on the industry we're working in, there could be other laws and regulations that we need to be familiar with.

When starting out, it is OK to make quick fixes for anything that is fundamentally broken and is causing severe issues, such as regulation non-compliance. We can always come back later to this particular aspect of the research process and practice, and improve the initial fix with something more effective, efficient and long-term. I say this on the assumption that multiple things will need attention, so we won't have the luxury of doing the best possible fix right now, but need to use a short-term first and a more permanent solution later.

Stage 1: Auditing all the things

It is unlikely that we will be starting from scratch, with a completely blank slate, unless we are joining a brand new start-up for example, or any organization that hasn't done customer research before. So if there are research artefacts and HR documentation, for example, lying around, they could be of use to us in establishing ReOps processes and practices.

This is the kind of thing that is going to be useful to us and support our work for quite some time, so it's probably a good idea to create our own framework to help us organize the audit. Having a list of artefacts is the first step in the auditing journey; finding and cataloguing the artefacts are crucial at this stage.

Please make peace with making a lot of use of spreadsheets while we are
working in research operations. Spreadsheets with lots of tabs.

In our search we may find:

Research infrastructure documentation

- guidance
- governance and policies
- templates
- frameworks
- process documentation
- job descriptions

We may have other tools suitable for cataloguing and auditing, but pretty
much everyone has access to spreadsheets. Whatever tool we use, the
framework is likely to be similar. There may be details that need to be
added or amended to suit our organization, department or circumstances,
but the basics of what we'll need for our initial audit can be seen in
Figures 2.1 and 2.2.

- **Basics:** Included is the document name, document type, location of document and short description about the document.
- **Access:** Last updated will help us start to understand if it's likely to still
  be relevant or potentially out of date, last accessed will help us understand if people are using it or not. There are many reasons why who has
  access to the document is useful to know, for example whether the people
  who need to use it, can use it. Conversely, if the documents contain
  participants' personal data, maybe too many people have access, which is
  why legal implications have been included as an element in the audit
  framework.

Figure 2.2 shows an example of what it might look like when we fill in the
spreadsheet.

FIGURE 2.1 Research process document audit framework

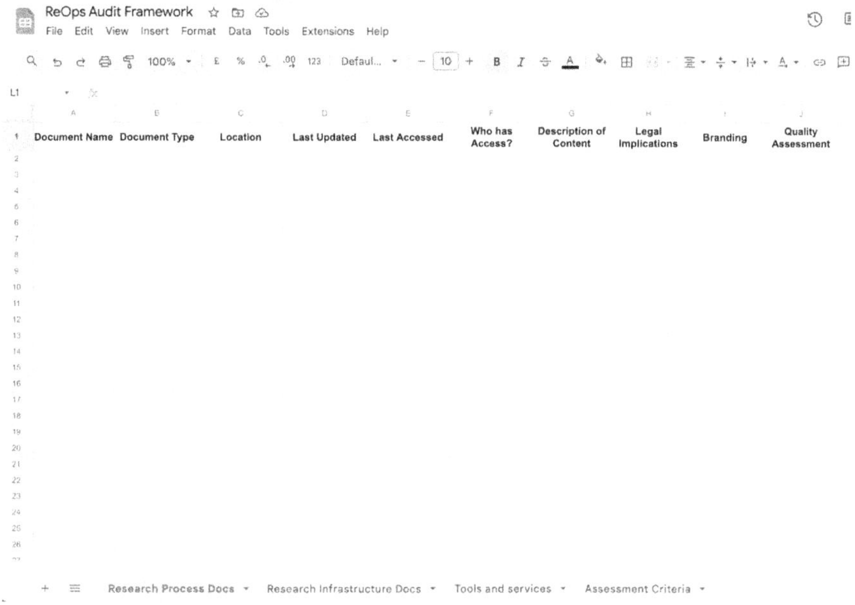

FIGURE 2.2 Example of research process documents audit form

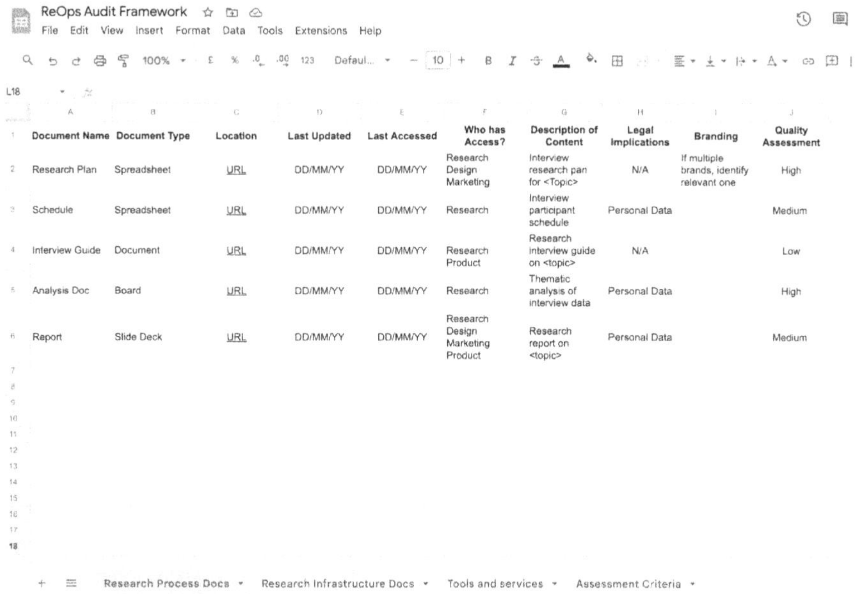

Research process documentation

- examples of research reports
- examples of surveys
- examples of interview guides

The audit framework for research process documents (Figure 2.3) is essentially the same with a couple of extra components; many organizations have multiple brands associated with them, so it could be useful (especially for reports) to note what brand the document is associated with. Quality assessment may not be part of our initial audit; it could be a component left for later in the process. In the context of research process documents, we can assess whether examples of reports and plans, etc., are of high quality and can be used as examples of best practice or they have elements that can be reused in future templates. The kinds of things we'll want to assess are that the examples: follow brand and tone of voice guidelines, contain expected information and metadata, are robust and of sound reasoning, are well written and have clear layouts.

FIGURE 2.3 Research infrastructure documents audit framework

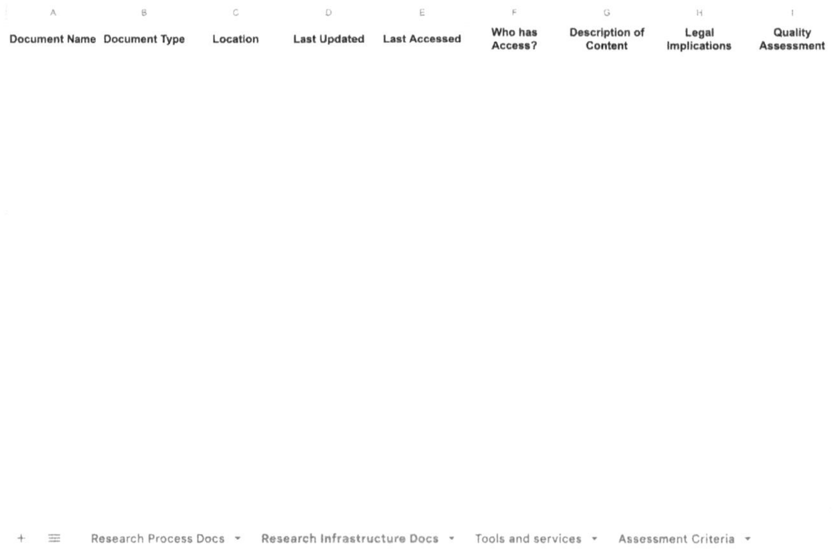

A	B	C	D	E	F	G	H	I
Document Name	Document Type	Location	Last Updated	Last Accessed	Who has Access?	Description of Content	Legal Implications	Quality Assessment

+ ≡ Research Process Docs ▾ Research Infrastructure Docs ▾ Tools and services ▾ Assessment Criteria ▾

Some of the examples we find may be poor examples that demonstrate the error we want to avoid (this could be useful for training purposes later on). At the beginning we may not be able to assess everything in terms of it being fit for purpose; we may not know enough about the research practice (and/ or organization) culture, expectation, etc., to make that judgement. At some point we will have that knowledge or we'll find the people to work with who have the knowledge to make appropriate judgement calls. And we probably don't have time to do a full audit in one go. The minimum requirement is finding and cataloguing the research artefacts. An example of what this could look like is laid out in Figure 2.4.

Tools and services used for research purposes

The next step is to audit and document tools and services (which includes participant panels). The framework is laid out in Figure 2.5.

- tools
- services
- participant panels

FIGURE 2.4   Examples of research infrastructure documents audit

FIGURE 2.5 Tools and service audit framework

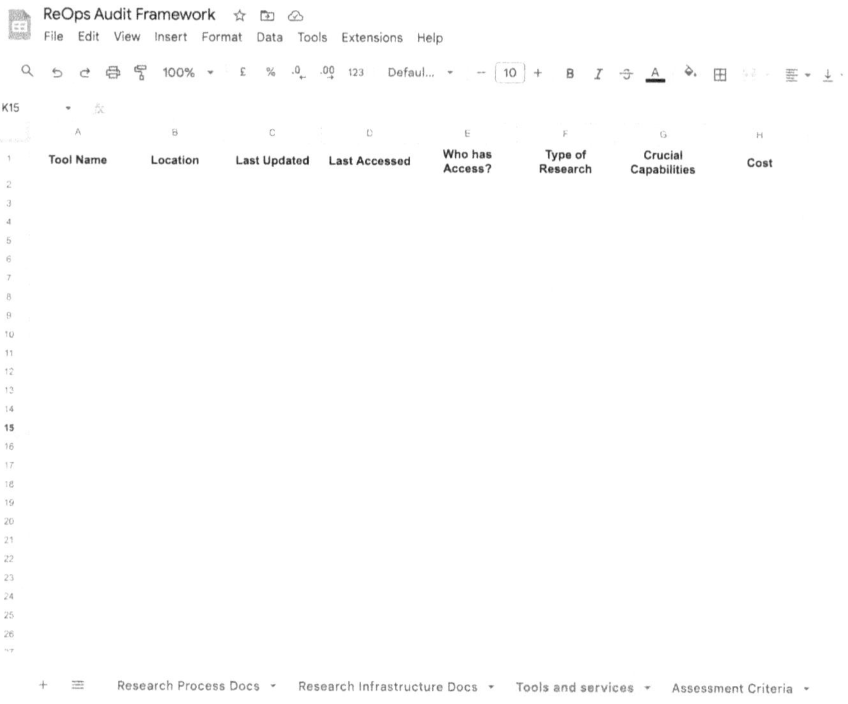

It is important not only to know what tools we have access to, but what those are tools for (do we, for example, have multiple tools that can do the same thing?), and, importantly, whether the tools we have access to comply with all the required laws and regulations. We will dive into this more at the end of the chapter.

As we go through the process of Stage 1, it's important to stop and fix any legal breaches we identify. We shouldn't be doing anything else until legal requirements are met, this could be removing data from a non-compliant tool or making sure that research data isn't accessible to the entire organization when it shouldn't be, etc.

Stage 2: Internal research

Once we are comfortable in the knowledge that laws aren't being broken, it's time to turn our attention to answering the question, what next? We can answer this question by doing internal research to understand the biggest pain points when our researchers are researching and experience in mapping the current research process with pain points.

Understand the experience of the people doing research and find the pain points

This is an important step to do, whatever the size and structure of the ReOps team, or if its researchers are doing it for themselves or on behalf of others.

Where we start depends on our familiarity with the research process in our organization. To cover as much as possible, let's assume we're a ReOps person new to the organization. This was me and the approach I took in November 2019 with a new job, new organization, new field, collaborating with my teammates, the research administrator and the head of user research.

What does the research process look like here?

At this point in time, the basic universal building blocks of the research process (whether user or market research) are well established. But there are nuances in the details depending on many things about the organization:

- the size and age of the organization
- how long there has been a research practice
- how long there has been a ReOps practice
- the industry(s) we work in
- where we and others in the organization are based, and where our audience/customers are located
- the size of the research team(s) and what department(s) we work in

> It's best not to assume too much about the research process, especially if we are new.

Research process mapping exercise

Journey mapping is a well-established user-centred design method and in 2024, at market research conferences I attended, I could see it was becoming more common in market research as well.

Invite the people who do research to participate in an exercise to map out the research process, using the mapping template in Figure 2.6.

Depending on how many people are doing research we may want to ask people to do this in groups in a workshop setting or individually in an interview setting.

If doing this in an individual setting, we can work with people to complete their map, asking them questions along the way. It is a useful artefact not only to have a visualization of their understanding and experience of the research process, but also to help structure our interview/conversation with them as we work to gain a deeper understanding.

If we are doing it in a workshop setting, allow groups time to discuss and complete the map together. Once the groups have finished, ask each group to present their map in turn and use key points as a basis for group discussion. In an ideal world each map will be relatively similar, so after the first group we want to encourage people to highlight any significant differences in their group's map.

Analysing our research process maps

The next steps once we've gathered our maps together are to:

- Create a summary map of the high-level process – aggregating where there is most agreement:
  - stages
  - tasks
  - tools
  - positives
  - negatives
  - opportunities.
- Taking the map to the next level of usefulness is to identify the impact of the things that are perceived as not working, and the things that are perceived as working, as shown in Figure 2.7.
- Identify where there are divergences in the process and why there are variations, and their impact. Are there differences in the research process or experience of the research process based on location? Or interacting with different teams and different stakeholders?

FIGURE 2.6 Template for research mapping process

Research process stage	Example	...	...	...
Tasks	Agree research objectives Choose methodology			
Who is involved	Marketing, Product			
Tools and services	Trello, Spreadsheet			
Guidance, templates available	Research plan template			
What is working	Shared tools			
What isn't working	Lack of confidence in choosing right method			
Opportunities	Provide support for choosing right method to answer the question			

FIGURE 2.7 Adding to the template for the research mapping process

Research process stage	Example	...	...	...
Tasks	Agree research objectives Choose methodology			
Who is involved	Marketing, product			
Tools and services	Trello, spreadsheet			
What is working	Shared tools			
What isn't working	Lack of confidence in choosing right method			
Opportunities identified by researchers	Provide support for choosing right method to answer the question			
Impact of positive experiences Why is it working	Shared tools support collaboration across different teams			
Why isn't it working	Instances of the wrong method being used, and the research can't be answered in a satisfactory way			
Size of negative impact				
Variations and divergence				
Opportunities identified by Ops				

Perception and the research process

Above I talked about the perception of things working or not working in the research process. This is not to throw doubt on the experience of people doing research, but is a way to describe the principle of what people say and what people do can be different things (as commonly understood by the user research profession). Rather than taking the experience at face value, we need to dig deeper to find the root cause of the experience.

People may have a negative experience for a multitude of reasons, which will require different actions to improve that experience. This is why it's important to have a (semi) structured discussion while people are making their research process maps, to understand why things are happening as well as what is happening. Table 2.1 shows a variety of reasons why something in the research process might be suboptimal, and potential actions to take to rectify this.

EXAMPLE SCENARIO

One likely place where researchers are feeling pain is the participant recruitment process. There is a lot of admin involved in recruiting the right participants and an appropriate number of them, and that's before considering GDPR and other procedures and regulations that may need to be complied with.

Sometimes the issues being experienced are that people don't know something exists or they don't understand it. Guidance on how to do a thing is a good example of both these things, as shown in Table 2.2.

Prioritizing opportunities and actions to be taken

How we prioritize what we are going to work on, and in what order, depends on a multitude of factors:

- Does it affect legal responsibilities (e.g. data protection)?
- Is it in our remit to change this thing?
- What are the size of the impact (urgent blocker or an annoying minor issue)?
- The amount of work required to fix the issue:
  - o Is budget required? Do we need to get approvals?
  - o Are other teams involved?
  - o Does it involve significant changes?

TABLE 2.1 Why people doing research may struggle with the process

Reasons for a negative experience	Potential actions to take
Aren't aware of process	Provide training and guidance
Don't understand the process	
Don't have access to the right tools	Work to provide the appropriate people, the appropriate access to the tools they need
The right tool or service isn't part of the process	
The process has blockers because of other teams	Work with the teams in question to remove the blockers
Key stages are missing in the research process	Work to implement the stage in the research process and support needed to complete the tasks within this stage
The research process isn't standardized	Work to implement a standardized research process that works in your organization's context
Aren't aware of a template	Work to make the research process and its materials accessible, and promote what is available for researchers to use
Aren't aware of a tool	

TABLE 2.2 Some examples of why researchers may struggle with participant recruitment

Reasons for a negative experience	Potential actions to take
Not everyone is aware of the participant panel they can utilize for recruitment	Provide the appropriate people, the appropriate access to the tools they need, and training and guidance in using these tools and services
Not everyone is aware of the approved list of recruitment agencies to partner with	
Everyone is doing their own recruitment, using their own particular process	Work to implement a standardized research process that works in your organization's context
If possible, another potential option would be to centralize all or part of the recruitment process as well as standardizing	

- Who is going to do the work? How much capacity do they have to do the work?

We can organize our priorities into short-term, mid-term and long-term work. Or MoSCoW: Must have. Should have. Could have. Won't have/right now.

There may be another step we need to take before we can effectively prioritize these research operations tasks… if we need to identify who can and will do the work. It will be useful to read Chapter 9 on different ways ReOps teams can be structured.

This isn't necessarily a one-time exercise. We can do this kind of reflection at any time, if we need a structured way to identify what isn't working in the research process, to go beyond anecdotal feedback.

Stage 3: Budget management

Interestingly, budget management currently isn't included in the skills requirements on many research operations job descriptions. It is also a training course that many ReOps people wish were available. There are many different ways that a budget might be structured and therefore managed, many of which I have experienced myself. Budgets can be siloed or centralized or a combination of the two, depending on the organization.

Step one. The first thing to understand is what kind of budget structure we are working with. Table 2.3 is another handy framework we may want to use to understand what budget(s) we have to work with, if any at all. I have yet to be in a job or meet a person working with an entirely centralized budget, but it could happen. Most common, I think, is the hybrid model where the ReOps team have control and management over some of the budget and will try to influence or help others spend their budget as wisely as possible.

Step two. Once we've identified which budgets we have control over, next is to understand what the size of the budget is, what it is being spent on, and when payments are due.

Step three. Understand the invoice payment process and how long it takes, so that all the bills are paid on time.

Step four. Understand what the budget approval processes are in our organization, who's involved (who we should work with), what

TABLE 2.3 Types of budget access

	No budget	Budget controlled by others	Influence	Manage on others' behalf	Control and manage budget
Participant recruitment					
Participant incentives					
Tools					
Services					
Hardware					
Agencies					
People [permanent]					
People [contractors]					
Travel and expenses					
Labs*					

information is required when we submit our request, for example, our annual budget. When submission deadlines are, and what timescale approvals have.

Step five. Identify potential budgeting improvements. It depends what access we have to budget and what our needs are in how we want to distribute such resources.[1]

If clarity is lacking in who and what is involved in budgeting and we are looking to connect with people in the know, the following teams could be involved in budgeting:

- finance
- compliance
- data protection
- legal
- procurement
- IT
- HR
- departmental leadership
- C-suite

I learnt budget management by doing it and not being shy about asking questions and for advice, as it's a lot of responsibility to properly manage a budget. I have had jobs where there was no budget, there was budget but I had no control or influence, I controlled and managed parts of the budget, I managed parts of the budget on other people's behalf, or I had influence over budget management, but didn't do it myself.

For each I have learnt what I can and cannot do in the circumstances and how to do that thing. Each organization is different.

Stage 4: Other considerations for successful research processes and practices

Onboarding and offboarding

ONBOARDING

Whatever the size of the organization and complexity of the industry and work, it's not a good idea to throw new team members in at the deep end and expect them to 'swim' (be an effective team member) immediately. Orientation and understanding take time. Having something to refer to, to guide them, makes a big difference to how smoothly their transition into a new job goes and how overwhelmed they are while going through it.

Having an onboarding template allows for a consistent onboarding experience with clear expectations and each new person to establish a consistent research practice. Such a template can be a document or it can be a Trello Board (which means people can move the cards they've completed to a 'done' column for a sense of progress).

Things to include in our onboarding template is shown in Table 2.4.

It is also useful to have an onboarding buddy – someone who knows the ropes and the new person can ask questions of. It's useful if this person is not the line manager, that way newbies can start getting to know multiple people.[2]

OFFBOARDING

Offboarding is not just about giving the leaver a proper send-off, but also making sure everything is properly handed over and all relevant accesses are revoked, for data security reasons for example.

Make a list of all tools the leaver has access to that they need to be removed from, then identify anything in research tools where they will need

TABLE 2.4 How to structure an onboarding table

Day 1	Week 1	...	...	Ongoing
Tech set-up HR orientation Systems to access Meet line manager Meet immediate team	People to meet Introduction to research process Useful documents about the organization Mandatory training	People to meet Shadow a team member to better understand research process Useful documents to read Mandatory training	Kick off first official project	Useful links
Version 1				
Tech	People	Training	Reading	
Version 2				

to transfer ownership, such as projects, data, etc. Next, make sure all document ownership has been transferred on shared drives (e.g. Team Drive or Sharepoint). Lastly, review whether the leaver has any documents stored on their personal drive or hard drive that shouldn't be there, then make sure they are stored in the right place.

Choosing the right tools for our organization

The tools we use during the research process are a key factor in an organization's research infrastructure. There are many factors to consider when choosing the right tools. Unsurprisingly, we need to consider many factors when choosing and managing tools for those doing research:

- What tools do we have? Are they supporting the things we need to do?
- Do we need to change tools?
- Do we need more or fewer tools?
- What budget do we have for tools?
- What methodologies and tasks do we need to support?
- Are there particular countries that we need our tools to work in? For example, some regions may have firewalls in place. Another example is, countries that have low bandwidth internet will need lightweight tools.

- Tools will need to comply with relevant laws such as GDPR.
- How do tools' AI functions use the data input?
- Are the tools accessible?
- Who will be using the tools? Levels of expertise in those using the tools will help us choose what kind of tools to use.

It is important to audit the tools we have first and then identify any potential gaps and needs for tools (framework shown in Table 2.5). Some tools do it all, but can be quite expensive; sometimes we need a few different specialist tools.

The size of the research need will help us determine, for example, whether we need an annual subscription or something more flexible like monthly subscription that can be stopped at any time. I've added examples of what this can look like in Table 2.6.

Tone of voice and brand guidelines

The tone of voice and brand aesthetic for all research communications with participants and all reports shared with stakeholders should be in line with organizational brand guidelines. I personally find it interesting that tone of voice and brand guidelines are consistently considered as a part of market research infrastructure and processes, but not that of user research. Yet both types of research should ensure that research and research communications are in line and consistent with branding requirements.

If we are working within a user experience team, for example, then it is unlikely that we will be involved in working on such guidelines, but we will need access to and familiarity with such things. If we're in a marketing department we might actually get to shape brand guidelines in a user-centric way.

TABLE 2.5 Framework for assessing tool gaps and needs

Research need	Size of need (number of teams, frequency of research)	Critical tool capability	Critical outputs	Stakeholders (and their research literacy)

SOURCE Inspired by Ola Trytek, Lead User Researcher at Springer Nature
NOTE Could be lab hire or building and/or running and maintenance of a lab.

TABLE 2.6 Example of how to assess tool gaps and needs

Research need	Size of need: • number of teams • frequency of research • criticality of product	Critical tool capability	Critical outputs	Stakeholders (and their research literacy)
Evaluation of the prototype before the development	6 teams Twice a quarter Medium income product	Accessible Compatible with figma Mobile testing function Use own participants	Usability metrics Screen recording Written responses Heatmaps	Product leadership
Updating information architecture to include new products	2 teams Twice a year High income services	Accessible Card sorting Tree testing Support multiple languages	Time of task Task pathway visualization Similarity matrix visualization	Innovation director
Project management	All teams Daily All products	Accessible Secure GDPR compliant Automation	Task tracking Task size estimation Sprint planning	C-suite

Change management

Whether we are creating new processes and practices, or improving existing ones, change management is an integral part of how we will create and embed or iterate, while ensuring that whatever research is being undertaken continues to happen as smoothly as possible. We will cover this in detail in Part Three: Advanced operations.

Important considerations when getting started

It may seem daunting to read this whole chapter and think about all the things that might need to be done to get started in ReOps. But getting started can mean different things, from starting a research process and ReOps practice from scratch, to onboarding into an established ReOps role in an established ReOps team. So there is a lot of variation in what we personally might have to do.

Another thing to consider is whether there is an established research process, with some ReOps tasks being done by the researchers and some being done by a ReOps person that is about to leave, for example. We will need to ensure that the research process still runs smoothly while we get up to speed, so this will be an important part of our prioritization process, when we are deciding what to do when. This experience will stand us in good stead when we're iterating and making improvements in the future, but we'll get to that later.

Conclusion

Establishing effective research operations begins with prioritizing key tasks such as ensuring legal compliance, understanding budget constraints and conducting thorough audits of existing resources. Key steps include:

- **Compliance:** Address legal and regulatory issues to prevent repercussions.
- **Auditing:** Systematically catalogue research artefacts and tools using spreadsheets to leverage existing resources.
- **Internal research:** Engage researchers to map out and understand the research process, identify pain points and inform improvements.
- **Budget management:** Understand and manage budget structures, expenditures, and approval processes.
- **Onboarding and offboarding:** Implement structured processes for smooth transitions and maintain data security.
- **Tool selection:** Regularly audit and choose tools that align with organizational needs and compliance requirements.

By laying a strong foundation through these steps, organizations can create a resilient and efficient ReOps function that supports high-quality research and strategic decision-making.

Useful resources

S Marsh. How our team got started in ReOps, Medium, 2019. medium.com/researchops-community/getting-started-with-researchops-f77cd6779554

Notes

1   L Birtley. Budgets: User research hierarchy of needs, UXR @ Microsoft Blog, 2023. medium.com/uxr-microsoft/budgets-user-research-hierarchy-of-needs-3b82f3fe4dcc (archived at https://perma.cc/KU2P-MWS4)

2   N Anderson. Building a team that wants to stay: Tips for properly onboarding user researchers. D Scout, People Nerds Blog, 2024. dscout.com/people-nerds/properly-onboarding-user-researchers (archived at https://perma.cc/QP88-8FY2)

3

Data compliance in research operations

There are all sorts of laws and regulations we may need to comply with when doing research, depending on the industry we're working in and the country in which we and our customers reside. So, legally and ethically, one of the first things we need to do in a research operations role is to review what laws and regulations we need to comply with and that the research practices in place or being developed comply with those laws and regulations.

This chapter will primarily focus on ensuring the research operations are set up so that the research process complies with data protection and data privacy regulations. But these are not the only laws that we need to consider. Increasingly, accessibility is being written into law; not just within disability anti-discrimination laws, but specific accessibility and digital accessibility laws, which we'll look at through the lens of participant recruitment in Chapter 4.

But first, with continuing fast-paced advances in technology, the need for data protection, and society's awareness of how their data is being used, continues to increase in prominence. The General Data Protection Regulation (GDPR) is probably the most familiar of these, depending on where we are in the world. GDPR covers Europe and the UK. Different states within the US have federal laws, such as the California Consumer Protection Act (CCPA). Where I currently work (2024), Springer Nature, a global science publisher, GDPR is used as a global standard. No matter where the customers are based that participate in our research and no matter in which country the people doing the research are, everyone and everything is treated to the same standard. There may be legal and regulatory requirements that we will need to comply with in addition to GDPR, such as data protection laws within China,[1] or New Zealand's 2020 Data Protection Act.[2] But, if we are complying with GDPR, then we're covering most data privacy and protection laws, as these are the strictest laws in the world when it comes to requirements for protecting citizens' and consumers' data.[3]

GDPR ensures data privacy and data security and applies to anyone processing the personal data of EU/UK citizens or residents. GDPR focuses on seven areas of protection:

1 Lawful, fair and transparent use of data.

2 Limiting data use to specific and defined purposes.

3 Data is stored for that specific purpose only as long as it's needed.

4 Minimizing the amount of data collected.

5 Ensuring data held about a person is accurate and up to date.

6 Data processing will ensure security, integrity and confidentiality.

7 Data controllers are held accountable to comply with regulations.[4]

By doing customer research, we will collect and create personal data. GDPR regulates how to manage personal data across all the different phases of research. By complying with the law, we are protecting the participants of our research, protecting the organization's reputation and protecting the people doing the research and handling the data.

What is considered personal data?

GDPR defines personal data broadly, including data such as online identification markers and location data.[5]

Personal data, also referred to as personally identifiable information, is that which when used alone or with other relevant data can identify an individual.[6] A useful example is to think about the information presented about you in your passport – this is personal information used to identify you, such as your name, address, date of birth, place of birth, etc.

We also need to pay attention to traceable data, which is also known as quasi-identifiers or indirectly identifying data. Not all personal data directly identifies a person, but collecting enough quasi-identifiers has a cumulative effect, and at some point we will be able to identify the specific individual.

It is useful to take scientists as a case study of this concept. Scientists are a relatively niche group of people. Current estimates suggest there are approximately 8 million scientists in the world, which is 0.1 per cent of the population. That may still seem like a big group of people, but those numbers decrease dramatically when considering different fields of study.

Table 3.1 contains details of two imaginary people. Example 1 is fairly anonymous; however, with a little effort we can identify who example 2 is,

TABLE 3.1 Traceable data depends on the context

	Example 1	Example 2
Role	High-school teacher	Principal investigator
Subject	Science	Snail paleobiology
Location	London, England	Perth, Australia

or at least greatly narrow down to a small pool of people, and with a little effort we will be able to find the name of the person in example 2.

IMPORTANT NOTE

In market research, in particular, there are a lot of quantitative surveys that are entirely anonymous; data protection doesn't apply to such studies.[7]

The level of GDPR risk that we are managing at each point in the research process depends on several factors:

- How many people have access to the personal data?
- How much personal data do we have about each person?
- How sensitive is the data?

GDPR risk is high when we are using or collecting raw personal data where potentially multiple people have access to this data. This includes potential/ participant contact details and personal details about them being used through the recruitment and selection process. It includes the data we generate through doing research such as video and audio recordings, screenshots or notes taken.

GDPR risk is medium when data is being processed and aggregated. At this point fewer people have access to the data and the work is being done to anonymize the data as much as possible. GDPR risk is also medium when we share research insights with video clips and quotes that aren't fully anonymized. So research participants' names can be seen and/or their face can be seen in a video.

GDPR risk is lowest when research data is fully anonymized, meaning it is not possible to identify individuals when working with the insights or the data itself. This is all visualized in Figure 3.1.

FIGURE 3.1 Data protection risk visualization

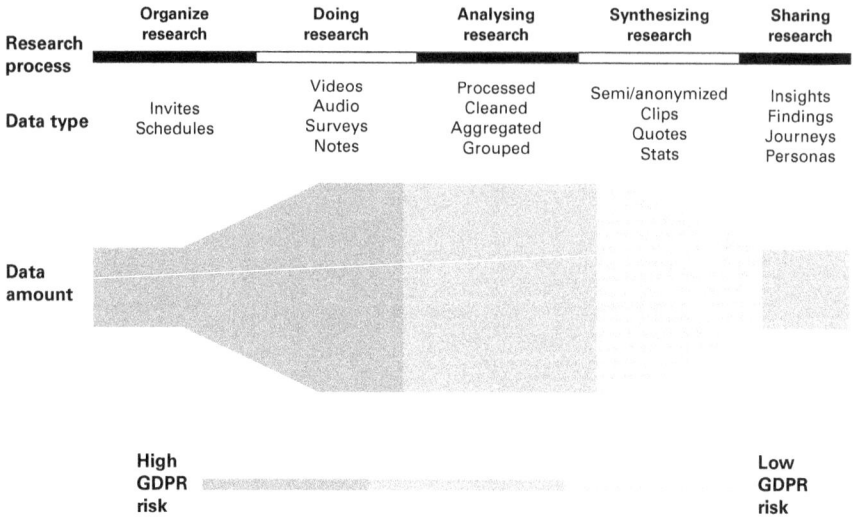

Research process	Organize research	Doing research	Analysing research	Synthesizing research	Sharing research
Data type	Invites Schedules	Videos Audio Surveys Notes	Processed Cleaned Aggregated Grouped	Semi/anonymized Clips Quotes Stats	Insights Findings Journeys Personas

Data amount

High GDPR risk

Low GDPR risk

How do we ensure GDPR compliance?

The people doing ReOps may be leading the effort to comply with regulations, but in truth GDPR compliance is everyone's responsibility. To support people fulfilling their responsibilities, very clear guidelines that are easily accessible are essential for ensuring that anyone who is doing research can comply. Providing training to anyone who will be undertaking research is also essential, certainly when onboarding people into our organization's particular research processes, but it is also useful to consider regular (perhaps annual) refreshers to help people to follow the rules. Refreshing people's understanding of how our organization complies with GDPR is particularly useful if any tools, for example, have changed or rules have been updated.

GDPR compliant tools, services and data storage

Tools, services and storage infrastructure must comply with GDPR at all times before, during and after research is done. We may have one tool to rule them all, or we may have different tools for each phase of research. Either way, we need to ensure that each tool is GDPR compliant if it is used for storing, capturing or processing research data that contains personal data.

GDPR compliance during planning

Make sure that we identify what data we need to collect in the planning stage of the research. To comply with regulations we need to collect only what we need and there is no 'nice to have' information. When formulating the recruitment strategy, if using internal databases of people, determine whether we have permission to access contact details for the potential participants. Do we have permission to contact those people?

Recruiting participants in a GDPR compliant way

If we're using internal data, rather than a recruitment agency to recruit, we need to make sure, if using a marketing list, that contacting people to invite them to participate in research is included in the terms and conditions they agreed to when they signed up to receive marketing emails.

IMPORTANT NOTE

We need to make sure any recruitment agencies we are using are adhering to GDPR and any other laws and regulations necessary.

GDPR compliance during data collection and analysis

User research data includes:

- notes from research sessions (typed or handwritten)
- photos, audio and video recordings
- information that participants enter into prototypes or test versions of services (usability research)
- information participants have told us or shown us during moderated research sessions, such as interviews and contextual inquiry
- paperwork that participants refer or respond to
- online identifier: IP address[8]

We will need to ensure that this kind of data is captured and stored in a GDPR compliant way. This goes beyond the tools used, and is inclusive of under what legal terms the data is captured (see details about legitimate interest and informed consent) and who has access to the data once it's captured and stored.

Being compliant means that the data is captured and stored in a secure way, we have only captured what we need and only the people who need access have access.

Sharing research with quotes and clips from participants

As long as it's included in our terms and conditions and consent form, we can include personal data while presenting and sharing the research. When discussing informed consent, we will see that we need to be explicit about what will be shared, with whom and how it will be shared. Generally, this will mean sharing video clips of interviews or usability tests to demonstrate the insights with impact, with the purpose of sharing insight to be actioned in improving our products and services or sharing contextual knowledge. If we plan to share clips, for example, more publicly we will need the participants' explicit consent for this.

Things to include in reports, if covered in consent forms:

- a participant list (to demonstrate the validity of our sampling)
- verbatim quotes
- photos of participants' faces
- audio clips
- video clips (with their name included – thanks Zoom and Google Meet)

There are things we can do to limit the amount of information we are sharing, such as blurring faces and names, not sharing particularly sensitive pieces of information and blurring form inputs if participants are using real data.

If our organization uses third parties in some capacity (agencies, consultants and contractors) and research data will need to be shared with them to carry out this work, we should also make this explicit – but we'll go into that very soon.

Participants' rights in GDPR

Another important aspect is the person's (participant's) right to access, right to be informed and right to be forgotten.

The right of access, commonly referred to as subject access, gives individuals the right to obtain a copy of their personal data, as well as other supplementary information that our organization holds about them. It helps individuals to understand how and why we are using their data, and check we are doing it lawfully.[9] This is done by the participant through a subject access request.

The right to be informed covers some of the key transparency requirements of UK GDPR, for example. It is about providing individuals with clear and concise information about what we do with their personal data.[10]

Under UK GDPR, for example, individuals have the right to have personal data erased. This is also known as the 'right to be forgotten'. The right only applies to data held at the time the request is received. It does not apply to data that may be created in the future. The right is not absolute and only applies in certain circumstances.

When does the right to erasure apply?

Individuals have the right to have their personal data erased if:

The personal data is no longer necessary for the purpose which we originally collected or processed it for; we are relying on consent as our lawful basis for holding the data, and the individual withdraws their consent; we are relying on legitimate interests as our basis for processing and the individual objects to the processing of their data, and there is no overriding legitimate interest to continue this processing; we are processing the personal data for direct marketing purposes and the individual objects to that processing; we have processed the personal data unlawfully; we have to do it to comply with a legal obligation; or we have processed the personal data to offer services to a child.[11]

These rights mean that it is essential that we know where research data is stored, and it is easily finable so that we can comply with requests. Thus, we need to have agreed storage and file naming conventions. We will go into this in Chapter 5.

Legitimate interest vs informed consent

There are two main concepts of data protection that we use in customer research: legitimate interest and informed consent. As already mentioned, if we don't collect any personally identifiable information, we don't need to gain consent or identify under what condition we are gathering the data.

Legitimate interest is the most flexible of GDPR lawful processing of personal data. Legitimate interest refers to an organization needing to collect or process personal data for a specific purpose, and the person whose data is being used would expect the organization to use their personal data in such a way. The processing should have a clear benefit and not have a negative impact on the person's data privacy and own interests.

For legitimate interest to be valid, how an organization collects data, for example on their websites, should be detailed in a publicly available privacy statement. There is no active opt-in to data collection when using legitimate interest, so it's important to consider whether this is the most appropriate basis with which to collect personal data from individuals. It tends to happen when cookies, for example, are accepted on a website.[12]

When the concept of consent is used in user research, people are actively opting in for their data to be collected. And it needs to be voluntary, specific and explicit, concise, clear and unambiguous, fair and easy to withdraw.

During moderated research, for consent to be informed, we need to share with the participant in a clear and understandable way:

- who is doing the research
- the purpose of the research
- what data we're collecting
- what will happen during the research
- who we'll share the results of the research with
- that their participation is voluntary, and that they can stop or withdraw their consent at any time
- how long their data will be kept
- what their rights are and how they can complain
- whether and how the session is being recorded
- whether the session is being observed (and who's watching)

Moderated research cannot rely on legitimate interest as a basis for collecting data, as participating in a research session cannot be considered as a 'normal' part of using the organization's product or services, for example. Written consent strengthens confidence that the participant's feedback won't affect their relationship with the organization, reducing bias in data collection. Therefore, informed consent leads to more high-quality research and more robust insights from moderated research.

For unmoderated research such as surveys that collect personal data, a data privacy statement can be provided that the participant agrees with, similar to the kind of consent statements available when signing up to a newsletter. Later in the chapter there are templates for both data privacy statements and informed consent forms.

TABLE 3.2 When to use informed consent and when to use legitimate interest

Low impact on privacy Legitimate interest (Data privacy statement)	High impact on privacy Informed consent (Signed consent form)
Written responses to questions asking for personal data or traceable data (not including sensitive data) that are used for trend analysis with aggregated data (automated statistical analysis).	Video and audio recordings of participants that are stored and indexed.
Contacting potential participants	Research where individual responses with personal data is analysed by a human.
Passive data collection that happens when individuals accept cookies are using a website as they normally would. Tools such as Google Analytics or Hotjar would be detailed in the organization's privacy policy.	Sensitive data collection of any kind (protected characteristics)

User research relies mostly on informed consent. Legitimate interest is not really discussed in the field of user research. Market research is much more aware of this concept.

- No UX research content on data protection discusses legitimate interest as an option for collecting and processing personal data for UX research purposes.
- Informed consent is standard in the field of practice of UX research across all industries and has been since before GDPR was enforced.

But, GDPR literature discusses legitimate interest and informed consent being the valid options that apply to collecting and processing personal data. It is necessary to have a clear framework for choosing the right option, shown in Table 3.2.

Consent forms

Consent forms must use understandable language, whatever language that may be, including sign language and braille – if appropriate to our organization.

EXAMPLE CONSENT FORM[13]

Your research session will be facilitated by [name of researcher].
Information we will collect

During the session, we might ask you:

- Questions to learn more about your [relevant topic 1], frustrations and other relevant topics related to your [profession, experience, etc.].
- To share your opinions and experiences with [relevant things to your organization].
- To do particular tasks relevant to our [product or service, etc.].

Privacy and confidentiality

How your data will be used

All personal data collected during the research will be treated confidentially. All parts of our research process conform to GDPR guidelines. Your data will be processed using GDPR compliant tools by the researcher(s) leading the project. Data may include screen, voice or video recordings and note taking.

No information, opinions or experiences you share with us, whether positive or negative, will impact any of your past, current or future [things you have with our organization].

How your information will be shared

Our research reports may include your comments and actions; however, we won't publish anything that identifies you personally outside our company. Neither will any third party partners working with us.

Freedom to withdraw

Your participation in this study is voluntary.

- You can refuse to take part at any time.
- You can take a break at any time.
- You can ask questions at any time.
- You can leave at any time without giving a reason.

By signing this document, you consent to the following:

- To take part in the research study.
- Recordings to be shared internally at [organization] and with third-party partners.

- You have read research [Terms and Conditions].
- You have read our [Organization's Privacy Policy].
- You understand that information shared with you during the session is [Organization]'s property and should not be disseminated, distributed or mentioned to anyone else.

Your agreement

To take part in the research, please sign this form showing that you consent to us collecting these data.

_____

I remember attending a UK government accessibility conference in Edinburgh, Scotland in November 2018; Snook (a service design agency) had an excellent case study of iterating their research consent form for a specific project to be inclusive as all the participants' language was British Sign Language (BSL). Unfortunately, I can no longer find the case study online, but this work had a great impact on me, as the work they did to understand the consent needs of these participants meant they significantly reduced the time of the consent video. The first iteration was a direct translation for written English to BSL and the video was around 18 minutes long; after working with BSL users, the consent form was improved and the video length was reduced to 8 minutes. This is the power and importance of user-centricity and inclusion.

Privacy policies and statements

The purpose of a privacy policy is to explain how a business collects, uses, shares and protects users' personal information and explains what control users have over that data.[14] Privacy policies are required under GDPR.

It is likely that there is a privacy policy already in our organization, unless it's a brand new start-up. Whether it already exists or we are starting with a blank slate, we need to make sure that our research activities are covered by the policy. Policies will cover analytics and other tracking-related activities for marketing and product development, but we can't necessarily assume that the privacy policy includes our kind of research activities, and any kind of personal data collection needs to be included.

Privacy policies need to include what data is being collected, how it's being collected, why it's being collected, and under what legal basis, who has access to the information, customers' rights and how they can act on them, contact details and how long the data will be held.[15]

If research activities aren't included in the privacy policy, we need to work with our legal and data protection teams to have them incorporated.

It is useful to have a data privacy statement to include in surveys, for example, when you are collecting personal data, that summarizes and reassures the respondent how data is being collected, stored and used and also links to the privacy policy and other relevant documents, if they need more detail.

Data privacy statement example

> Your details will only be used for customer research purposes. Your data will be stored in a secure database and will not be shared externally. For more information on how we treat your data read our [Privacy Policy]. To know about our customer research activities with us check [our website].
>
> You can opt out at any point or email us at [email@email.com]. This will not affect any [products/services/subscriptions] you have with [our organization].
>
> I understand.
>
> _____

Adding research activities to terms and conditions

Do we have the right to recruit people from internal systems? Have people on the marketing communication list opted in to being contacted about participating in research? If not, only the owner of the database could email people on our behalf, or perhaps they can't be contacted at all for our purposes. See Chapter 4 on recruiting best practice for more information.

Other explanatory documents we may need

Terms and conditions

If our research practice includes moderated research, we'll need research terms and conditions. As well as acknowledging our organization's responsibilities in conducting moderated research, these should include any expectations of the participant:

- language proficiency
- the kind of technology they need access to, to participate in the research
- what is acceptable or unacceptable behaviour
- honesty (no false claims, just to participate in the research)

These are needed, for example, as a form of protection for both our organization and the participant – so everyone knows what is expected. A worst case scenario would be, for example, if we need to end a research session early because the participant is being abusive, or they have clearly lied on the screener survey and are not a suitable candidate to participate. Having terms and conditions clearly laid out means the researcher has the right to end the session and not pay the participant the incentive as the terms and conditions have not been met. Equally, if the researcher were to behave badly while moderating the session, the participant is protected under the terms and conditions, and has a basis for complaint. Hopefully we will never need to use the terms and conditions in such a way, but they need to be in place, in case they are needed.

Prize draw rules

If large-scale and in depth surveys are a part of our research practice, prize draws are a cost-effective incentive method for encouraging people to participate. If we're running a prize draw we will need a publicly available document explaining the rules of participation and winner selection.

In any document like this, we need to include who is and isn't eligible to participate, including any age restrictions, location restrictions, for example if our organization doesn't work with countries under international economic sanctions, and details for incentive payments (tax considerations, for example).

We should work with our legal and data protection teams to ensure these are correctly worded and contain the right information for our organization.

Collecting sensitive data

How and why sensitive data needs to be handled differently

The European Commission defines personal data that is considered 'sensitive' and is therefore subject to specific processing conditions to be:

- personal data revealing racial or ethnic origin, political opinions, religious or philosophical beliefs

- trade union memberships
- genetic data, biometric data processed solely to identify a human being
- health-related data
- data concerning a person's sex life or sexual orientation
- any (alleged) criminal offences[16]

In the UK, for example, these are referred to as protected characteristics and are protected by law under the Equality Act 2010 (which was updated as of June 2024).

Most organizations will not need to collect this kind of sensitive personal information on a regular basis. But it very much depends on what our organization does. If we are in the field of healthcare or prison reform, for example, we probably will collect such information in all our research.

If we do need to collect sensitive data during research, we should coordinate with our legal, data protection, and diversity, equity and inclusion (DEI) teams, to make sure we are collecting data in the correct and most sensitive way.

We'll need to restrict access to sensitive data more than we would do with other personal data we have collected during the research process. See Chapter 6 for more details.

Liability in data protection

The EU Commission defines a personal data breach as a breach of security leading to the accidental or unlawful destruction, loss, alteration, unauthorized disclosure of, or access to, personal data transmitted, stored or otherwise processed.

If one of the third party tools we use to conduct our research is hacked, the vendor is responsible for notifying us as soon as they become aware of the breach, and we in turn will need to inform the affected people. However, it is the vendor that has legal liability for the breach.

If a breach is caused by our organization, we will have 72 hours to notify the supervisory authority. If the organization's systems have been hacked, for example, the organization is liable for the breach.

If you lose your laptop, it is stolen or you leave it somewhere and you have participants' personal information stored on the hard drive or if you use a tool that isn't GDPR compliant and is not approved by your organization which has a subsequent breach, you can be held personally liable and could be personally fined for a breach. If your organization can show they did everything in their power to protect against a breach, and it is your behaviour as an individual that caused the breach, that is where personal liability comes in.

We are all accountable

Depending on the type of issue, should a data breach happen each of us is accountable and our responsibility as an individual will be evaluated and taken into account; things that will be considered are money lost, wasted employee time, wasted participant time, research wasted, legal and HR involvement, code of conduct issues for the employee and company reputation and risk to people's privacy.

Data protection bad practice is different; it won't necessarily be liable for a fine but it greatly increases the potential for data breaches and non-compliance with regulations. For example, gaining a signature on a consent form retroactively isn't necessarily finable, but it's not actual informed consent, which requires people to opt in to the terms of the session before the session happens, and it can easily lead to no consent being gained – processing people's data without consent is GDPR non-compliance.

Beyond data protection

There may be other regulations that we need to adhere to. The best advice I can give for the long term is to put the effort into having a good working relationship with the relevant teams that are experts in these areas and can provide the necessary support, whether that is legal, risk, compliance.

This is important in the short term as well. If we are reassured that any relevant laws and regulations are being complied with, we can then move on to understand what other operations work is required. It doesn't have to be perfect, but it does need to be good enough, and we can return to these practices and processes in the future to improve them.

Conclusion

Protecting our participants' (past, present and future) data is a legal requirement and is also the ethical thing to do. Data protection strictness varies from country to country. I recommend using the strictest regulations as a standard in all the countries the organization operates in for typical personal data. And when sensitive information is being collected, we have to elevate our protection processes further.

It can be difficult to retain so much information about laws and regulations if you aren't thinking about it on a daily basis. Operations people do tend to think about data regulation and compliance on a daily basis. Whether people are doing research regularly or occasionally, such requirements apply the same. It's important to have documentation/guidance available and support channels for questions to support those doing research to ensure they are compliant during the whole research process.

Such compliance is everyone's responsibility, but operations people tend to lead the charge on this. This means we should also keep up to date with any changes in laws and regulation to assess if processes and practices need to be iterated to comply and then support those doing research to adjust.

Notes

1 C Murray. US data privacy protection laws: A comprehensive guide, Forbes, 2023. www.forbes.com/sites/conormurray/2023/04/21/us-data-privacy-protection-laws-a-comprehensive-guide/?sh=5944b0e05f92 (archived at https://perma.cc/V5HD-Z2R3)

2 S De Silva. New Zealand: Data protection overview, OneTrust Data Guidance, 2023. www.dataguidance.com/notes/new-zealand-data-protection-overview (archived at https://perma.cc/A7A2-FG6Q)

3 B Wolford. What is GDPR, the EU's new data protection law? GDPR.EU, 2024. gdpr.eu/what-is-gdpr/ (archived at https://perma.cc/WC6T-56CZ)

4 B Wolford. What is GDPR, the EU's new data protection law? GDPR.EU, 2024. gdpr.eu/what-is-gdpr/ (archived at https://perma.cc/WC6T-56CZ)

5 ICO. What is personal information: A guide, Information Commissioner's Office, 2024. https://ico.org.uk/for-organisations/uk-gdpr-guidance-and-resources/personal-information-what-is-it/what-is-personal-information-a-guide/ (archived at https://perma.cc/R8YG-QS35) All text content is available under the Open Government Licence v3.0 (www.nationalarchives.gov.uk/doc/open-government-licence/version/3/ (archived at https://perma.cc/6ZTS-9EDT))

6 J Frankenfield. Personally identifiable information (PII): Definition, types, and examples, Investopedia, 2023. www.investopedia.com/terms/p/personally-identifiable-information-pii.asp (archived at https://perma.cc/2WL5-N3LX)

7   Intersoft Consulting. GDPR Recitals No. 26, Intersoft Consulting, 27 April 2016. gdpr-info.eu/recitals/no-26/ (archived at https://perma.cc/6D9Y-3BZ3)

8   Service Manual Team. Managing user research data and participant privacy, GOV.UK, 2018. www.gov.uk/service-manual/user-research/managing-user-research-data-participant-privacy (archived at https://perma.cc/Z2R5-AMTY) All text content is available under the Open Government Licence v3.0 (www.nationalarchives.gov.uk/doc/open-government-licence/version/3/ (archived at https://perma.cc/6ZTS-9EDT))

9   ICO. Right of access, Information Commissioner's Office, 2024. https://ico.org.uk/for-organisations/uk-gdpr-guidance-and-resources/individual-rights/individual-rights/right-of-access/ (archived at https://perma.cc/Q26F-W86Y) All text content is available under the Open Government Licence v3.0 (www.nationalarchives.gov.uk/doc/open-government-licence/version/3/ (archived at https://perma.cc/6ZTS-9EDT))

10   ICO. Right to be informed, Information Commissioner's Office, 2024. https://ico.org.uk/for-organisations/uk-gdpr-guidance-and-resources/individual-rights/individual-rights/right-to-be-informed/ (archived at https://perma.cc/9HS9-NZNA) All text content is available under the Open Government Licence v3.0 (www.nationalarchives.gov.uk/doc/open-government-licence/version/3/ (archived at https://perma.cc/6ZTS-9EDT))

11   ICO. Right to erasure, Information Commissioner's Office, 2024. https://ico.org.uk/for-organisations/uk-gdpr-guidance-and-resources/individual-rights/individual-rights/right-to-erasure/ (archived at https://perma.cc/WK6W-2BD3) All text content is available under the Open Government Licence v3.0 (www.nationalarchives.gov.uk/doc/open-government-licence/version/3/ (archived at https://perma.cc/6ZTS-9EDT))

12   L Irwin. What is legitimate interest under the GDPR? IT Governance, 2024. www.itgovernance.eu/blog/en/the-gdpr-legitimate-interest-what-is-it-and-when-does-it-apply (archived at https://perma.cc/33UH-R7EY); ICO. Legitimate interests, Information Commissioner's Office, 2024. https://ico.org.uk/for-organisations/uk-gdpr-guidance-and-resources/lawful-basis/legitimate-interests/ (archived at https://perma.cc/93BX-4PH5) All text content is available under the Open Government Licence v3.0 (www.nationalarchives.gov.uk/doc/open-government-licence/version/3/ (archived at https://perma.cc/6ZTS-9EDT))

13   Consent Kit. The informed consent checklist for Research Ops people, Consent Kit Resources,2024. consentkit.com/informed-consent-checklist (archived at https://perma.cc/2TFU-CZEC); D Travis. Anatomy of a user research consent form, User Focus, 2018. www.userfocus.co.uk/articles/anatomy-of-a-consent-form.html (archived at https://perma.cc/5SEF-4AQ7)

14   M Komnenic. How to write a privacy policy in 9 easy steps, Termly, 2023. termly.io/resources/guides/how-to-write-a-privacy-policy (archived at https://perma.cc/9Y3F-HE6N)

15 M Komnenic. How to write a privacy policy in 9 easy steps, Termly, 2023. termly.io/resources/guides/how-to-write-a-privacy-policy (archived at https:// perma.cc/9Y3F-HE6N); ICO. Create your own privacy notice, Information Commissioner's Office, 2024. https://ico.org.uk/for-organisations/advice-for-small-organisations/create-your-own-privacy-notice/ (archived at https://perma. cc/9ZA4-7SHG) All text content is available under the Open Government Licence v3.0 (www.nationalarchives.gov.uk/doc/open-government-licence/ version/3/ (archived at https://perma.cc/6ZTS-9EDT))

16 Intersoft Consulting. GDPR personal data, InterSoft Consulting Key Issues, 2024. gdpr-info.eu/issues/personal-data/ (archived at https://perma.cc/3ET4-X5SY); ICO. Special category data, Information Commissioner's Office, 2024. https://ico.org.uk/for-organisations/uk-gdpr-guidance-and-resources/lawful-basis/special-category-data/ (archived at https://perma.cc/N6F8-9XWL) All text content is available under the Open Government Licence v3.0 (www. nationalarchives.gov.uk/doc/open-government-licence/version/3/ (archived at https://perma.cc/6ZTS-9EDT))

4

How to recruit participants

Models for best practice

Without the right participants research of value cannot be done. This chapter will provide templates and guidance on THE effective recruitment of research participants. We will cover:

- deciding the best recruitment method for us
- templates
- guidance
- screener questions
- governance (who can we contact and how)
- panel management

We may think that participant recruitment is very much part of the research process, which it is, but I also see it as part of the infrastructure for a few reasons. Whether we are working with agencies or maintaining our own participant panel, ongoing engagement and strategizing is required to enable consistent and effective recruitment that works for the researchers and the participants alike.

What do we need to do to support participant recruitment?

Participant recruitment, depending on the user target audience, is often time-consuming and perceived as the most burdensome part of the research process. So, however we are able to support recruitment, we need to balance speed with data protection and finding the right people.

What can we do, from the minimum to doing the most? The answer depends on the set-up of the ReOps function; who is doing it and how many, and the number of people doing research. Some research teams are lucky enough to have a recruitment specialist working with them to cover the majority of recruitment tasks and participant engagement work; that is the dream. But if we aren't so blessed, we will need to decide what level of recruitment support is viable.

Another scenario may be one ReOps person to 50 researchers. However superhuman that ReOps might be, they won't have the capacity to recruit participants for 50 people's research as well as doing a multitude of other ReOps work. In this case, providing templates and guidance that researchers can use to self-serve in recruitment is the most practical and pragmatic approach.

We may think in Table 4.1 there is actually a lot of work even in giving the least amount of support when it comes to participant recruitment. It's true that if templates, governance and guidance aren't available, it represents a heavy workload upfront to put such things in place. But there are many reasons why we may want to prioritize this work over other kinds of ReOps work.

TABLE 4.1 Different levels of support you can provide to recruit participants

Doing the least --------------->	--------> intermediate ------->	----------> Doing the most
Providing templates • common screener questions • consent forms • data privacy statement • recruitment brief • recruitment communications • schedule template Governance and guidance • standardized incentive amounts • approved tools • list of approved recruitment agencies	Templates, governance and guidance Aspects of panel management • segmentation • consent management • paying incentives • consent review management	Templates, governance and guidance • full panel management Manage recruitment process start to finish: • agree segmentation • agree schedule • find and screen • invite and book • participant coordination • all logistics • any follow up

Once the templates, etc., have been established, it makes recruitment easier for everyone doing research, reducing the amount of administrative work required, and supporting a consistent recruitment process which benefits everyone. This consistency is important because it reduces GDPR risks. Participants know what to expect, no matter who in the organization is contacting them to participate in research. All potential participants and actual participants will receive the same information, in the right tone of voice for the organization which will comply with regulations and support the building of trust between participant and researching organization.

Templates will need to be reviewed, maintained and updated, but this is much easier to do once the initial infrastructure is in place.

Consent form and data privacy templates can be found in Chapter 3.

What are the best methods of recruitment for us?

There are many recruitment strategies at our disposal. Which one will work best for us will depend on the type of participants we are looking for, as well as the time and budget we have available. Table 4.2 lays out various recruitment strategies, what they are good for and what to consider if we are going to employ these strategies.

TABLE 4.2 Recruitment strategies

Recruitment method	What it is good for	Things to consider
Professional recruitment agency	Specialized users General users if you can't do it yourself Potential customers	Expensive Low effort for you Speed of recruitment will depend on the type of person you are looking
Automated recruiting platforms (external)	General users	Medium cost, relatively quick recruitment but only for the most general characteristics
Intercepts (in person)	Specific people in a certain location, e.g. industry event	High effort Time consuming Won't necessarily get the right people

(continued)

TABLE 4.2 (Continued)

Recruitment method	What it is good for	Things to consider
Intercepts (digital)	Specific people currently using your digital products and services or prospective customers	Low cost, low effort, but focuses on people who are already aware of the organization
Internal participant panels	Specific people who currently or previously have interacted with your organization	Low cost, medium effort and speed in recruitment turnaround time
Referrals	Specific people/specialized users	Asking current participants to refer colleagues, family, friends is likely to produce quick results with relevant people but if it's your only recruitment method it is likely to be relatively biased sampling
Marketing and sales lists	Specific people who currently or previously have interacted with your organization	Low cost, medium effort and speed in recruitment turnaround time but you must have permission to use these lists
Cold calling and cold emailing, cold messaging on social media, online forums and community groups	People with specific characteristics Potential customers	High effort for potentially low reward. Risk annoying people with unsolicited contact – needs a communication template to ensure the right information is included Contact details need to be publicly available

Things we will need, whatever recruitment methods we are using

Recruitment brief

This is useful for any circumstance, whether a recruitment agency will be doing the recruitment, someone internally is supporting the recruitment process fully, someone internally is supporting the recruitment process partially or the researcher is doing the recruitment themselves and this is part of the documentation process so research can be reused in the future.

TABLE 4.3 Recruitment brief template

Research details	
Dates	
Location	
Length (of research session or survey, etc.)	
If applicable, session times to schedule in people	
If applicable, incentive amount	
Participant characteristics required Qualifying criteria Disqualifying criteria	
Number of participants needed (altogether and per identified user group)	
Description of research purpose	
Contact details of researcher or ReOps person	

Table 4.3 includes the most common components to include in our recruit-ment brief. It's not an exhaustive list, but it's a good place to start.

We may want to provide a sample size calculator to support robust recruitment.

Participant characteristics that we are looking for will inform the screener questions we need to ask. Under GDPR, we only ask for the information we need, so we need to think about what the important characteristics are for our participant wish list. This will depend on the purpose of the research and the intended user group:

- **Demographics:** Not all demographic elements may be important to who we want to be involved in the research. Does age, gender or location matter? If yes, then include them in our recruitment criteria; if not, we don't need to ask about them.
- **Behaviour:** What types of tasks/actions do we need our participants to typically do or not do for the purposes of the research?
  o We may need to ask about *confidence levels* in doing these actions.
  o We may need to ask about *experience levels* in doing these actions.
  o Level of confidence and level of experience aren't necessarily synonymous.

- What **technology and devices** will be used to do these tasks and actions?
- **Language proficiency level** – do we need to include the use of interpreters for certain participants to participate, for example?
- **Access needs:** Do we need to make any adjustments for participants to be able to participate, or are we doing specific accessibility research in which we need a certain type or range of access needs?

Screener questions

Having standardized screener questions helps us to ensure that the right kinds of participants are being recruited and the potential for bias is reduced, because everyone is using robust, well-worded screener questions.

First we need to work out what are the common questions the researchers need to ask. There will always be additional questions for specific research objectives, but there will be questions that are always relevant to the research our organization does, as shown in Table 4.4.

TABLE 4.4 Examples of screener questions

Tell us about yourself	Description
Name	Consider using one field for name as not every culture has first and last names
Contact details	Ask for email or phone – only the one you need
I am currently based in (territory/ country):	Being geopolitically sensitive means acknowledging that not all locations where people live are considered a country
I prefer to use this device for doing [x] task	Give options in closed questions where possible, rather than it being all open text fields, which takes more time for the participant to fill in and more time for you to process
Language proficiency	The Common European Framework of Reference for Languages (CEFR) is useful for understanding what languages people are comfortable with and at what level
	It presents 34 scales of listening, reading, spoken interaction, spoken production and writing activities

SOURCE Council of Europe. Self-assessment grid – Table 2 (CEFR 3.3): Common reference levels, Council of Europe, 2024. www.coe.int/en/web/common-european-framework-reference-languages/table-2-cefr-3.3-common-reference-levels-self-assessment-grid

The tone of voice used in all forms of communication with participants will depend on the organization we work for/with and the nature of the research. Where possible, and if appropriate, use conversational design to help put participants at ease. We do this because sharing personal information at any stage of the research process can feel like a vulnerable position to be in.

Sensitive information and protected characteristic screener questions

Asking for sensitive data during the screening process is when it is most important to have standardized questions that have been approved by the relevant legal and DEI teams, depending on the type of data we need.

If we are asking sensitive questions for the first time, the Office for National Statistics (ONS) in the UK is an excellent resource for guidance on how to ask sensitive questions. They have done extensive research to run the UK population census every 10 years. They cover, among other characteristics, questions on:

- sex
- gender identity
- sexual orientation
- living arrangements
- ethnicity
- health status

The ONS also provides guidance for survey respondents on how to answer particularly sensitive questions, such as those about sex and gender. How the ONS ask their questions may not be suitable for our participant populations, but it is a good starting point for considering how to most appropriately and sensitively ask questions (www.ons.gov.uk). If we aren't in the UK, there is likely to be a similar organization in our location.

The most important thing to remember is sex and gender are two different things and we must respect how people identify – people are who they say they are. Sexual orientation is not related to people's sex or their gender. Labels are ever evolving, and that's a good thing. Language is not static and neither is our understanding of the spectrums people live on. So we need to know how to talk about things like sex and gender and sexual orientation sensitively and respectfully. Even the most sensitive and empathic of us can find it difficult to adjust to new things and not make assumptions about who people are. But we can't assume who people are and how they identify by how they look, what they sound like, their name, their age, their mannerisms and their gender performance.

Because language is still evolving, that means we need to check in with such screener questions we might need to use on a relatively regular basis, because what is appropriate now may not be as appropriate in two years' time.

Being diverse and inclusive from the start

Diversity and inclusion falls into two main categories when it comes to research operations, internal and external – both are fundamentally necessary.

External diversity and inclusion

By this I mean the infrastructure is set up to enable research with external customers to be done in a diverse and inclusive way:

- We are actively recruiting for different kinds of access need.
- We are actively recruiting for a range of experiences.
- We have tools, etc., that enable anyone to participate in research, whoever they are.

Internal diversity and inclusion

By 'internally' I mean that research practice is designed to be inclusive of the needs of people doing research and diversity and inclusion are core to the recruitment processes when building our teams. Internal DEI is covered in Chapter 2 and Part Two. It is very hard to do external diversity and inclusion if we don't have internal diversity and inclusion.

There have long been laws against discrimination for what in the UK are called 'protected characteristics'. This is covered by the UK Equality Act. Not discriminating against people in the digital world, for example, has been written into law in some countries for about a decade now, and it's becoming increasingly prominent.

For example, the UK government requires their services to be accessible to all those who need them, and in the EU the European Accessibility Act is coming into force in 2025.[1]

It's important to acknowledge if our organization has a lot of legacy systems (and tech debt) that aren't accessible by design; it requires a lot of effort, time and money to rectify. It's important to do so, which is why more and more laws are being enforced, to ensure that organizations are non-discriminatory.[2]

Accessibility and access needs

An access need can be considered anything a person requires in order to fully participate in their environment or community. Access needs can be physical, mental or emotional and may require changes to the standard practices of our organization. Remember, all access needs are valid and must be respected.[3]

When we are recruiting for access needs, we have to think carefully about what information we need to know about a person's needs in order to enable them to participate in the research.

If we don't need to know about specific disabilities and conditions, then don't ask, because this is sensitive data and will need to follow the specific processes of collecting sensitive data (see Chapter 3). And not all access needs and adaptations that people use are related to diagnosed conditions. Rather than asking about why someone might need to use a device or change settings from the standard to make things easier to use, ask them about what changes they make and how they make the changes.

For example, ask them what they use to make it easier to use the internet and computers, which devices, software and extensions they use to browse, if visual adaptations are for reading, how they use devices and software to interact with others and which other adaptive devices they may use (such as head pointers and keyguards).

We can ask questions about:

- **What software or devices do people use to help them browse the internet?** This could include, screen readers, screen magnification, speech recognition, captions or translation tools.

- **Do people change the appearance of websites to make them easier to read?** Are they changing font type, font size, colour contrast, or screen overlays?

- **Do people use devices or software to make it easier to interact with people online?** These might include speech generating devices, fluency assistance, text to speech, or voice typing systems.

- **Do people use adaptive devices?** They could be using an alternative mouse and keyboard, key guard, vibration feedback, eye gaze tools or head-pointers.

We may also consider using something like the Digital Inclusion Scale to help us understand how much people do or don't do online.[4]

As with the Common European Framework of Reference for Languages that I referenced when talking about language proficiency screener questions, it is better to give people a range of scenarios for how they do something or how comfortable or confident they feel doing something than to simply rate their confidence level. Identifying what scenario resonates with them will give us a more accurate assessment of their capabilities than a self-assessment of rating our confidence from 1 to 5, as people will tend to over- or underestimate themselves.

An example of this is asking people to assess how confident they are about reading in a particular language.

Rating scale version:

Rate your confidence in reading in English with 1 being not confident at all and 7 being very confident.

Scenario version:

Rate your confidence in reading in English:

1 I can't comfortably read the language, even if I'm comfortable with the spoken language.

2 I can recognize familiar names, words and very simple sentences.

3 I can read simple content on personal topics and longer work-related material.

4 I can read everyday personal content and well-structured job-related material.

5 I can read lengthy work-related articles and understand contemporary informal writing.

6 I can read specialized articles, technical instructions, and complex factual and literary content.

7 I can effortlessly read virtually all forms of written language.

This is based on work I did with Rita Duarte in 2024, based on the Common European Framework of Reference for Languages for screening research participants at Springer Nature.

We should think broadly about where those access needs arise. The best description I have found is the Microsoft Inclusivity Toolkit (inclusive. microsoft.design) as mismatched human interactions which can be permanent, temporary or situational (as shown in Table 4.5).

TABLE 4.5 Permanent, temporary and situational access needs

	Permanent	Temporary	Situational
Touch	A person who has one arm	A person with a broken arm	A person holding a baby
Sight	A person who is blind	A person with cataracts	A person distracted while driving
Hearing	A person who is deaf	A person with an ear infection	A person trying to hear in a loud environment
Speaking	A person who is non-verbal	A person who has laryngitis	A person trying to talk in a loud environment
Cognition	A person with a learning disability	A person with concussion	A person who is very stressed

SOURCE Adapted from: Microsoft. Inclusive Microsoft design, Microsoft, 2016. inclusive.microsoft. design/tools-and-activities/Inclusive101Guidebook.pdf

When we look through this lens we all need support to go about our lives at one time or another, or throughout our lives. Therefore, everyone has access needs and it's not in fact a small percentage of our customer base, but all of them, and we can add another dimension for a more in-depth understanding of how people are interacting with our products and services by combining it with the (digital) inclusion scale. If our products aren't digital we can make it any kind of inclusion scale that is appropriate for the context (see Figure 4.1).

Adding the needs and inclusion together, we create a matrix which we can plot participants on for a particular research project. Another way to use the matrix is to plot personas in particular scenarios and use these scenarios to test how accessible our product or service is, as demonstrated in Figure 4.2.

We can repurpose the matrix to consider and visually plot environmental access needs, for example (see Figure 4.3). There are multiple ways the matrix could be adapted, again depending on circumstances. Environmental access needs are pertinent for my work within the field of science.

Imagine Grayson, who is a geologist, and is currently out doing fieldwork in a remote mountain range. They are connected to the world by running their laptop and smartphone off a solar powered battery pack and an intermittent 4G hotspot. Grayson has received feedback after peer review about a journal article they submitted from their previous fieldwork trip. To enable

Grayson to make updates to that journal article a publisher needs to provide a lightweight online service for them to do that, with their current set-up in the field. Otherwise, Grayson may miss a deadline, or the process will be significantly delayed because Grayson must wait until they have finished their fieldwork and are back in a place with a reliable internet connection and power supply.

FIGURE 4.1 Assistive needs template

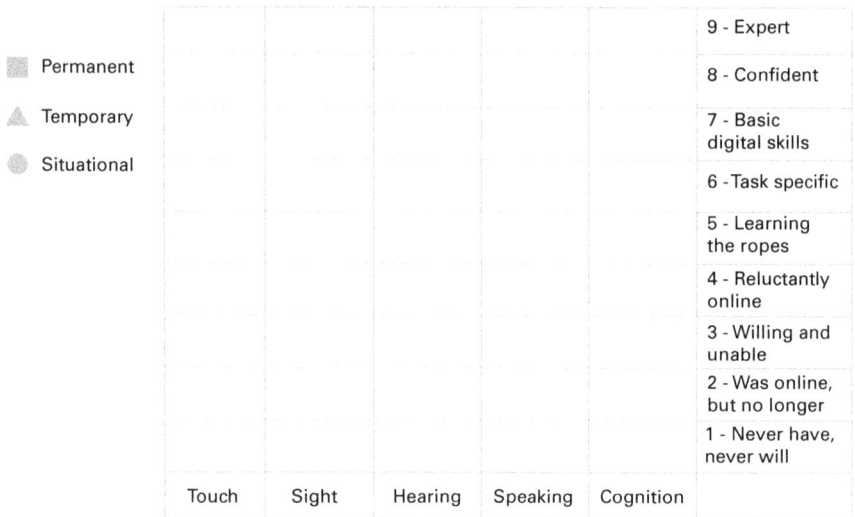

FIGURE 4.2 Example of mapping participants on the assistive needs matrix

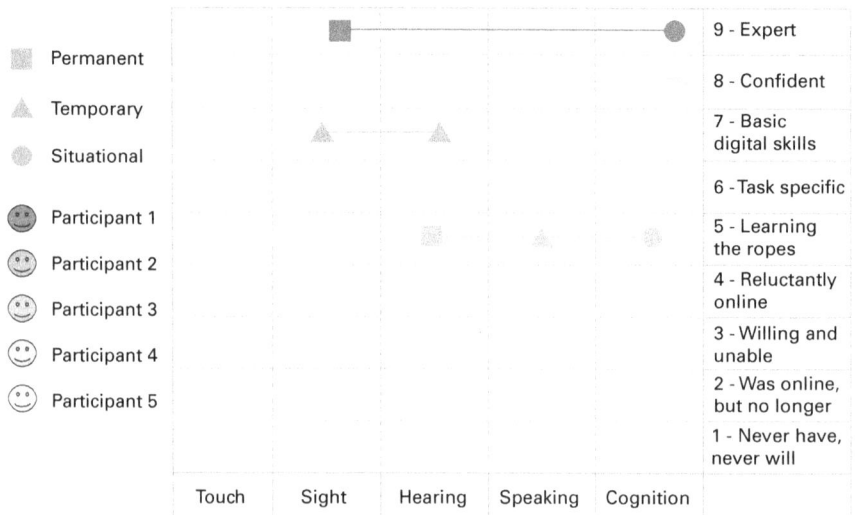

FIGURE 4.3 Assistive needs matrix adapted

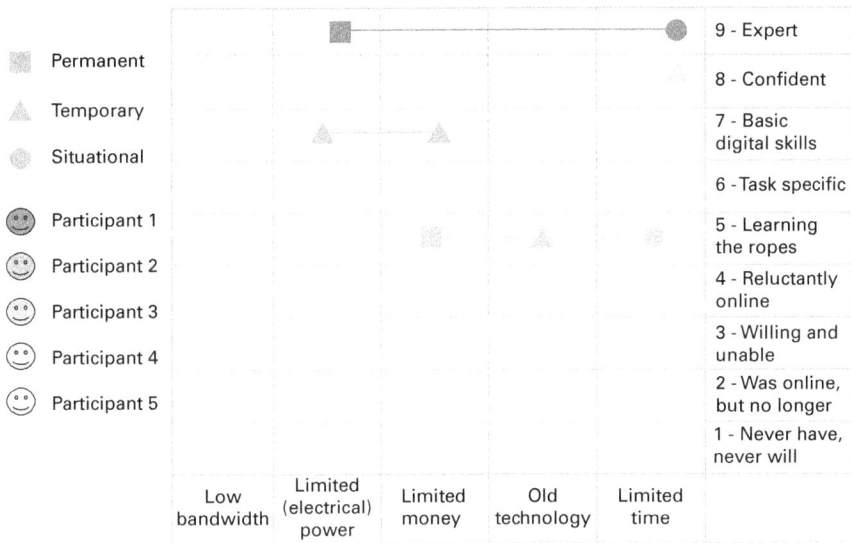

Permanent

Temporary

Situational

Participant 1

Participant 2

Participant 3

Participant 4

Participant 5

9 - Expert

8 - Confident

7 - Basic
digital skills

6 - Task specific

5 - Learning
the ropes

4 - Reluctantly
online

3 - Willing and
unable

2 - Was online,
but no longer

1 - Never have,
never will

Low
bandwidth

Limited
(electrical)
power

Limited
money

Old
technology

Limited
time

Using proxies as participants

In certain circumstances it may not be possible to talk directly to the intended user group, or the impacted user group. People with chronic illnesses, for example, may not be able to participate in a research session or complete a survey, but their carer may be an appropriate proxy to understand the person who is living with chronic illnesses' experience.

Recruitment communication templates

In order to provide a consistent experience to all participants and potential participants through the recruitment process, it is useful to have templates available for each type of communication that is needed. These include:

- invite and screener
- successful screening and next steps (unmoderated study)
- successful screening and next steps (moderated study)
- unsuccessful screening with thanks
- thank you for participating in the session (and incentive details)

Table 4.6 documents the kind of information that needs to be included in each of these communication templates.

TABLE 4.6 What to include in recruitment communication templates

Template	What to include
Invite and screener	**Eyecatching subject** to get attention **General topic** but not too much detail at this point to avoid bias in participants' screener question answers **Date range** of research so participants can determine whether they are available and it's worth applying to participate **Effort required to apply to participate** (e.g. 2 minutes to answers some questions and the research session will be 45 minutes) **Benefits of participating** (e.g. incentive amount) **Link to screener** [clear call to action]
Successful screening and next steps (unmoderated)	**Subject line** that clarifies successful screening and call to action **Set expectations** of the unmoderated study (type of study, type of tech they need, e.g. will they need to download a browser extension) **Deadline** – when does the study close? **Reminder of incentive** **Link to study**
Successful screening and next steps (moderated)	**Subject line** that clarifies successful screening and call to action **Link to calendar** to book a session **Set expectations** of the study (type of study, type of tech they need, e.g. will they need to download a browser extension?) **Deadline** – when does the study close? **Reminder of incentive**
Confirmation of session booking	**Subject line** that clarifies moderated research session has been booked **Confirmation** of time and date of session and session length **Set expectations** of the study (type of study and topic) **Add to calendar link**, with tool link (e.g. Zoom link) **Reminder of incentive**
Unsuccessful screening	**Subject line** that clarifies unsuccessful screening **Thanks** for taking the time to apply
Thank you for participating	**Subject line** that say thanks and a call to action to claim incentive **Thank you message** **Link to incentive/incentive details**
[Optional] Reminder email – participation	It's best not to book sessions too far in the future. However, if this is unavoidable have a reminder email set up for 1 or 2 days before the session takes place or the unmoderated study closes to remind people of the details – which can include the same information as the confirmation emails
[Optional] Reminder email – screener	If you are experiencing a low response rate, you can send one reminder email for those who haven't responded to the screener. Leave a reasonable amount of time before sending

SOURCE L Burnam. How to write compelling research invite emails (with templates and examples), User Interviews, 2023. www.userinterviews.com/blog/research-invite-email-examples-templates

Governance

What kind of governance might we need? That will depend on the context of our organization and our research. There are a few elements that are probably true for everyone, such as how often we can contact any one potential participant in a quarter or year, to invite them to participate in research. For example, if someone has participated in research, they cannot be invited again for 90 days, if appropriate.

It is important to have governance around who we can and cannot contact. There are a lot of potential internal resources to recruit from but the first thing to do is to make sure that whoever is doing the recruitment can access internal data and can legally contact people contained in the internal databases.

Terms and conditions of signing up to a product need to include a clause that by signing up the person consents to being contacted about research participation invitations. But we also need to give people the ability to opt out of being contacted subsequently. We must check whether the terms and conditions allow for this. If not, we can work with the owners of the data, to see if they can contact potential participants on our behalf and the potential participants can actively opt in to us having their details to invite them to participate in the research.

Standardized incentives

Incentivizing participants to take part in research is industry standard for both user and market research. To make incentivizing participants fair and consistent, it is useful to have a framework for how much to incentivize a participant, perhaps depending on the time and effort required to participate in the research, for example. So participating in a one-time 30-minute interview will be incentivized differently to participating in a 10-day diary study, where diary entries are required each day and the participant will also be interviewed before and after the diary study period takes place. User Interviews (a research participant platform) has a very useful guide and incentive calculator we can use to determine what incentives we should be providing.[5]

There are various platforms that can be used to pay incentives, such as Tremendous, which doesn't require us personally expensing the cost of the incentive, but all of them come with restrictions in terms of countries that

they serve. If there is a circumstance where we do need to expense participant incentives because the only available method was a bank-to-bank
transfer, it is likely that we will need to provide a clear explanation as to
why we are personally sending a past, current or potential customer money.
To reassure the finance department that we aren't bribing people or commit-
ting some kind of fraud, we should provide them with the details of the
research and the person's participation. It is important to clarify that
research incentives aren't gifts but are reimbursement for the person's time.
There are different tax rules for gifts and reimbursement. There may be
other details that our finance department needs. If possible, talk to them
before paying the incentives that need to be expensed so they know it will
happen and we know what information we need to provide them.

There will be certain circumstances when we are not able to incentivize
participants. We may have no budget to provide incentives. Or if the participant is a public servant and they are taking part in the research in this
capacity, many countries have rules that mean public servants cannot receive
'cash gifts', even though the incentive is not actually a gift, it's included in
the restrictions. Therefore, we may have to consider alternatives to cash
incentives. If we have an incentive budget available, we can offer to donate
to a charity on the participant's behalf. It may be that we can let the participant choose the charity, or it may be best that we choose an appropriate
charity; it's best to check with our compliance department to ensure no
conflicts of interest. If we do not have a budget available for incentives,
consider producing (relatively) regular newsletters for participants to share
what the research insights have been used for (within reason, e.g. don't share
commercially sensitive information). It's not free as it will take someone
time and effort to produce a decent newsletter, but demonstrating to participants they have provided valuable insight and made a difference to whatever
our organization does can be an effective incentive.

List of recruitment agencies

If working with recruitment agencies is something that our organization
does on a regular basis, it is worth maintaining a list of approved agencies
and what kind of recruitment they are good for. Not all research recruitment
agencies were created equal, and we need to make sure that we work with
reputable agencies that comply with laws and regulations and find high-
quality participants in an appropriate way.

Participant panel management

What is a participant panel?

A research panel is a list of people who have opted in to being contacted and participating in our research and they have agreed for us to hold a certain amount of information about them. Panels can be large or small. We may use a relatively small panel for a limited time – for example 30 people to participate in a diary study or a private beta phase. We can contact them on a regular basis to share feedback, but once the specified period has come to a close, these participants shouldn't be invited to participate in research for a period of time, to avoid bias. A large participant panel, often referred to as a participant database, has thousands of opted-in members. Members of databases can remain there for as long as they want, or as long as they are still a part of the target audience for research. Because we are sampling from a larger group, there is less risk of bias and participant fatigue.

When to build our own panel

Depending on who our intended customer group is for participants and the topic of research, it can take a lot of time and effort to find the right people. Frequency, subject matter, scope and scale are all areas of consideration as to when a panel may be needed. If the organization has the need for regular recruiting of niche criteria over a longer period of time, this is the time to consider building our own panel.[6]

Where I work at the time of writing, Springer Nature (a science publisher), is an excellent example of a genuine need to build our own participant panel. The organization has more than 10 researchers and more than 30 designers that do research on a regular basis, with an audience of scientists submitting to publish their research. With approximately 8 million scientists in the world, this is a niche group of people, considering the (very roughly) approximate number of people of working age in the world is 5.4 billion.

THE BENEFITS OF MANAGING OUR OWN PANEL

You have the ability to recruit niche participants quickly; as we have an engaged audience that have signed up to be contacted and if doing multiple research projects per month, the cost of managing your own panel, compared with always working with a recruitment agency, is much lower.[7]

WHAT WE NEED TO KNOW BEFORE BUILDING OUR OWN PANEL

We will need someone with the right expertise and enough time to manage the panel. We will need recruitment strategies in place to keep replenishing the panel with the appropriate mix of people, otherwise we risk participant fatigue if users are contacted too frequently about participating in studies. We risk bias in our data collection if we are sampling from too small a pool of people.

WHAT IS NEEDED FOR MANAGING A PANEL?

- *A GDPR compliant tool* that will allow us to manage people's personal data: contact details, demographics and other criteria it's essential for us to hold about the people who have signed up to our database.

- *A sign-up form* to collect those essential details and allow any panel members to read the relevant terms and conditions, that will set the expectations to being a part of the panel. A panel sign-up form will most likely be made up of your common screener questions. Ensure there is a mechanism to allow panel members to keep their details up to date and accurate.

- *A process for conducting consent reviews* on a regular cadence (for example, annually), to ensure that people still want to be members of the participant panel.

- The ability to *provide support to researchers* who are using the panel for recruitment and panel members, if they have any questions or concerns.

- As mentioned previously, *recruitment strategies* will need to be implemented to ensure there is a regular influx of new panel members.

- A deep *understanding of the make-up of our customer population*, so that recruitment strategies can be tailored to ensure the panel members are a relatively accurate representation of the customer population.

- A clear understanding of what our panel size needs to be, again depending on our customer population.

- And someone to remove the low-quality participants from the database.[8]

Recruitment tools

There are many tools out there that can help us with our research recruitment. Some tools support all the recruitment related tasks:

- participant panel management

- inviting, screening and scheduling research sessions
- delivering consent forms
- paying incentives

If we have the budget, it is very effort effective to have a tool that can do it all. It cuts down on the amount of administration that is required and it reduces the number of places that participants' personal details are stored. There are also tools that can do each of these tasks individually. If we don't have the budget for the tool that does everything, audit the internal tools to see what can be used for our purposes and what gaps we are left with.

A common scenario, depending on the type of organization we are working in, could be that we can make use of *an internal CRM* (customer relationship management system) to manage the participant panel, *a digital contract signing tool* (being used by HR) to manage consent forms, *a calendar app* such as Calendly to book meetings with clients can be used for booking research sessions and *a survey tool* and email client for inviting and screening.

In this scenario the only tool gap that exists is a way to pay participant incentives and there are many low-cost options out there for this task. As we can see, it is possible to create a recruitment process based on tools the organization already has, but it will require more effort to train people doing research to use the process, and to document the process, and it will take more effort to do the recruitment itself. Any tool we use must comply with data protection regulations that we need to follow. And in this scenario each tool itself is GDPR compliant, but using multiple tools in this way does require a lot more data management to keep track of where participant details are stored, and if a participant makes a GDPR erasure request, for example, we need to audit every tool for their details to remove them.

Effective recruitment of research participants is vital for valuable research outcomes. In this chapter we have looked at comprehensive guidance and templates to streamline this process, from deciding on the best recruitment methods to maintaining participant panels and managing governance. Successful participant recruitment involves balancing speed with data protection, ensuring inclusivity, and maintaining consistent and respectful communication. By establishing robust templates and strategies, we can reduce administrative burdens, enhance the participant experience, and uphold data security and compliance standards. Ultimately, the goal is to create a sustainable and efficient recruitment infrastructure that benefits both researchers and participants.

Notes

1   European Commission. European Accessibility Act: Q&A. Employment, Social Affairs & Inclusion, European Commission, 2024. ec.europa.eu/social/main.jsp?catId=1202&intPageId=5581&langId=en (archived at https://perma.cc/LR8V-YF2T)

2   Level Access. Navigating international accessibility laws, Level Access, 2024. www.levelaccess.com/blog/navigating-international-accessibility-laws/ (archived at https://perma.cc/QU4F-U27H); B Gokulnath. Accessibility laws around the world: A comprehensive overview, Hurix Digital, 2024. www.hurix.com/accessibility-laws-around-the-world-a-comprehensive-overview (archived at https://perma.cc/4AXV-T3DR); S Fjeld. Accessibility laws worldwide, Eye-Able, 2024. eye-able.com/blog/accessibility-laws-worldwide (archived at https://perma.cc/J94Z-LA8B)

3   Youth Friendly. How to meet access needs through outreach, Youth Friendly, 2016. www.youthfriendly.com/blog/access-needs-youth (archived at https://perma.cc/MN2M-XACV)

4   A Collins Rees. Reflecting on how we developed the digital inclusion scale, User Research in Government Blog, 2019. userresearch.blog.gov.uk/2019/02/22/reflecting-on-how-we-developed-the-digital-inclusion-scale/ (archived at https://perma.cc/UXU2-XEH5)

5   User Interviews. User research incentives, User Interviews, 2024. www.userinterviews.com/ux-research-field-guide-chapter/ux-research-incentives (archived at https://perma.cc/ZK9B-ZFSN); User Interviews. The user research incentive calculator, User Interviews, 2024. www.userinterviews.com/lp/ux-research-incentive-calculator (archived at https://perma.cc/9Q3C-DDSH)

6   D DeSanto. Creating and managing a research participant panel, The GitLab Handbook, 2024. handbook.gitlab.com/handbook/product/ux/ux-research/research-panel-management/ (archived at https://perma.cc/NZ96-4D7J)

7   P Hesketh. Research panel management: The complete guide to building and managing research panels. Consent Kit, 2023. consentkit.com/research-panel-management (archived at https://perma.cc/MW27-S9XW)

8   P Hesketh. Research panel management: The complete guide to building and managing research panels. Consent Kit, 2023. consentkit.com/research-panel-management (archived at https://perma.cc/MW27-S9XW)

5

How to manage data, information and knowledge

Like all aspects of research and research operations, there is a range of activities and strategies that we can focus on when it comes to data, information and knowledge management, depending on our capacity and capabilities.

From my experience and knowledge, and working with knowledgeable people who are specialists in the area, we need to start with data and information management to create the building blocks of good practices that will enable us to do effective and sustainable knowledge management. Knowledge management is some of the most sophisticated work we can do when it comes to research operations.[1] To me this means there is a lot of groundwork to do before we are ready to start embedding governance and practices related to knowledge management, as shown in Figure 5.1.

FIGURE 5.1 Building blocks of knowledge management

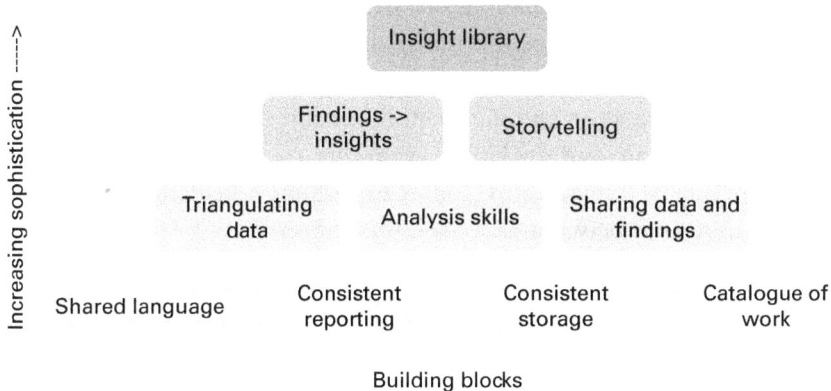

Data and information management are the foundation, but they're also a necessity for doing compliant research. But, let's start with some definitions.

What is data management?

Data management is the practice of collecting, processing (organizing and analysing), storing, accessing and maintaining data securely, efficiently and cost effectively for use in informing business decisions.[2]

What is information management?

Information management is the collection, storage, curation, dissemination, archiving and destruction of documents, images, drawings and other sources of information.[3]

What is knowledge management?

Knowledge management is the practice/discipline of identifying, creating, organizing, storing, using, accessing and retrieving, evaluating, and sharing knowledge within an organization to improve efficiency, decision-making and innovation.[4]

As you can see, the definitions of the management of data, information and knowledge are very similar. The activities of management of these things are in essence the same. But data, information and knowledge are different things, so the management of one, is not necessarily the same as the management of another. When I started writing this, I didn't think we'd get to this place, but here we are.

Let's define what data, information and knowledge themselves are, to help us understand what is required to manage them. What is data? Data is factual information such as facts or numbers (e.g. measurements and statistics), which are collected, examined and used to help decision-making.[5] What is information? Information is facts, news or knowledge about a situation, person or event. Information is knowledge obtained from investigation, study or instruction.[6]

So data is information and information is data? And information is also knowledge? Does anyone else have a headache?

Before we make things more complex by defining knowledge, let's understand the difference between data and information.

What is data?

Data is raw facts, that is, unprocessed and unorganized; it has not yet been interpreted in any way. Data is an individual unit. A raw fact, a measurement, is an individual unit of data.

What is information?

Information is data that has been processed, organized and interpreted to add meaning and value. Information depends on data to exist, and the actions that are taken with the data create information, including grouping data together and giving context to create meaning.[7] So now we have a clearer picture of data and information.

What is knowledge?

The dictionary definition of knowledge is the state of knowing about or being familiar with something, gained through experience or association.[8] For the purposes of knowledge management, there are two key types of knowledge:

o tacit knowledge: gained through experience and intuitively understood

o explicit knowledge: documented and shared with others

We use information to gain knowledge of a thing. We process data to create information and we process information to create knowledge. So knowledge management, for us in the context of research operations, is the process of taking tacit knowledge gained through doing customer research and making it explicit knowledge for an organization to use.

You may be wondering why I have got into the weeds of these definitions. I do this not just because I have information science degrees, but because it's very common for people to jump straight to solutions and tools. 'We need a tool to manage our knowledge' (you can replace knowledge with insights, which we'll get into later). Or, 'We need a tool to manage our data' etc., etc. But if we jump straight to a tool, we will likely end up with something that is unmanageable and unused. A tool is a means to manage these things, not the thing itself (thing being data, information and knowledge). We need to understand the things we are trying to manage and how to manage them, because they need different means of management (tools, governance and practices). DiLeo describes this as magical thinking.[9]

In research operations we need all three of these practices – data, information and knowledge management – and we will consider all three in turn, starting with data management (circling back to where we started, before going on a definition side-quest).

Data management for research operations

Whether covering data collection, processing, storage and access, and maintenance and archiving everything must be done considering compliance. This means data security, privacy and protection are considered in every step. In essence the tools, processes and practices we are using for data management must be GDPR compliant.

Data collection in customer research

These are the specialist tools we use in research to collect customer data (whether that data has personal identifiable elements or not, see Chapter 3). This will include tools for both passive and active data collection.

ACTIVE DATA COLLECTION TOOLS

These are those tools where customers actively and intentionally decide to share things about themselves with us. They include:

- survey tools (digital and physical)
- tools to record moderated research sessions (remote meeting tools, recording tools, etc.)
- unmoderated research tools that record screens, as well as voice and face (such as UserTesting, UserZoom, Loom, Indeemo, Loop11, etc., many of which also have functionality for moderated research)
- participant management tools (also data storage tools) for collecting details about people who choose to engage with our research on a semi regular basis
- feedback tools and suggestion boxes

PASSIVE DATA COLLECTION TOOLS

These are tools that customers opt into or out of depending whether they accept cookies on a website, if we are thinking digitally. Tools such as:

- passive screen recording (e.g. Hotjar)
- A/B and multivariate testing tools (e.g. Optimizely)
- digital analytics (e.g. Google Analytics)
- monitoring tools (e.g. social media, trend analysis)
- observation (in physical spaces – paper, tablets, etc.)

Where does observation and ethnography sit? I think in terms of customer research data collection this is a combination of active and passive interaction with the researcher, but the 'research subject' is aware and has consented to participate in the research.

Data processing in customer research

Data processing involves techniques and tools we use to turn our individual units of data into information (and subsequently into knowledge).

This section will focus on data that we have collected ourselves to process.

In terms of customer research, data processing includes data cleaning, organizing and analysing and visualization. We use different tools for this depending on the type of data we've collected:

- statistical analysis tools (e.g. Q Research)
- qualitative data analysis tools (Notion, Miro, for video e.g. Dovetail, for content e.g. Condens)
- data visualization tools (e.g. Tableau, Hotjar heatmaps)
- spreadsheets can be used for data cleaning and analysis

Data storage in customer research

We can store digital data in tools such as Google Team Drive and Microsoft Sharepoint. Physical data should be stored in a locked cupboard or filing cabinet.

TOOLS THAT DO IT ALL IN CUSTOMER RESEARCH

There are many tools that span data collection, processing and storage groups or processing and storage, such as survey tools, or specialist tools such as Optimal Workshop, Dovetail or Hotjar.

Data management, GDPR and data ethics

Data management and managing the research process are intrinsic to each other (see Chapter 5). Part of tracking the research process and all the passive and active research data collection that is happening at any one time gives us important information for our data management.

- We need to know that only tools that meet organization standards for accessibility, security, privacy and protection for collecting data, processing and storing are being used.
- We need to know what tools are being used at any one time to minimize the impact on customers. Particularly in terms of digital experiences, we want to avoid using too many tools that are going to slow down and disrupt what they are doing, such as using tools that require extra processing or having five different pop-up requests and messages for feedback and research participation in one session.

- We need to know that data is being collected in an ethical way that does no harm.
- We need to know where the data is stored, so that it can be accessed and deleted when requested by customers (see Chapter 3).
- We need control over the budget spent on tools.

What do we need to do to support data management?

We need to provide governance and guidance regarding the data management processes and tools that we are going to use in our organization. This is actually what will become our information management practices and processes, and will be covered later in the chapter.

It's important to highlight here that data can also get trapped in silos, in the different tools we use to do the research, of which there are often many, one tool for card sorting and tree testing, another for running usability and interview sessions, a tool for surveys, etc. It's not always easy to, and depending on data processing agreements and regulations we may not want to move data from one tool to another. So what happens if we need to store our data in multiple places? This is tricky and I don't have a good answer, but one thing we can do is link them together. As in, document where the data is stored and where it can be accessed.[10]

Information management for customer research

For me, information management for research operations is ensuring that all the supporting documentation, governance and guidance to enable people to do research is stored in a known place, is easily accessible and understandable by those who need it and conforms to agreed standards, meaning it will meet the needs and expectations of those using it.

I think of this place where we curate the supporting documentation as a research repository. This is a tool, but it is also more than a tool. There are also policies and practices that are required for successful information management.

A research repository can be as simple as a spreadsheet with a list of links and descriptions to the supporting documentation available, or it may be one folder in a shared drive where everyone knows they go for supporting documentation. However, we can also use specialist tools such as Guru or Confluence, etc., which will enable us to implement our policies.

What policies do we need to have documented when it comes to data and information management?

- an agreed cadence for reviewing, updating or archiving data and information
- governance on which tools are approved for data collection, processing and storage
- a process for when a tool functionality gap is identified
- policy for who can access raw data and what for
- guidance on which tools should be used when (e.g. this tool is good for that technique)
- how-to guide(s) (if appropriate) on data collection and processing
- information architecture for data storage places and naming conventions for research artefacts stored in them
- defined and agreed metadata for describing research artefacts
- GDPR and ethics policies
- participant recruitment policies and guidance
- templates used in the research process
  - brief and plan
  - discussion guides
  - reporting

To help everyone use information that will become knowledge, we need a shared research vocabulary, which needs to be logical, memorable, easy to integrate into current workflows and processes, can be used by everyone (researchers and non-researchers alike), follows existing standards and avoids jargon.

Having a shared language requires consistency; this makes things easier to find and evaluate whether it's the thing you are looking for. This evaluation is easier to do when something, a report for example, contains the information expected, and you don't have to learn something new each time you look for a piece of research. It also needs to be understandable to all, especially if non-user research experts are using research artefacts and repositories.[11] To ensure all content on a relevant topic could be found by a library user, we need to populate most fields in the library using consistent language, controlled by taxonomies or term lists, to describe the content.[12]

NAMING CONVENTIONS FOR RESEARCH ARTEFACTS AND VERSION CONTROL[13]

[Business Unit] [Type of Work] [Specific Thing] [Version]

Definitions:

[Business Unit]: Department, Team, Programme of Work

[Type of Work]: Plan, Usability Testing, Personas

[Specific Thing]: Focus of Work or Type of Document

[Version]: 1 = original, 1.1 minor change, 2 = major change. Major change = a change that breaks something.

Let's imagine that a Support Charity website is redeveloping its payment function for online donations. We can create folders and files using these conventions. Start by creating folders somewhere we and those who need to can access them. For example, within your shared drives set up these folders:

- Shared drives > Donations Team > User research data > Website > Payments

All the research data for a recent round of prototype testing research might be stored in a folder, which would live within the Payments folder, as shown above, called:

- > Donations Team – Online Payments Prototype Usability Testing – Round 1 Q2 2024

The research data, consent form and research extracts for a participant in that round of research might be named:

- Donations Team – Session Notes P1 Sam Smith – Online Payments Prototype Usability Testing – Round 1 Q2 2024.docx

- Donations Team – Recording P1 Sam Smith – Online Payments Prototype Usability Testing – Round 1 Q2 2024.mp4

- Donations Team – Consent Form P1 Sam Smith – Online Payments Prototype Usability Testing – Round 1 Q2 2024.pdf

- Donations Team – Analysis – Online Payments Prototype Usability Testing – Round 1 Q2 2024.xlxs

- Donations Team – Final Report – Online Payments Prototype Usability Testing – Round 1 Q2 2024.pptx

We need clear file names to understand what the files contain and which project they are related to. In fact, it's more important to have clear and understandable file names if they aren't all in the same folder. Not having everything in one place is useful if we don't want all the artefacts to be accessible to all. We may not want everyone to have access to the raw data or all the details you have collected about the participants.

METADATA FOR RESEARCH ARTEFACTS

The global ResearchOps community has done extensive work on how to name things, and what should be included in a taxonomy for research arte-facts. Elements of the Minimum Viable Taxonomy Level 1 include:

- project title/project code or identifier
- date
- name of product, service or problem space
- topic(s) or research question
- target audience(s)
- report deliverables
- researcher name/research team
- sample size
- access level
- research method(s)
- related/cited research

These are the essential elements for a research artefact to be understandable.[14]

Building a research repository

The purpose of a research repository is to provide infrastructure for the research process; a centralized place for research materials and artefacts.

To be effective, as discussed above, we will need to implement naming and description conventions by defining and applying standard descriptions for research assets. And we'll also need to define the scope of the repository, what the boundaries are and what people should expect to find there, and what it won't include.[15]

STARTING SMALL

To start small with a research repository, we can start with a spreadsheet list, using the MVT from the ResearchOps community as described above.

It is a common problem in many organizations. I have experienced it in several organizations and Jones also described the experience; people are the main source of information and knowledge management.[16] Although it is perceived to be the most reliable and time-saving approach, it is in fact inefficient, unreliable, incomplete and inevitably a lot of valuable knowledge is lost, whether that is research insight itself or related to research infrastructure. The main benefit of having research repositories and insight libraries is to have a known single version of the truth and avoid duplication.

Knowledge management in customer research

Knowledge management supports discovering previously unseen connections between research content from different research projects, thereby surfacing new connections and insights.[17]

As with everything in research operations, there are different levels of knowledge management that can be implemented and practised within an organization, depending on our capacity and capabilities.

Reporting templates

If we have the time and ability to do one thing in the knowledge management space, report templates are a good option. We can have reporting and knowledge sharing templates and guidance to ensure consistency in how we are sharing both quantitative and qualitative research. Consistency is important for building trust with the stakeholders and whoever is using the knowledge gained from research. Templates enable us to consistently meet the expectations and needs of those consuming and using the research.

We can include governance around branding and tone of voice of research reports; that is one kind of consistency. However, the most important is what information should be consistently included and how it should be included to make reports accessible and usable.

The metadata in research reporting is there to ensure traceability of research, so that those making decisions with the knowledge now and also in the future can do so with confidence.

The following content is based on internal knowledge management discovery research I did with Claire Alexopoulou and Rita Duarte in 2022 and internal data storage research we did in 2023.

There are many reasons why people do secondary research using our past research, to:

- understand context
- avoid duplication
- help shape research ideas
- triangulate data
- make decisions

How people look for past research will depend on how much information management we have in place. If information and knowledge management practices are not consistent, people become the main resource for finding past research, as discussed above. People will also search and browse the places they know research is kept, if they have access to them. When a research report, for example, is found, they need to be able to assess that this is the source of truth they are looking for and they need to assess the quality, relevance and suitability to use for their purposes.

In order to assess the quality and relevance of a piece of research for potential reuse, the report needs to contain certain expected elements:

- dates – when the research was done, when the report was last updated
- who did the research
- the purpose of the research
- study design and methodologies used
- participant criteria and sample size
- key findings
- key constraints
- links to raw data

These are the trust and relevance criteria that people are using to assess the suitability of the research. Other elements include:[18]

- product/service name or focus area of the research
- study status (e.g. stand alone project or part of an ongoing research programme)
- link to project plan

Supporting those doing research to effectively communicate research insights with impact means we need to support the communication of insights that are actionable and understandable. Communication to a wide range of stakeholders who aren't experts in research is a skill in itself but is often an afterthought and rushed. Just because the research has been done, doesn't guarantee that it will be used, successful communication of insights is pivotal to research return on investment. There are templates and guidance we can provide for this.

Reports made in slide decks and documents are the classic way of sharing and documenting what we have learnt from research. Now, the documentation may happen in an insight library, but this may not be the best way of sharing with those who need to know. It really depends on the organization and the level of research literacy. It's more than likely there will be presentation versions and written/reading versions for sharing the research.

GUIDANCE ON WRITING REPORTS: READING/FULL DOCUMENTATION VERSION OF THE RESEARCH (IF CONTAINED IN A PRESENTATION FORMAT)

- It's OK to have more words on the slide when it's for reading. But still try to avoid overloading a slide.
- Make use of the speaker notes section to add detail. Or consider using more slides with less information or whether fewer words could be used to get the point across.
- Where possible and appropriate use visuals and graphics.
- Consider what additional slides are needed to set the context of the work, if someone is reading this report in two years' time.

GUIDANCE ON WRITING SHAREBACK AND PRESENTATION VERSIONS OF THE RESEARCH

- Minimize the number of words on the page.
- Where possible and appropriate use visuals and graphics.
- Aim for one point per slide, we can use more slides if we need to.
- If we need the detail written down to present it, many of us do, add it into the speaker notes rather than having it on the slide.
- What additional slides do we need to set the context of the work for stakeholders, if they haven't been directly involved in the work itself?

Alternatives to written sharebacks include:

- infographics
- videos
- comics
- interactive workshops[19]

How we share our findings depends on many things.[20] If we have multiple audiences to share the insights and findings with, we need to have multiple versions of the narrative. We're not telling different versions of the truth but prioritizing information to align with what the audience's priorities are. Each version of the artefacts shared needs to be clearly labelled.

REPORT TEMPLATES: WHAT TO INCLUDE

There are many different types of research reports, but generally their structures are pretty consistent. Here are some of the most common types of research reports:

- **Usability reports** share key findings about users' behaviour, expectations and challenges.
- **Analytics reports** share analysis of past performance and what insight can be gained from this, and provide recommendations.
- **Market research reports** evaluate data related to customer perceptions of brands, products etc., report on market structures and opportunities.
- **Competitive analysis** outlines the competitive landscape, industry trends and overall outlook.
- **Qualitative research reports** are reports written for studies using qualitative methods, such as interviews, contextual inquiry or diary studies, etc.
- **Quantitative research reports** are written for studies with quantitative methodology, such as benchmarking, first click tests or A/B tests.[21]

Whatever format we agree is the best way to communicate the research, there are some essentials to be included to communicate effectively and for the full documentation version to enable it to be reused later:

1 The first thing to consider with report and shareback templates is to make sure it is in line with the brand identity and tone of voice of the organization.

2 Have an executive summary version – if the audience only reads one page/slide, what do we need them to know?

3 Information to include in a research report (to have impact):

o why the research was done (what we needed to learn/why the audience needs to pay attention)

o top insights and opportunities, and what business goals they are relevant to

o metadata: method, participant segmentation/sample and size and when the research was done

o quotes and highlight reels (seeing and hearing directly from the customer)

o infographics to summarize

o conclusions and next steps – what will we do? What do we need the audience to do?

o active language, plain language (if we need to use jargon, be sure to clearly explain it).[22]

REAL-WORLD EXAMPLE

Creating a research output repository: Home Office Digital UK

The Home Office is the UK government department that leads on work around policies and services related to immigration and passports, and crime, counter-terrorism and policing. The Home Office Digital team created a repository of user research outputs. This was achieved by a couple of people going through all the raw data themselves to identify user needs in a consistent way, which is quite an undertaking. The repository included:

- links lists of user needs that don't change very often and give a real feel for the context
- links to experience maps and user journeys
- anonymized interview transcripts
- research brief, research questions and debriefs
- types of users
- anonymized case studies
- anonymized highlight videos
- summary slide decks of insights
- photos of research happening and being synthesized, to give a sense that it's real[23]

Repository governance: Ofsted

Ofsted is the Office for Standards in Education, Children's Services and Skills in the UK. While working there, Salma Patel used governance to have a community-sourced research library, encouraging teams to add their own research into the library and the description into the catalogue. Some of the instructions listed after the contents page in the catalogue included:

- which files should be placed in the catalogue
- how to anonymize participant data adequately
- which naming structure they should use to add files and folders to the catalogue
- how to link the catalogue to the new files they have inserted
- how to share the files in the library
- how and from whom they can request access to edit the catalogue[24]

What we haven't found so far is any information about how other organizations handle the contribution process for adding insights to the library. Who is responsible for what? We might want to take inspiration for GDS Design System governance and other design systems.[25]

Research reports can and will share a combination of findings and insights. But they are different things; the most impactful and useful thing we can share, with the biggest return on investment, is actionable insights. The next section in this chapter will look at the difference.

Findings and insights in customer research

Table 5.1 summarizes the difference between data, findings, insights and actionable insights.

As we have prescribed a structure for effective reporting of research, to consistently meet the needs of research consumers, we need to prescribe a structure for effective insight sharing. Insights can be contained within a particular research report, but they can also stand alone as a self-contained narrative to be understood in isolation, as well as being triangulated from multiple pieces of research and stored in an insight library. The elements included increase the value and usability of the insight, allowing insight users to learn, prioritize and take action based on their own goals. And they enable us to track the impact of the insights.

TABLE 5.1 The difference between findings and insights

Data	Raw numbers, notes, videos – data that has been captured but not analysed	
Findings	Observations of behaviour, interactions, issues, perceptions, opinions and attitudes	What
Insights	Observation + understanding [motivation, why something is happening, context]	What + why
Actionable insights	Observation + understanding + business knowledge to identify opportunity for action	What + why + action

What to include in an insight?

- Insight part 1:
  - What is happening? Description of observation.
  - Why is it happening? Description of reasons/context behind the behaviour/issue.
  - Why is it important to the organization? How is it impacting the business?
  - Relevant business goal/OKR/metrics.
- Insight part 2:
  - What should we do about it?
  - What are the opportunities we've identified?
  - What is the impact of taking this opportunity?
  - What work would need to happen to take the opportunity?
  - What is the risk if we do nothing? What is the risk of not taking the opportunities identified?
- Insight part 3:
  - What we actually did about it: what action has been taken based on the insight?

(Tracking the impact of research is covered in Part Three.)

This is based on work I've done over the years at Springer Nature, some of it shared at conferences – ConveyUX 2021 for example – and on my personal Medium blog. I have had feedback and support from many people on this work: Claire Alexopoulou, Rita Duarte, Angela Collins Rees, Ola Trytek, Tania Ramos, Rain Thompson-Brody, Susana Vilaça, Rita R Silva and other colleagues.

Building an insight library

Insight libraries' usefulness has been hotly debated over recent years, but I think we have turned a corner in widespread appreciation of their importance. The concerns are well founded, knowledge management is a lot of work, and data, information and knowledge can quickly become out of date.

A lot of consideration is needed to create a repo or a library; it's unwise to jump straight into it. They present a huge opportunity for surfacing relevant insights from different projects, study design, business functions and disciplines. However, they are often poorly implemented, they are laborious and siloed.

We need to think about:

- the infrastructure first
- and the tooling second

Maintaining an insight library is one of the most sophisticated things you can do in your user research and research operations practices. I am an advocate of starting with building a simple spreadsheet list then scaling a research repository before undertaking the construction of an insight library.

When discussing the sharing of research/findings/insights more effectively, it often quickly turns to tools as solutions to doing this. As I'll talk about later, there are other cheaper, less risky ways to start this process than buying a tool or building one in house.

There is also the risk of not having something with which to collate your research, which means extra work for the researchers and not getting the maximum value out of the research done. As we've discussed previously, one of the benefits of curated insight libraries is that you get to capture all those insights you've gathered that aren't directly relevant to the current research question being focused on. These 'secondary' insights are usually forgotten and lost, but can be put to good use in an insight library. A curated and well-maintained insight library supports people doing secondary research. Secondary research is the prime use case for libraries.

Secondary/desk research is the searching for, finding and using already existing data and insight. During secondary research we take (mostly) primary research, edit, redact, reformulate and represent for new work, or for other new purposes with our teams, stakeholders, departments, clients, etc. Whereas with primary research we're creating new datasets (doing research with participants).[26]

A library is a repository, but a repository is not always a library. Using the analogy of physical shared spaces, the difference between visiting a repository and a library is that a library is intended for public use for research and leisure, and (usually) allows items to be checked out with a library card; it's a place to access knowledge. A repository is a location for storage, often for safekeeping or preservation, stored information for use by the public or qualified people, for data and information but not knowledge.

START SMALL WHEN BUILDING AN INSIGHT LIBRARY

A low-effort, high-impact way to make research more easily accessible is a simple list (catalogue) of research done, so work can be accessed with just enough context to know that you are accessing the right thing.

This would be writing a list we can group into high-level themes. There are varying amounts of detail we can include in our list – e.g. title, data, link, methodology, findings, outcomes.

A research report repository is both just a list and not just a list. It is a consistent place to go for research outputs. Things that we'll need to create the list:

- consistent naming conventions
- know where the reports are located

Things that will enhance our list:

- unique identifier for each project (like an ISBN for user research)
- using repo functions of existing tools
- make it someone's job to maintain the list[27]

A research report repository is not an insight library. An insight library is a collation of knowledge, insights that have been extracted from the research data, not links to reports. That's not to diminish the usefulness of a research report repo, but insight libraries are more sophisticated and require a lot more work. We can't have a quality insight library without quality insights. This means that robust analysis is a cornerstone of any high-quality user research, but I include it here because it's really hard. Analysis is a skill in itself and it's quite easy to do an unintentionally bad job of it. Robust analysis is a sophisticated skill, and a necessary skill to be able to share high-quality research insights.[28]

To build an effective insight library, first we need to:

- Define the scope of the insight library (what we will include and what we won't include).
- Gather needs and expectations for the different user groups (researchers, Ops, marketing, product, etc.).
- Understand the current practices to sharing and accessing insights, pain points, things that are working.
- Prioritize requirements.
- Identify how to measure success.[29]

Next we will need to review tools. We may be purchasing a new tool or customizing an existing tool. We may not be using a dedicated tool, but repurposing a tool that we think will meet our needs. Whatever the circumstances, we will need to deep dive into the tool to find out which features and functionalities would support the 'must haves' of this library.[30]

- Deciding the scope will identify:
  - what files are going to live in the repo
  - what is going to live in the insight library

Auditing and gathering

People related

We will need to identify:

- who needs what level of access and types of permission
  - administrator/manager
  - contributor/editor
  - viewer/consumer
  - no access
- whose responsibility is access and permission management

Knowledge related

We will need to audit and gather the relevant research that is going to be included in the insight library.

Decide structure and taxonomy

If we are moving from research reports to insights in a library, one of the most time-consuming parts of the process of building an insight library will be translating what is documented in research reports into consistently structured insights. How long this takes will depend on how research is documented in the first place, and how much consistency this has. Assuming that research has been done and reported long before the building of an insight library and implementation of knowledge management practices, this will take a long time. A big question those doing the work will have to ask themselves is, what to do with those not using the template? It is relatively easy to rename a file, it is a lot more work to reformat a research report. I would suggest that research with longevity should be reformatted, but we may not want to put the effort into shorter-lived research.

We will need to agree upon the information architecture of the library and metadata to be used to describe the context of each piece of research; as discussed previously, we know what elements people reusing research consider important – this will become our metadata.

Knowledge management practice guidance and training

When moving documents and insights to their respective resting places, we need to ensure that the people doing research are following the established naming conventions and using the designated templates, for example. Through the work I have done at Springer Nature with Claire Alexopoulou and Rita Duarte, we have identified the most effective way to change how people work in terms of the research process, and knowledge management is a combination of written guidance and hands-on training (we'll look at this in more depth in Part Three), either one on their own, is unlikely to lead to practice change.

WHY INVEST IN AN INSIGHT LIBRARY?

Investing in an insight library will allow us to:

- properly categorize research insight
- find insight easily
- understand the provenance, context and limitations of research
- discover patterns
- support an evidence-based approach to the organization's work[31]

Summarizing past research

In the circumstances that we don't yet have a fully established insight library, we may take a different approach to secondary research. There are many reasons we might want to bring together all the past research on a particular topic in one place and make it easy to consume. A good example is communicating to senior stakeholders and interested teams what we already know when a new project is being kicked off, so that the team(s) working on this aren't starting from scratch. And it helps to avoid research being duplicated. Depending on the need and what the summary is for we might need a high-level summary; this is the 'too long, didn't read' (TL;DR) version summarizing the essence of what we know. These can be one-pagers that are easy to read and disseminate to interested parties. Figure 5.2 shows a template for a high-level summary. This is where we focus on what has been learnt from the research (with citation to which pieces of research the insights have come from).

Another simple format we can use for high-level summaries of research is based on work I did at GDS with the service communities team in 2018/19. Service communities are networks of people in different public sector departments who work together to design and deliver an end-to-end service, like starting a business or getting health benefits.[32] Such tasks in the UK require a person to interact with multiple different government departments to achieve the outcome they need. At the time this work was being done, it was

FIGURE 5.2 High-level past research summary template

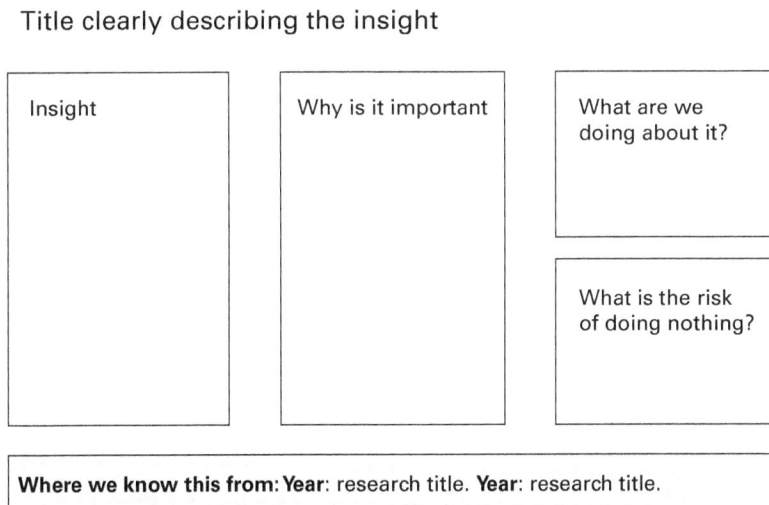

Title clearly describing the insight

Insight	Why is it important	What are we doing about it?
		What is the risk of doing nothing?

Where we know this from: Year: research title. **Year**: research title.

not easy to share research findings between different government departments. Sharing insight with a different department was considered making the insight public, which has a lot of data protection connotations.

We identified the basic elements that are important to share to make the information useful to others but also easier to share, without having information sensitivity concerns. These categories can essentially be used as a crib sheet or a summary sheet that the researcher can complete:

- context (such as service, phase of development)
- research questions
- sample size
- user groups/persona summary
- research methodology used
- ethical considerations and consent
- materials and artefacts used in the research
- summary of findings and insights

Constraints are not just around the sensitivity of data but also the platform that we share on. There was no one secure tool that all government departments were using to share this kind of information. Rather, many different tools were used in different departments. We created and iterated a user research summary sheet; sort of a simple hybrid between a repo and a library. Through iteration of the crib sheet, we removed all jargon so it could be used by anyone.[33]

We may need more in-depth summaries of research on a particular topic, still gathering together multiple pieces of research into one place, but more detail on each piece of research including key metadata such as methodologies, segmentation and sample sizes as well as the insights gained from the research.

Guidance on what to include within an in-depth summary of past research

It is important to note that summarizing past research around a particular topic (done by multiple people) is time-consuming, especially if there is no research insight library.

Step 1: Identify all the potentially relevant past research.

Step 2: Read all the research thoroughly. And assess whether the research is robust and relevant. You may need to review documentation and raw data as well as the research report.

Step 3: For each piece of research included in the summary include:

A summary of:

- o research goals
- o methodology details
- o one sentence for each of the top three findings
- o one sentence for each of the top three key opportunities.

Step 4: As many slides as are needed to capture the key findings and insights.

Step 5: Ensure links/access to each piece of research summarized and each person involved in the research are included and have been properly credited.

This is based on work I did with Claire Alexopoulou in 2023.

As we have seen, there is a lot for both the researcher and the Ops person to do during the process of doing a research project. Even after all the reporting and sharing has been done, the job isn't over. It is important to find ways to track the impact the research made, to be able to demonstrate research return on investment. And demonstrate the value of ReOps return on investment. We will look at this in Part Three: Advanced operations.

Information and knowledge management is not a part-time job

Collections of unapplied insights build up quickly in organizations. As more and more research is conducted, key insights for better serving customers that are not currently an organizational priority are too easily left on the cutting room floor, piled away in locations our stakeholders do not frequent.[34] This is one of the key challenges in customer research knowledge management and needs a person or people, not just tools, to maximize the use of insight.

Who is going to manage the data, information, knowledge?

We have focused a lot on the building of research repositories and insight libraries but this is only part of the story. Once these things are built, there is still a lot of work to be done. Such as:

- maintenance tasks
- iterating templates
- iterating metadata

- data gardening (include archiving)
- tracking impact of research, as well as data, information and knowledge management practices and tools
- knowledge management practice training; there could be multiple phases of training, particularly if we are using a powerful tool with a steep learning curve (such as dovetail)

Once the infrastructure has been built there is still:

- library management
- research management
- taxonomy management with some content describing capability
- knowledge management[35]

This kind of work is labour-intensive and time-consuming. It is important to do this work in a sustainable way and set stakeholder expectations really clearly.[36]

It takes time to change the way people work, especially when it comes to information and knowledge use. Kiernan and Sutton advise to communicate about it, a lot.[37] Keep reminding people it's there. A repository needs to continuously evolve. Make it part of the onboarding process (not just for researchers, designers, analysts, etc., but product and marketers, etc.).

When we don't have dedicated resources to manage information and knowledge for customer research we run into very familiar problems:

- **time wasting, because research is not easy to find:**
  o knowing the research exists, but being unable to find it
  o struggling with the scale of research going on in an organization and not being able to keep track of it all
- **money wasting because research is siloed:**
  o research groundhog day; having to cover the same ground regularly without the opportunity to learn from what is already known
  o research is only used once or not at all
- **inability to measure ROI:**
  o losing control of the research by emailing it or printing copies (finding others using the research out of context and without our knowledge)
  o having difficulty measuring or showing the impact of research[38]

Conclusion

We have considered the many complexities of data, information and knowledge management in this chapter. These are disciplines in themselves with whole degree courses dedicated to them. Which makes it an even greater speciality to be knowledgeable about these disciplines and customer research. I end this chapter with this thought to really emphasize the skills required to manage research data, information and knowledge. Such skills are essential to the effective and efficient conducting and subsequent use of research. The amount of work necessary to do this should not be underestimated.

Notes

1 S Marsh. Working towards user research and insight libraries. UX Collective Medium Blog, 2020. uxdesign.cc/working-towards-user-research-and-insight-libraries-1c618bcec565 (archived at https://perma.cc/3CHF-BMVG)

2 Oracle. What is data management? Data management, defined, Oracle, 2024. www.oracle.com/uk/database/what-is-data-management/ (archived at https://perma.cc/CM7N-JNVB); J Holdsworth. What is data management? IBM, 2024. www.ibm.com/topics/data-management (archived at https://perma.cc/G33D-TKAP); C Steadman and J Vaughan. What is data management and why is it important? Full guide, TechTarget, 2024. www.techtarget.com/searchdatamanagement/definition/data-management (archived at https://perma.cc/9FD7-PD27); Salesforce, Inc. Data management: What it is, importance, and challenges, Tableau from Salesforce, 2024. www.tableau.com/learn/articles/what-is-data-management (archived at https://perma.cc/5W7V-LRAY); SAP SE. What is data management? SAP, 2024. www.sap.com/products/technology-platform/what-is-data-management.html (archived at https://perma.cc/6B7A-86AD)

3 Association for Intelligent Information Management. What is information management? AIIM, 2024. www.aiim.org/what-is-information-management (archived at https://perma.cc/ZN5L-E692); Association for Project Management. What is information management? APM, 2024. www.apm.org.uk/resources/what-is-project-management/what-is-information-management/ (archived at https://perma.cc/8KGU-PYMQ)

4 IBM. What is knowledge management? IBM, 2024. www.ibm.com/topics/knowledge-management (archived at https://perma.cc/YW4Y-VACB); C Richardson. What is knowledge management? Guru, 2019. www.getguru.com/reference/what-is-knowledge-management (archived at https://perma.cc/BEG8-TNCE); Koenig MED. What is KM? Knowledge management explained. KM World, 2018. www.kmworld.com/About/What_is_Knowledge_Management (archived at https://perma.cc/RD6F-4J5S)

5   Cambridge University Press and Assessment. Data. Cambridge Dictionary, 2024. dictionary.cambridge.org/dictionary/english/data (archived at https://perma.cc/C2TC-9FWE)

6   Merriam-Webster, Inc. Information, Merriam-Webster, 2024. www.merriam-webster.com/dictionary/information (archived at https://perma.cc/EQ64-FEYZ); Cambridge University Press and Assessment. Information, Cambridge Dictionary, 2024. dictionary.cambridge.org/dictionary/english/information (archived at https://perma.cc/92H3-9XMR)

7   BYJU'S. Data and information, BYJU'S, 2024. byjus.com/biology/difference-between-data-and-information/ (archived at https://perma.cc/ESC4-9LAA); S Jain. What is data vs. what is information? Bloomfire, 2023. bloomfire.com/blog/data-vs-information (archived at https://perma.cc/MSX6-5V4S)

8   Cambridge University Press and Assessment. Knowledge, Cambridge Dictionary, 2024. dictionary.cambridge.org/dictionary/english/knowledge (archived at https://perma.cc/2SK9-GV6C); Merriam-Webster. Knowledge, Merriam-Webster, 2024. www.merriam-webster.com/dictionary/knowledge (archived at https://perma.cc/BZ5V-NPC9)

9   E DiLeo. Repositories in practice: Using knowledge management to create research stories, ResearchOps Community, 2023. medium.com/researchops-community/repositories-in-practice-using-knowledge-management-to-create-research-stories-6c6cfcd98efa (archived at https://perma.cc/HUR3-46DC)

10 S Marsh. The building blocks of libraries and repositories in user research, Springer Nature UX Research Medium Blog, 2021. medium.com/springer-nature-ux-research-team/the-building-blocks-of-libraries-and-repositories-in-user-research-9a02779a75ec (archived at https://perma.cc/43TA-VRWJ)

11 A Jones. Dialogues on a digital library: Co-designing the Atlassian Research Library, ResearchOps Community, 2023. medium.com/researchops-community/dialogues-on-a-digital-library-co-designing-the-atlassian-research-library-6cc443864e8 (archived at https://perma.cc/XMQ3-L5AZ)

12 A Jones. Dialogues on a digital library: Co-designing the Atlassian Research Library, ResearchOps Community, 2023. medium.com/researchops-community/dialogues-on-a-digital-library-co-designing-the-atlassian-research-library-6cc443864e8 (archived at https://perma.cc/XMQ3-L5AZ)

13 Based on work I have done at Springer Nature, and S Marsh (2022) *User Research: Improving product and service design and enhance your UX research*, 2nd edn, Kogan Page, London

14 E DiLeo. Introducing the Minimum Viable Taxonomy Level 1, ResearchOps Community, 2022. medium.com/researchops-community/introducing-the-minimum-viable-taxonomy-level-1-63d13589fdcb (archived at https://perma.cc/K7YN-95M4)

15 E DiLeo. Repositories in practice: Using knowledge management to create research stories, ResearchOps Community, 2023. medium.com/researchops-community/repositories-in-practice-using-knowledge-management-to-create-research-stories-6c6cfcd98efa (archived at https://perma.cc/V4TG-EXXD)

16 A Jones. Dialogues on a digital library: Co-designing the Atlassian Research Library, ResearchOps Community, 2023. medium.com/researchops-community/ dialogues-on-a-digital-library-co-designing-the-atlassian-research-library-6cc443864e8 (archived at https://perma.cc/XMQ3-L5AZ)

17 A Jones. Dialogues on a digital library: Co-designing the Atlassian Research Library, ResearchOps Community, 2023. medium.com/researchops-community/ dialogues-on-a-digital-library-co-designing-the-atlassian-research-library-6cc443864e8 (archived at https://perma.cc/QZT9-8CXL)

18 R Miles. Managing research insights at a portfolio level, ResearchOps Community, 2020. medium.com/researchops-community/managing-research-insights-at-a-portfolio-level-45585c9594d8 (archived at https://perma.cc/ 6MPX-UZHX)

19 A Mastalerz. 8 creative ways to share your user research, Marvel Blog, 2019. marvelapp.com/blog/8-creative-ways-share-user-research/ (archived at https:// perma.cc/DAE3-VGAW)

20 Service Manual Team. Product and service community, GOV.UK Service Manual, 2017. All content is available under the Open Government Licence v3.0. www.gov.uk/service-manual/communities/product-and-service-community (archived at https://perma.cc/LY33-ZMGR)

21 User Interviews Inc. Writing UX research reports and presentations, User Interviews, 2024. www.userinterviews.com/ux-research-field-guide-chapter/ how-to-write-effective-reports-and-presentations (archived at https://perma.cc/ P2SY-97ZL)

22 User Interviews Inc. Writing UX research reports and presentations, User Interviews, 2024. www.userinterviews.com/ux-research-field-guide-chapter/ how-to-write-effective-reports-and-presentations (archived at https://perma.cc/ B4D3-EAB3)

23 S Marsh. The building blocks of libraries and repositories in user research, Springer Nature UX Research Medium Blog, 2021. medium.com/springer-nature-ux-research-team/the-building-blocks-of-libraries-and-repositories-in-user-research-9a02779a75ec (archived at https://perma.cc/3LSU-J7DU)

24 S Marsh. The building blocks of libraries and repositories in user research, Springer Nature UX Research Medium Blog, 2021. medium.com/springer-nature-ux-research-team/the-building-blocks-of-libraries-and-repositories-in-user-research-9a02779a75ec (archived at https://perma.cc/PB4X-AXF9)

25 GOV.UK Design System team, Design System Working Group, GOV.UK Design System, 2024. All content is available under the Open Government Licence v3.0. design-system.service.gov.uk/community/design-system-working-group/ (archived at https://perma.cc/QYA2-KFKW)

26 S Marsh. The building blocks of libraries and repositories in user research, Springer Nature UX Research Medium Blog, 2021. medium.com/springer-nature-ux-research-team/the-building-blocks-of-libraries-and-repositories-in-user-research-9a02779a75ec (archived at https://perma.cc/PB4X-AXF9)

27 S Marsh. The building blocks of libraries and repositories in user research, Springer Nature UX Research Medium Blog, 2021. medium.com/springer-nature-ux-research-team/the-building-blocks-of-libraries-and-repositories-in-user-research-9a02779a75ec (archived at https://perma.cc/J6YB-MBEX)

28 S Marsh. Working towards user research and insight libraries. UX Collective Medium Blog, 2020. uxdesign.cc/working-towards-user-research-and-insight-libraries-1c618bcec565 (archived at https://perma.cc/3CHF-BMVG)

29 L Van Ekeren. Building a repository in SharePoint, Part 1: Groundwork and preparations. ResearchOps Community, 2023. medium.com/researchops-community/building-a-repository-in-sharepoint-part-1-groundwork-preparations-3baf06630be (archived at https://perma.cc/NYE5-UGWU)

30 L Van Ekeren. Building a repository in SharePoint, Part 2: Development, maintenance and beyond, ResearchOps Community, 2023. medium.com/researchops-community/building-a-repository-in-sharepoint-part-2-development-maintenance-beyond-5b15dbb8b9b (archived at https://perma.cc/7GCS-UZ8R)

31 A Jones. Dialogues on a digital library: Co-designing the Atlassian Research Library, ResearchOps Community, 2023. medium.com/researchops-community/dialogues-on-a-digital-library-co-designing-the-atlassian-research-library-6cc443864e8 (archived at https://perma.cc/M2GW-6FT2)

32 Service Manual Team. Product and service community, GOV.UK Service Manual, 2017. All content is available under the Open Government Licence v3.0. www.gov.uk/service-manual/communities/product-and-service-community (archived at https://perma.cc/5VFK-BTC4)

33 S Marsh. The building blocks of libraries and repositories in user research, Springer Nature UX Research Medium Blog, 2021. medium.com/springer-nature-ux-research-team/the-building-blocks-of-libraries-and-repositories-in-user-research-9a02779a75ec (archived at https://perma.cc/3LSU-J7DU)

34 J Burghardt. Activating insights to overcome common barriers to product impact, ResearchOps Community, 2022. medium.com/researchops-community/activating-insights-to-overcome-common-barriers-to-product-impact-ec534ffe0c1a (archived at https://perma.cc/UN27-P3MU)

35 A Jones. Dialogues on a digital library: Co-designing the Atlassian Research Library, ResearchOps Community, 2023. medium.com/researchops-community/dialogues-on-a-digital-library-co-designing-the-atlassian-research-library-6cc443864e8 (archived at https://perma.cc/WE76-G3AT); L Van Ekeren. Building a repository in SharePoint, Part 1: Groundwork and preparations. ResearchOps Community, 2023. medium.com/researchops-community/building-a-repository-in-sharepoint-part-1-groundwork-preparations-3baf06630be (archived at https://perma.cc/NYE5-UGWU); L Van Ekeren. Building a repository in SharePoint, Part 2: Development, maintenance and beyond, ResearchOps Community, 2023. medium.com/researchops-community/building-a-repository-in-sharepoint-part-2-development-maintenance-beyond-5b15dbb8b9b (archived at https://perma.cc/7GCS-UZ8R)

36 A Kiernan and L Sutton. 5 ReOps learnings at the UK Department for Education. ResearchOps Community, 2022. medium.com/researchops-community/5-ReOps-learnings-at-the-uk-department-for-education-8c93ec7e66f1 (archived at https://perma.cc/9UQ7-RSEZ)

37 A Kiernan and L Sutton. 5 ReOps learnings at the UK Department for Education. ResearchOps Community, 2022. medium.com/researchops-community/5-ReOps-learnings-at-the-uk-department-for-education-8c93ec7e66f1 (archived at https://perma.cc/9UQ7-RSEZ)

38 Team ReOps. Research repositories: A ResearchOps community program of work, ResearchOps Community, 2022. medium.com/researchops-community/research-repositories-a-researchops-community-program-of-work-811b2ba3638f (archived at https://perma.cc/8879-FV2M)

6

Supporting and managing the research process

No matter the field or type of organization we are working in, there will be a way of tracking the progress of projects. Research is no different. Tracking the progress of a research project becomes increasingly important, the more people that are involved in the research. Who may need to know or be aware of the progress of a piece of research or multiple pieces of research?

- ReOps people
- people doing the research
- people directly impacted by the research (for example, marketing and product teams)
- business stakeholders interested in the outcome

So even if we are a research and operations team of one, we will have people that are interested and invested in the status of our research. Therefore, an essential part of managing the research process is tracking the status of all the research happening at any one time. For those in ReOps roles, this helps us be aware who needs what support on any given work day, depending on the remit of our Ops roles. And if there are many people doing research, there will be a lot of context switching to make sure everyone gets the support they need.

I have heard on more than one occasion individuals saying documenting research is not important to them, which is why they leave it until the end of a project as it's constantly deprioritized. And, sometimes it is never done at all, as they move on to the next piece of research. I appreciate that, in the moment, it may not seem important to document our research if we can hold all the moving parts in our head before, during and after the research has happened.

But I hope this scenario shows that we need to document our research for others, those supporting us to make the research happen and those wanting to reuse it effectively in the future. Without proper documentation, ReOps people cannot provide the necessary support efficiently and effectively. Meaning more questions and back-and-forth are needed to provide the right support, and no one is really satisfied.

Have a way to track the research process

There are many project management tools out there, and it's likely that we will already have access to something that is fit for purpose without allocating part of our budget to it:

- we could use a spreadsheet if we are desperate; it is far from ideal but better than nothing
- Trello is a common tool to enable collaboration and project tracking
- Confluence
- Jira
- Asana
- AirTable
- and many others

Let's assume a scenario of using a Trello board – we will use lists (columns) to represent each stage of the research process. We can use the stages of research as our Trello column lists:

- planning
- segmentation and sampling
- recruitment
- doing research
- analysis and synthesis
- sharing
- implementation
- done
- blocked/paused

Within our Trello research tracking board, each piece of research is represented by a card that we can move from column to column depending on the status of the research. On each card the title should be the name of the research and we use labels as a quick way to summarize what this particular piece of research is about.

Labels can include:

- people working on the research
- broad topic
- type of research (quantitative, qualitative, mixed methods)

Within the card we need to link the relevant documents, again depending on the status of the research, for example:

- brief and plan
- schedule
- analysis doc
- reports

We can use the '@' function in the comment fields to communicate with each other, to let others know when something has happened or something is needed. For example, '@ReOps_Person – Participant 1 has completed their session and the incentive needs to be sent'.

Obviously, Trello is just one option for tracking research. We don't have to use this particular tool; I use it in this scenario as I am familiar with it. We just need to find the tool that works for us for tracking and collaboration. Collaborating and tracking are particularly important when the research isn't entirely linear, for example recruitment of participants and conducting research sessions are happening simultaneously.

Planning research for the best outcome

Planning is the foundation on which impactful research is delivered. It is hard to produce high-quality research without robust planning. Documenting the planning of research helps us solidify the purpose and logistics of the research being done, communicates to others these details and enables others in the future to understand if they can use it in secondary research.

It is useful to provide one or two templates for planning research: 1) brief/proposal, and 2) detailed plan. Sometimes this is the same document; depending on what approval is needed, we may need to make them separate documents.[1]

The brief is a high-level summary or pitch that describes the intention of the research. A research brief should include the following information:

1 Context: What is the opportunity or issue? [User need]

2 What do we need to learn? [In order to maximize the opportunity or fix the issue]

3 What is the business driver? Why do we need to learn this? [Business need]

4 Who are the relevant customer groups?

5 What are the timescales?

6 What budget is needed?

7 What is the intended outcome? What actions will be taken?

8 What do we already know?

Through experience I have learnt that it is important to use language that everyone can understand rather than more technical (research and UX) terms – it can easily confuse people who are both research literate and non-literate if we ask them what are the research objectives and research questions? Even research professionals can find it difficult to articulate the difference between the two. But if we ask people to answer the eight questions above we are well on the way to doing impactful research. If the person doing research cannot articulate what needs to be learnt and why we need to learn it, the research results from this kind of vague proposal will not be particularly useful, if they are used at all.

The research plan will build on the brief, adding necessary detail to enable the research project to actually happen. We don't need to duplicate what we already have in the brief, but we should build upon it:

• What specific questions will be answered?

• How will the questions be answered? [Research methodology]

• Who are the participants? [Segmentation/sample criteria]

• How many participants are needed? [Sample size]

• How will participants be recruited?

• Who are the stakeholders?

• What are the constraints and dependencies?

• Are there any risks associated with doing this research?

• What is out of scope for this research?

• What are the deliverables?[2]

Answering questions, rather than just having section titles, encourages people to be more descriptive and add detail when completing the brief and plan.

There may be other relevant questions to ask for planning research, but these are the fundamentals of the things that need to be agreed and planned, to enable efficient and effective research to happen. Having everything documented makes each decision traceable if someone were to question why something was done, for example. It allows the ReOps and research people to plan and prioritize what exactly needs to happen and when it needs to happen. Answering these questions will expose any gaps or risks; for example, ensuring that we have access to the right tools to do the research, or if recruiting a hard-to-reach customer group, and that this is accounted for in the time scales.

Other support artefacts for planning research:

• Guidance on how to choose the right method.
• See Chapter 4 for templates, governance and guidance related to participant recruitment.

Choosing the right method

Assuming primary research is needed, as the questions we have can't be answered by existing data (see Chapter 5), then people tend to jump straight to a method and we'll hear them say, 'We need to do some usability testing', for example. But is that actually the right thing to do? It's easy to get stuck in a rut of using only a couple of methods because they lend themselves to faster turnaround times or people are simply familiar with the method, regardless of what is actually needed.

The key to choosing the right method is to first understand a few key things, and then select a method:

1 What do we need to learn?
2 At what point in the development cycle are we?
3 What constraints are we working with?

Some high-level examples of things we may want to learn are listed below. Some of these questions are about context, some are about behaviour, some are about perception:

• Who are the customers?
• What is the size of the market?

- What is the size of this opportunity?
- How do customers behave in a particular situation?
- What's the customers' attitude towards this service?
- What are the customers' wants and needs?
- What do the users expect?
- What do we know about the users using the product/service?
- Do we have known knowledge gaps?
- What is the business goal?
- What is the size of this problem?
- Are we making the right decision?
- Are our assumptions valid?
- What was the quantitative and qualitative impact of a change?

Asking what needs to be learnt clarifies the purpose of the research. If there is no clear purpose, it is difficult to do actionable, insightful research. Some of the questions lend themselves to quantitative research methods and some to qualitative methods. Often it is ideal to take a mixed methods approach using both quantitative and qualitative methods, for robust results.

Table 6.1 shows the different methods that are appropriate at different stages of the development cycle. Although using this table can help those doing the research be more confident in choosing the right method, we can't always use the ideal method. Sometimes we need to use a method that is good enough because it works best within the constraints of the situation. Some barriers to doing customer research include:

- lack of budget
- lack of resources
- limited time
- an inaccessible customer base
- lack of stakeholder buy-in
- ethical issues
- lack of understanding

Even when using a good enough method, we still need to do robust research. But we can do robust research while being pragmatic.

TABLE 6.1 Choosing the right customer research method matrix

	Learn and discover		Analyse and scope		Design, develop, iterate		Deploy and measure	
Types of things to learn about	Market size and structure. Who are customers? What are they trying to achieve? What are their experiences and barriers? What's missing, opportunities? What is the context of their actions? What are their attitudes and opinions?		Constraints: economy, technology, legislation. Potential impact and consequences. Attitudes and perception of concept. Attitudes and opinions of potential pricing. Feasibility [cost/benefit]		Choose potential solutions. Design potential solutions. Prototype and test solutions. Learn and iterate (with increasing fidelity). Satisfaction		Deliver solutions [gradual or full roll out]. Measure what's important: does it meet the need? Does it meet expectations? Are customers satisfied & loyal? Is marketing effective? What is the brand impact? Is pricing competitive?	
	Qualitative	Quantitative	Qualitative	Quantitative	Qualitative	Quantitative	Qualitative	Quantitative
Method	Desk research, Interviews, Contextual Inquiry, Ethnography, Pop up/hall test, Focus groups	Surveys	Diary studies, Contextual interviews, Participatory design, Stakeholder interviews, Stakeholder Workshops, Desk research	Analytics	Usability testing, Interviews, Content testing, Pop up/hall test	A/B testing, Card sorting, Tree testing, Impression Testing, Usability metrics, Desirability Studies, Surveys	Interviews, Contextual Inquiry, Ethnography, Pop up/hall test, Focus groups, Diary studies, Participatory design, Stakeholder Workshops	A/B testing, Card Sorting, Tree testing, Impression testing, Desirability Studies, Surveys, Analytics, Benchmarking, NPS/CSAT Usability metrics

Here are some examples we can share with those doing research of the kind of compromises that can be made, depending on the constraint:

Scenario 1

- o Scenario: How does customers' use of the product change over time in [a particular] context?
- o Ideal methodology: Ethnography.
- o Business constraint: Time.
- o Methodological compromise: Conduct a diary study or context inquiry.

Scenario 2

- o Scenario: The analytics show the shop cart abandonment has increased for x product.
- o Ideal methodology: Moderated usability testing with incentivized participants.
- o Business constraint: Money.
- o Methodological compromise: Conduct pop-up research.

Scenario 3

- o Scenario: Can we build an app that deletes yourself from someone's contacts for people fleeing domestic violence?
- o Ideal methodology: Contextual inquiry.
- o Ethical constraint: Can't talk to potential users.
- o Methodological compromise: Desk research; forums analysis, social media, competitor analysis.

Scenario 4

- o Scenario: What is it like to make an insurance claim in stressful circumstances?
- o Ideal methodology: Contextual inquiry.
- o Ethical constraint: Can't talk to existing users.
- o Methodological compromise: Internal research – talk to customer services, review their data.

Once we have chosen the appropriate research method(s), we can start to prepare for actually doing the research.

How involved ReOps are in the planning of research will depend on the skillset and scope of the ReOps person/people. At a minimum, ReOps need to be aware that research is being planned, even if they are not actively involved in shaping the details of the research. This allows ReOps to plan ahead themselves in terms of resources available for supporting the set-up and conducting the research.

Support to provide for setting up and doing research

To support both the preparation of and then conducting of the research, there are several templates and key guidance that we can provide that will make it easier and quicker for people to start actually doing the research.

It depends on what the most common types of research being done are, to what templates we should focus on creating first. But it is a fair assumption that if moderated research is being done there will be regular interviews, focus groups, hall tests and usability tests. So if this is a brand new customer research department, these four staple qualitative moderated methods are a good place to start.

It is worth providing templates for these moderated methods not only for efficiency, but to provide some consistency in participants' experience when interacting with researchers. This will help ensure that each participant hears the same information regarding consent and data protection and therefore the research being GDPR compliant. We can also manage the tone of voice and language the organization prefers to use (as long as it's understandable to the users). Including this content in templates means researchers don't have to think about rewriting it with each moderated research project or copying and pasting from a previous project. The templates are also useful for consistency in terms of how research is structured, however experienced or inexperienced the person doing the research is, as the templates outline the expected structure a research session will take; such as including both warm-up and wrap-up questions, enabling consistency in research across the board.

Templates to provide

Each of the templates presented here includes the basic structural elements that each research session should include, and example warm-up and wrap-up questions.

INTERVIEW GUIDE AND USABILITY RESEARCH PROTOCOL TEMPLATE

Study detail

Study name:

Date:

Participant number:

Moderator:

Observers:

Introduction

Details that need to be shared with every participant to set the context.

Read a prepared script to ensure consistency.

Thank you for participating in this study.
[Introduce yourself and any observer present.]

Today, your honest feedback on [xxxx] is needed. This is not a test, and you can't do anything wrong. You've already signed a consent form, but before we start, do you have any questions or concerns you'd like to raise?

Today you will be helping me to understand [brief sentence on the context of the study].

Please think out loud, giving honest feedback, both positive and negative. I didn't work on what you are interacting with/discussing today, you won't offend me with any feedback that you have.

Is it OK if I record the session? So I don't miss any important details?

[Press record] Once recording, note the live recording indicator and the observers' presence [if live streaming], explaining they won't interrupt. Explain who the observers are [which team they are from] and why they are observing.

Warm-up questions

[Example] Please can you briefly introduce yourself, tell us about your role, what you are working on at the moment.

Main focus of research

[Add interview questions or usability tasks here]

Wrap-up questions

Ok, we've looked at everything I was hoping to go through today. I just want to ask you a few questions. From what you have seen and experienced today...

[Add final summary questions here]

Are there any final thoughts that you'd like to share today?

Wrap-up statement

We've completed the session. Thank you very much for taking the time to take part and help us [xxxx]. It's been great to talk to you.

We send incentives [on a particular day] so you should receive yours shortly. Should you have any problems do not hesitate to contact me.

Do you have any questions for me before you leave?

FOCUS GROUP INTERVIEW GUIDE TEMPLATE[3]

Study detail

Study name:

Date:

Participants:

Moderators:

Observers:

Introduction

Good [morning/afternoon/evening], everyone!

Thank you all for taking the time to join us today. My name is [XXX], I'm a [role] and I'll be facilitating our discussion. This is my colleague [XXX] who will be helping me today.

Our goal for today is to have an open, honest and engaging conversation. We've invited you here because your perspectives and insights are incredibly valuable to us as we [state the purpose of the focus group and the intended outcome of the work]. There are no right or wrong answers and we want to hear from each of you.

To help us all create a safe and comfortable environment for us to talk, we have a few guidelines that we need to share before we begin. And please remember as stated in the consent form, everything discussed here is confidential.

Please speak one at a time so everyone has a chance to be heard.

Feel free to share your thoughts, even if they differ from others.

Please respect each other's reflections, even if you don't agree.

We may invite specific people to answer a question first, to ensure everyone can contribute.

If you don't feel comfortable answering a question, please say so. Do not feel obliged or pressured to answer a question you are not comfortable with.

If anyone is disrespectful, the discussion will be paused and they will be asked to leave.

We'll be together for about [duration]. If you need anything in the meantime, please feel free to let me or my colleague know.

Once again, thank you for being here. Let's get started!

Before we dive into the discussion, let's take a few minutes to introduce ourselves. I'm going to ask each person to give a short answer to [ice-breaker question].

Warm-up theme

Question 1: [add question here]

Observations:

Common responses:

Atypical responses:

Key quotes:

Theme 1

Question 1: [add question here]

Observations:

Common responses:

Atypical responses:

Key quotes:

Wrap-up theme

Question 1: [add question here]

Observations:

Common responses:

Atypical responses:

Key quotes:

High-level summary and final thoughts

[Share any final thoughts that might be appropriate]

The time for our discussion has come to an end. Thank you very much for taking the time to take part and help us [understand a topic]. It's been great to talk to you.

We send incentives [on a particular day] so you should receive yours shortly. Should you have any problems do not hesitate to contact me.

HALL TEST/POP-UP RESEARCH GUIDE TEMPLATE[4]

Study detail

Study name:

Date:

Location:

Moderators:

Participant details:

Logistics: consent form signed [ ], incentive paid [ ]

Introduction

Hi, I'm [name] doing research for [organization]. Could I take a couple of minutes of your time to ask you about [topic]. There will be a [incentive] for you to answer a couple of questions.

We're here to learn from you – there are no right or wrong answers. And you can stop at any time. If you are interested, we have a short form for you to review and sign which tells you about our data collection and what we do with the data.

Do you have any questions before we get started?

Research focus

Warm-up question:

Main question:

Ok, we've looked at everything I was hoping to go through today. I just want to ask you a few questions. From what you have seen and experienced today...

Wrap-up question:

End of the session
We greatly appreciate your time today. [Add any final logistical or wrap-up comments].

Capturing issues and themes collaboratively

If we are taking an agile and collaborative approach to usability testing or interviews it is useful to have a template to share with observers to capture issues and themes during research sessions that can be compared, synthesized and discussed after each session or after all the sessions.

A framework such as that shown in Table 6.2 can be used for this purpose. This is useful for consistency in what people are taking note of. However, if

TABLE 6.2 Template for capturing issues or themes

Issue/ themes	Category	P1	P2	P3	P..	Quotes P1: P3:	Priority	Actions

moderators and observers don't have a lot of experience it is useful to provide guidance on how to take notes and what to take note of. We might be supporting people to do research who are not experienced in research, so we should be providing guidance with the templates we use.

Templates for quantitative and unmoderated research

Providing templates for quantitative research is much more high-level here, because it is very dependent on what we are researching and how we are researching it. But we can provide guardrails for consent and data privacy information, and if there's other information (e.g. an introduction with the right tone of voice) or particular questions that need to be consistently included (outside of screener questions, see Chapter 4 for more information).

Data privacy statements for surveys and unmoderated research can be found in Chapter 3.

We may want to provide examples of quantitative research introductions to demonstrate good practice of providing the context of the study but not biasing the participants to answer in a particular way (i.e. they think we want a particular type of information, so they will skew their answers in this way).

The introduction will be dependent on what we are trying to learn and the research methodology being used. People are familiar with completing surveys online and offline, but are often less familiar with methodologies such as unmoderated usability tests and benchmarking, so it can be useful to set some expectations of what the experience of participating in the research will be like. The following are instructions for the most common unmoderated research methodologies: card sorting, tree testing and unmoderated usability research (Figures 6.1–6.5 are visual representations of the instructions provided for card sorting, and Figure 6.6 visualises the tree testing instructions).

CARD SORTING INSTRUCTIONS

This task is known as a card sorting exercise where we ask people to organize labelled cards into intuitive groups. It helps us to understand how you relate things to each other.

It will take you x – x minutes to complete.

Each card contains a title or a description of a thing.

We'd like you to sort these cards into groups, grouping together cards you think are similar in theme or closely related to each other. Group the cards in a way that makes sense to you.

You will find the cards in a list on the left-hand side of your screen. To group similar cards together, you can drag and drop each card into the main area of the screen.

[Closed sort instructions]

Use the group titles provided, drag and drop cards relevant to the group title into the appropriate column.

[Open sort instructions]

Create your groups by dragging and dropping an item from the left into the space on the right and adding related cards in the same column.

Please name your groups before finishing the exercise, in a way that makes the most sense to you.

[Hybrid sort instructions]

Use the group titles provided, drag and drop cards relevant to the group title into the appropriate column. You can also create additional groups of your own by dragging and dropping an item from the left into the space on the right and adding related cards in the same column.

Please name your groups before finishing the exercise, in a way that makes the most sense to you.

[For all sorts]

There is no right or wrong answer. Just do what comes naturally. When you're done click 'Finished' at the top right.[5]

FIGURE 6.1 Card sorting instructions step 1

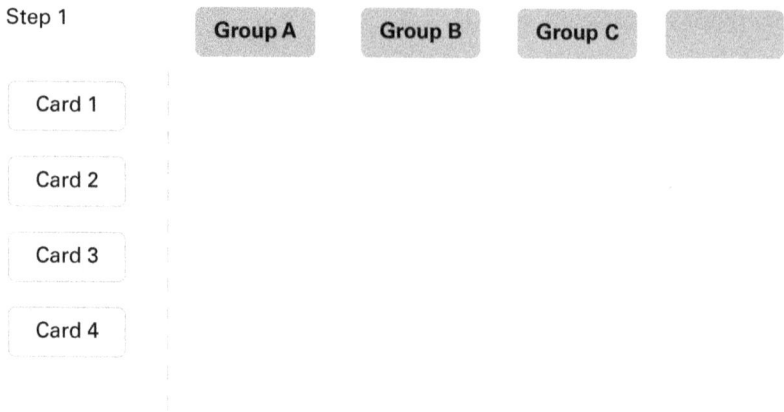

FIGURE 6.2 Card sorting instructions step 2

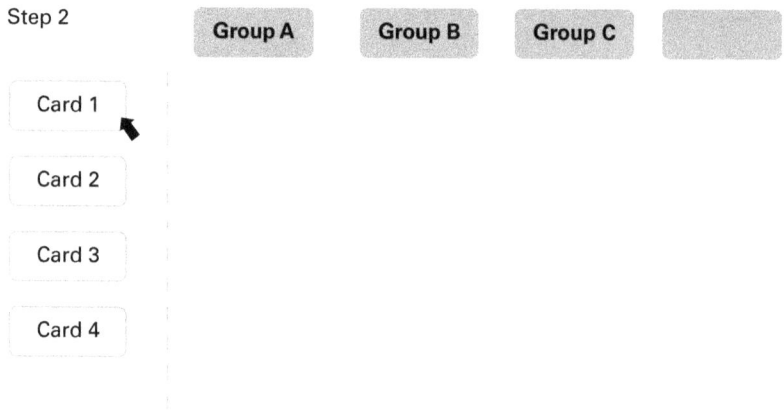

FIGURE 6.3 Card sorting instructions step 3

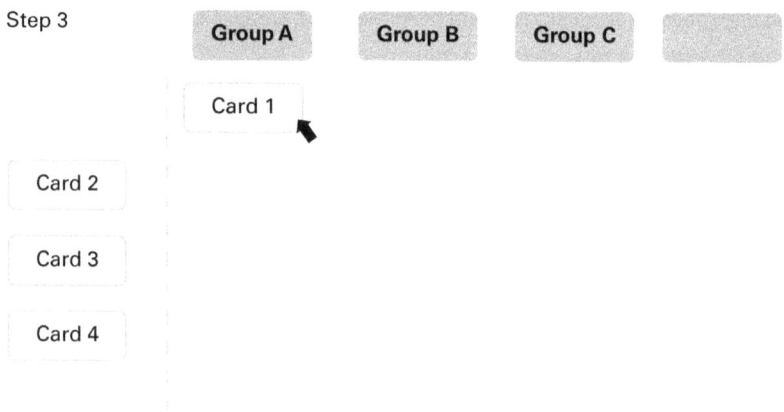

FIGURE 6.4 Card sorting instructions step 4

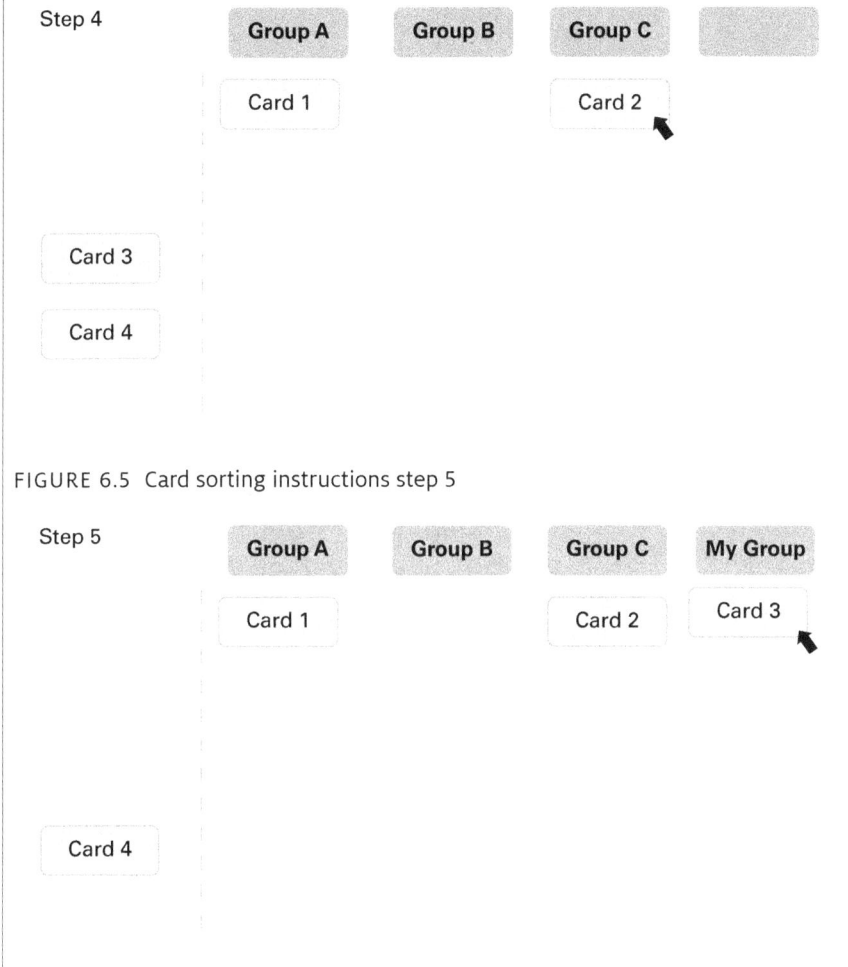

FIGURE 6.5 Card sorting instructions step 5

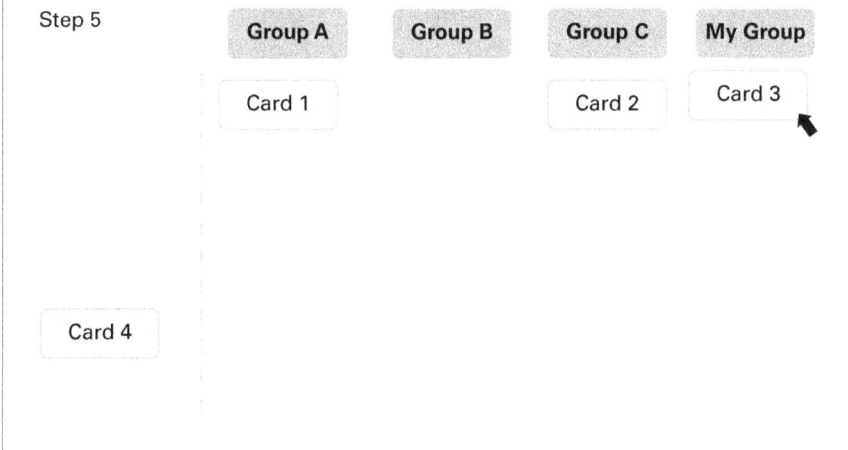

TREE TESTING INSTRUCTIONS

This task is known as a tree testing exercise. We ask people to show us where they would intuitively find information within a website, for example, using only the names of the content or pages.

It will take you 5–15 minutes to complete.

1   You will be asked to find a certain item and be presented with a list of links.

2   Click through the list until you arrive at one that you think helps you complete the task.

FIGURE 6.6 Tree testing visual instructions

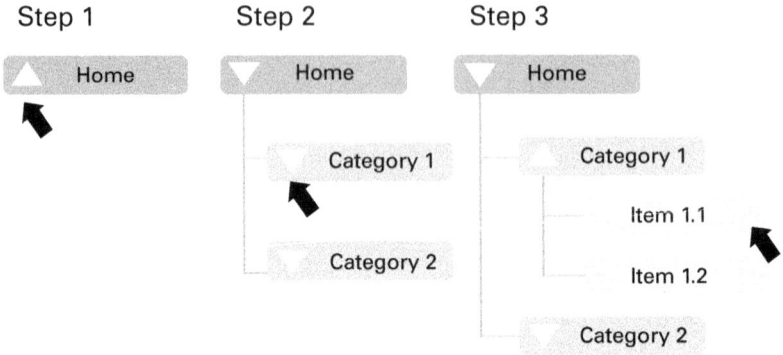

3   If you take a wrong turn, you can go back by clicking one of the links above.

This is not a test of your ability – there are no right or wrong answers.[6]

UNMODERATED USABILITY TASKS AND BENCHMARKING INSTRUCTIONS

Unmoderated usability test set-up for researchers:

- Tasks for unmoderated studies need to be more detailed and carefully written as there is no one to ask for clarification.
  - o Write tasks that cover your objectives.
  - o Write realistic tasks.
  - o Write actionable tasks.
  - o To help participants understand the tasks, give them a scenario of why they are doing the task.

Scenario: You have been invited to a wedding in August in England. You need a new outfit to attend the wedding, as the event has a dress code of 1920s flappers.

Task 1: Starting from the homepage, find an appropriate article of clothing that matches the wedding dress code, in your size. You have a budget of up to $250. Once you have found an appropriate item, please add it to the shopping cart.

Post-task questions[7]

- To what extent do you feel confident that you successfully completed the task? (1 = not confident at all, 7 = very confident)

- Overall, how easy or difficult was it to perform this task? (1= very easy, 7 = very difficult)
- Please provide feedback about completing the task (optional) [Open-ended question]

Instructions for participants

Thank you for participating in our study. This is a usability test, which means you will help us understand how real users interact with our product. Your feedback will help us improve the product to meet your needs.

You can complete this study in your own time and in your own environment. You will be given tasks to complete, your screen and actions will be captured while you are doing the task. Once you feel you have completed the task, you will be asked a couple of questions about your experience.

Before we start

- This study will require up to 15 minutes of your time.
- Choose a quiet, comfortable place to complete the study.
- Ensure your device and browser meet the requirements [requirements].
- Make sure you have a stable internet connection.
- Read the instructions for each task carefully.
- [If applicable] Please think aloud as you do the task. Talk about what you are trying to do, how you are trying to do it and what kind of experience you are having as you carry out the task.
- If you are stuck and unable to complete the task, please press the 'skip' button. You will be asked to describe why you couldn't proceed with the task.

Guidance we can provide

If we have a range of experience and capabilities in the team of those doing research, not only should we provide templates, but also guidance on best practice to again support the research done to be ethical, legally compliant, consistent and robust. Again, we will need to assess the situation, when starting to prioritize what guidance to provide in setting up and doing the research. The following are examples of the kind of guidance that is commonly required.

Guidance on note taking during research sessions

LOGISTICS

We can take brief notes ourselves, and ideally invite an observer who can also act as a note-taker. This will allow us to focus on the participant and not capture everything they say, but key things we may want to refer to later.

Focus on observations – recording what the participant is saying and doing and avoid trying to interpret what is happening.

Ask observers to look for:

- things people do: processes, tasks, tools, problems and barriers
- how they think: including their goals, triggers, choices, reasons, knowledge and gaps
- how they feel: their motivations, reactions, fears and frustrations

Taking good notes is a skill that needs to be developed over time, so give team members lots of opportunities to practise.

USING STICKY NOTES

For agile and lean research observers, they can write observations directly onto 'sticky notes' (virtual or physical). This saves time in later research analysis. These notes have to be kept brief and allow for fast analysis when thematic analysis of transcripts isn't possible within the timescales (although this should not be the only type of analysis we should ever use, but combined with other rounds of more robust research).

Ask observers to make notes that are:

- written clearly so they're easy to read
- brief
- based on a single point or observation, so they're easy to analyse and sort
- labelled with the relevant participant and session number

We could also ask observers to use colours consistently so we can sort the notes into observations, findings and actions, which would all be assigned different colours.[8]

Competitor analysis template and guidance

Competitor analysis is used to identify the strengths and weaknesses of our products and services and that of our major and minor competitors, enabling better ideation of strategies to stay competitive through improving or repositioning existing products and services as well as identifying gaps in the market that have not been filled yet or have not been filled effectively by others.

This should be done with our existing product or service, or the intended product or service. And then a SWOT analysis can be made analysing and synthesizing the strengths, weaknesses, opportunities and threats to our organization's proposition (see Table 6.3 for a competitor analysis template).[9]

Setting up and conducting research is the most dynamic time in the research process; it is where ReOps provide the most active support, in terms of working with the people doing research, as well as the templates and guidance we can provide. Although we are less actively involved in the next phases of doing a research project, there is still a lot of guidance that can be provided to support analysis and synthesis, which is often the stage of research that people feel the least confident about, and then sharing the research with impact.

TABLE 6.3 Competitor analysis template

Element	Description of element
Competitor name	Who is the competitor?
Mission and objectives	Organization intention
Product or service name	What proposition are we focusing on for the analysis?
Value proposition	Demonstrable benefits of product or service
Target market	Who are the groups of customers this proposition is for?
Market share	What is the size of this competitor's market share for this proposition?
Pricing	What pricing models are they?
Journey steps Journey usability	Documenting journeys of interest within a proposition Analysing the usability of each step in the process
Feature descriptions Feature pros and cons	If there is not a journey involved, e.g. tasks to do on a digital service, describe the features of the product and their pros and cons, when for example using a physical product
Marketing strategy online Marketing strategy offline	How is the proposition marketed online and offline – style of campaign on the relevant channels, is there consistency for a mutli-channel approach?
Key differentiators	What positively sets this proposition apart from others?
Key detractors	What negatively sets this proposition apart from others?

How to analyse and synthesize our findings

Analysis and synthesis of data is often the most daunting stage of the research process. Data and knowledge management practices are an important part of this stage in the research process (see Chapter 5). There aren't a lot of templates we can provide for this stage. It may be something that we consider as part of our training strategy for those who are less experienced. We can provide guidance on the analysis methods available, depending on the type of research being done. Best practice in research advises us to choose our analysis method as we are deciding our research method. This is because we may need to structure our data collection methodology in a particular way to enable us to do analysis in a particular way to answer our research questions in the most robust and actionable way possible.

Guidance on the types of analysis methods available: Analysis for qualitative research

CONTENT ANALYSIS/THEMATIC ANALYSIS

Content and thematic analysis is a way to codify and categorize qualitative data. It is a rigorous but interpretative art, putting things in systematic order based on themes relevant to our research objective. Thematic analysis, also known as grounded theory, allows us to go beyond the basic ordering and grouping to a deeper understanding of what the data is telling us.

This type of analysis is suitable for data generated from qualitative methods such as interviews, contextual inquiry, ethnography and diary studies, usability testing and open text field survey questions, too. Thematic analysis can be used in agile and lean environments.

We use thematic and content analysis if we need to identify patterns in qualitative data, and summarize by counting the patterns/various aspects of the content. We can make sense of large amounts of qualitative data.

Patterns (regular, repetitive, consistent occurrences) can be characterized by:

- similarities
- differences
- frequency
- sequence
- correspondence

AFFINITY DIAGRAMMING

Affinity diagramming is another useful method for identifying patterns from qualitative data. The difference between affinity diagramming and thematic analysis is that affinity diagramming is much more visual and participatory. It can be done using physical or digital sticky notes to write down ideas and then group similar things together. Thematic and content analysis is considered more rigorous and tends to be done by an individual. Affinity diagramming is a visual method of analysis, done through collaboration and physically moving pieces of data around into groups.

This method is suitable for agile and lean ways of working. It's a useful way of getting a first cut of findings to show stakeholders and get them on board with research themes early and then an individual can do the more robust thematic analysis to ensure the themes identified in the affinity diagramming are robust. This approach of affinity diagramming in the open was shared by Amy Stoks of Good People (www.wearegoodpeople.nz). A collaborative/open approach has the advantage of everyone engaging with the themes early, increasing a sense of ownership in the analysis and potential solutions, seeing things through to implementation. Early engagement helps with cross-organization storytelling and amplifying the intended outcomes, rather than stakeholders and colleagues being blindsided or overwhelmed by research results that are only shared at the end of the research process when the insights are fully formed.

Advice for analysing large amounts of qualitative data

When handling a lot of qualitative data, for example 20 transcripts for one-hour interviews, it will take a relatively long time to do this analysis and it can often take multiple rounds of analysis and synthesis before we truly understand what the data is telling us. For every one hour of interview, it could require multiple hours of analysis.

Usability research analysis will not require as much analysis time, for example, as exploratory interviews combined with ethnographic observation. The amount of time set aside for analysis really depends on the type of data we've collected, the type of thing we are trying to learn and what stage of the development process we're at. If we're doing a large discovery project to really understand the landscape and opportunities available, we need to make the time to do rigorous analysis, to be confident that we are making a decision to develop a product or service based on high-quality robust insights. If we are doing multiple rounds of research on prototypes, the analysis process can be more agile and lean (while still being robust), with each round of analysis being relatively short. *Just Enough Research* talks about having just enough data and insight to confidently make the next decision.[10] So it depends on what the stakes of that decision are. Are we making a decision to change a particular interaction on one webpage or are we making a decision to redefine an entire product journey or service experience? We will need more data to confidently make a decision on the latter scenario, compared to the former.

CATALOGUING ISSUES AND POSITIVES

If the aim of our work has been to identify, catalogue and prioritize issues with our product or service, identifying issues requires different processes depending on whether we have gathered qualitative or quantitative data – or we may be combining the two. We'll look at quantitative data shortly. This method is suitable for data generated from small-scale usability testing, pop-up testing and content testing (not to be confused with content analysis!). We use this method when we want to identify usability issues and user needs from our data.

AGILE ANALYSIS

We may be in a team environment that is using agile or lean UX ways of working and already have research included in the sprint planning process. If research isn't already included, it can be very difficult to get user research done and used in an effective way with the cadence of work. It can be at odds with the agile development process. However, the agile development process can include user research throughout, not just at the end to validate what has been done, but also during sprints to solve user problems.[11]

Analysis for quantitative research

- Usability metrics: There are two main types of metrics we can use to measure the experience of our product/service.
  - Objective metrics measure behaviour. These metrics are measured through observation and tracking. This includes time taken, success and failure rate, number of errors made, effectiveness and efficiency.
  - Subjective metrics measure attitude, opinions and perception. These are self-reported metrics, measured through survey questions. This includes satisfaction, Single Ease Question, Net Promoter Score (NPS).

- Combining subjective and objective metrics: It is useful to combine these metrics to understand whether the participant's perception matches reality.

If we need to understand the size of something, we will need to include large-scale surveys as part of our methodology, and plan for enough response for results to be statistically significant. MeasuringU.com has a lot of great resources and training on planning, collecting, analysing and understanding quantitative research data.

Triangulating data guidance

Triangulating data is where we gather multiple sources together on the same topic. We are often combining primary and secondary research techniques when we triangulate our data. For example, we are using web analytics shared from our data and performance analyst colleagues to demonstrate the potential scale of problems we have identified in usability research.

Or we are combining statistically significant attitudinal data from market research surveys with insights of behaviour from contextual user research. Combining different types of data makes our insights more robust, giving qualitative and quantitative perspectives on the research topic – covering the what and why of the thing we are learning about through the research and creating a holistic, evidence-based narrative. Before triangulation and synthesis are undertaken those doing research will need to assess each source of data to assess whether it is suitable and compatible to use in this particular project. We can use the essential knowledge management elements outlined in Chapter 5 to assess whether we can confidently combine multiple datasets.

Analysis infrastructure

If we are supporting qualitative research, then analysis infrastructure is something that is worth developing. Whether using a specialist data analysis tool or repurposing other tools already in our toolbox (such as Trello), consistent and robust analysis is essential to delivering high-quality and trustworthy insights. Something that it will be extremely useful to establish is a shared taxonomy. This is metadata that is relevant to the organization's vision, goals and strategy, that covers topics and elements that have the potential to come up in each and every, or at least many, of the research projects that happen. Having a consistent way to name patterns and trends that we are identifying becomes increasingly powerful over time and it enables us to triangulate more effectively across multiple research studies, over many years. We can see current trends and past trends – behaviours, perceptions, motivations, attitudes and how they changed over time.

Let's imagine we are working for a charity (Support Charity) and we are doing both market research for positioning the charity's next campaign and user research for the charity's website. We can use a shared taxonomy to analyse qualitative research. Table 6.4 demonstrates what our Support Charity shared taxonomy might be.

As we can see, the shared taxonomy is quite high-level and is designed to be broadly applicable to all research and tie it to the organization's vision. A shared organizational taxonomy alone is not enough for robust and detailed analysis of qualitative research. So we need to enable flexibility, which means that people doing research are not constrained to only using the shared taxonomy but they make use of this and add local taxonomies – there may be a taxonomy that is specific to the focus of a specific programme of work and then taxonomies that are specific to a research project.

Market research example

The marketing team are looking to understand better what motivates people who have recently donated for the first time to make one-off vs monthly donations, to be able to tailor marketing to encourage people to subscribe to direct debit monthly donations. With this research objective, we can see

TABLE 6.4 Example of a shared taxonomy for Support Charity

Pains	Gains	Organization values identified
Ethical concerns	Ethically sound	Dignity
Uncertain	Transparent	Empathy
Confusing	Clarity	Practical
Unaware	Awareness	Activism
Expectations not met	Expectations met	Positivity
Biased	Objective	People-orientated

that the global taxonomy won't be enough to analyse the focus group data solidly. The project itself may need its own unique taxonomy. But we can easily imagine that this is research that will be run more than once, maybe even on an annual cadence. Therefore, we can build a taxonomy that is specific to this research focus, as shown in Table 6.5.

User research example

The online donations team needs to understand why conversion rates are not meeting targets. They may do multiple types of research to understand how to improve their online donation conversion rates, such as contextual enquiry, usability research and unmoderated screen recordings, etc. Table 6.6 demonstrates the kind of taxonomy we might want to use for this user research focus.

I'm not saying this is a ready-made taxonomy to use in real-life projects, but it's useful as an illustration for the different levels of taxonomy we may need.

How to share our research with maximum impact

This is covered in detail in Chapter 5 – data, information and knowledge management.

TABLE 6.5 Example of a specific market research taxonomy for Support Charity

Promoters	Detractors	On the fence
Relatable stories	Unrelatable stories	Already volunteering
Elicit sense of altruism	Elicit sense of guilt	Donate goods/food instead
Sense of purpose	Finances too tight	Lack fund use transparency
Clear identity	Unclear impact	Apathetic
Sense of impact	Lack connection to purpose	Giving to other charities
Strong connection	Lack of trust	Participate in fundraising events

SOURCE Charity Link. Why don't people give to charity? Ten reasons for not donating. Charity Link, 2024. www.charitylink.net/blog/why-dont-people-give-to-charity-ten-reasons-for-not-donating; S Allen. Ten ways to encourage people to give more, Greater Good Magazine, 2017. greatergood. berkeley.edu/article/item/ten_ways_to_encourage_people_to_give_more

TABLE 6.6 Example of a specific user research taxonomy for Support Charity

Promoters	Detractors	Tasks
Information architecture understandable	Confusing call to action	Research charity
Clear call to action	Confusing navigation	Pick charity
Attractive design	Cluttered interface	Sign up to newsletter
Mobile friendly	Slow loading speed	Create account
Confidence in security	Accessibility issue	Check out as guest
Strong branding	Broken links	Add bank details
Key content surfaced	Security concern	Add credit card details
Easy transaction	Irrelevant pop-ups	Set up direct debit
Easy to find contact info	Key content missing	Choose donation amount
Understandable labelling	Not mobile friendly	Choose monthly or one off donation

Centralized research prioritization

How research is prioritized can depend on how research teams and research operations teams are structured within an organization (which we'll look at in Part Two).

Researchers may be embedded in marketing and product teams; in such situations what research takes priority will be decided between team leadership and the researcher. If researchers are working agency-style in a centralized team, it is likely that a variety of teams across the organization will make research requests, requesting time and resources from the research team to focus on their research need. If this is the case, something that research operations can work with the researchers to set up and manage is a research request process.

There are multiple reasons to set up a standardized research request process and a research backlog:

- track research demand
- track research questions
- consistently receive necessary information to enable effective research prioritization
- manage research resources

- increase research transparency
- increase rigour of research question asked
- surface past research findings and insights to teams, where primary research isn't required[12]

Several teams may unknowingly be requesting the same type of question to be answered.[13] If it is not prioritized the first (few) time(s) the research is requested, if we have a backlog of research questions this will help identify not only a research priority but also the opportunity to bring multiple teams together to work on strategic research for example, breaking down organizational silos.

Managing research requests and questions

One way to manage research requests is to have an intake form that anyone can use to request research or pose a research question; these requests will go into the research backlog to be evaluated and prioritized.[14]

What to add to a research request form:

- Name and contact details of requester.
- Name of team/department requesting research.
- Is there a sponsor for the work?
- What do they want to learn?
- Is there a particular customer group they want to focus on?
- Is there a specific product/service/business area the research needs to focus on?
- What are the relevant business goals?
- How do they intend to use the research insights?
- What is the intended impact on the customers?
- Known risks and constraints.

It is best to focus on what they want to learn and let the experts decide what kind of research is needed, if any. This approach is useful to enable anyone, however research literate or not, to request research services and support.

Conclusion

Who creates the templates and guidance will very much depend on the skills of the ReOps person/people. What I have shared here is a foundation on which to build, but undoubtedly needs to be iterated and detail added depending on our organization context.

If the ReOps people are Ops but not research professionals, collaboration is needed to ensure the templates and guidelines are as accurate and useful as possible. Bringing together research and operations expertise is necessary to provide the right things to those doing the research.

This also means some negotiation may be required for researchers to take time out of doing research, in the short term, to work on building the operations infrastructure that will benefit everyone in the long term.

Notes

1 M Mintjes. UX research briefing template, UX Insight, 2021. uxinsight.org/ ux-research-briefing-template/ (archived at https://perma.cc/668L-B9X6); P Hague (2022) *Market Research in Practice: An introduction to gaining greater market insight*, 4th edn, Kogan Page, London; L Buley (2013) *The User Experience Team of One: A research and design survival guide*, Rosenfeld Media, New York; E Hall (2019) *Just Enough Research*, 2nd edn, A Book Apart, New York

2 M Mintjes. UX research briefing template, UX Insight, 2021. uxinsight.org/ ux-research-briefing-template/ (archived at https://perma.cc/668L-B9X6); P Hague (2022) *Market Research in Practice: An introduction to gaining greater market insight*, 4th edn, Kogan Page, London; L Buley (2013) *The User Experience Team of One: A research and design survival guide*, Rosenfeld Media, New York; E Hall (2019) *Just Enough Research*, 2nd edn, A Book Apart, New York

3 A J Beltis. How to run a focus group for your business, HubSpot, 2022. blog. hubspot.com/marketing/how-to-run-a-focus-group (archived at https://perma. cc/5DEX-RWB8)

4 A J Beltis. How to run a focus group for your business, HubSpot, 2022. blog. hubspot.com/marketing/how-to-run-a-focus-group (archived at https://perma. cc/5DEX-RWB8); Service Manual Team. Doing pop-up research, GOV.UK Service Manual, 2017. www.gov.uk/service-manual/user-research/doing-pop-up-research (archived at https://perma.cc/S3GQ-VNZN) All text content is available under the Open Government Licence v3.0 (www.nationalarchives.gov. uk/doc/open-government-licence/version/3/ (archived at https://perma.cc/55XA-5HP5))

5   Optimal Workshop. Introduction to card sorting, Optimal Workshop, 2024. www.optimalworkshop.com/101guides/card-sorting-101 (archived at https://perma.cc/XK4R-3ECX)

6   Optimal Workshop. Tree testing overview, Optimal Workshop, 2024. www.optimalworkshop.com/101guides/tree-testing-101 (archived at https://perma.cc/FU8Q-7H5S)

7   K Whitenton. Unmoderated user tests: How and why to do them, Nielsen Norman Group, 2019. www.nngroup.com/articles/unmoderated-usability-testing (archived at https://perma.cc/4HWA-CZ4Y)/; T Adamjak. What is unmoderated usability testing? w/examples. UXtweak, 2024. blog.uxtweak.com/unmoderated-usability-testing-101/ (archived at https://perma.cc/QF6H-TTZ9); Maze. A beginner's guide to usability testing. Chapter 11: 5 Real-life usability testing examples and approaches to apply, Maze, 2024. maze.co/guides/usability-testing/examples/ (archived at https://perma.cc/Q4VE-BVM3)

8   Service Manual Team. Taking notes and recording user research sessions, GOV.UK Service Manual, 2017. www.gov.uk/service-manual/user-research/taking-notes-and-recording-user-research-sessions (archived at https://perma.cc/YXR4-NME7) All text content is available under the Open Government Licence v3.0 (www.nationalarchives.gov.uk/doc/open-government-licence/version/3/ (archived at https://perma.cc/7VDV-9EFW))

9   Lucidchart Software Inc. Competitive analysis, Lucidchart, 2024. www.lucidchart.com/pages/templates/competitive-analysis (archived at https://perma.cc/SFL8-72CA); Qualtrics. Competitor analysis using market research, Qualtrics, 2024. www.qualtrics.com/en-gb/experience-management/brand/competitor-market-research/ (archived at https://perma.cc/4MSR-GL44)

10 E Hall (2019) *Just Enough Research*, 2nd edn, A Book Apart, New York

11 Z Cabrera-Mieles. The rainbow sheet: a visual method for research analysis, UX Collective, 2019. uxdesign.cc/the-rainbow-sheet-a-visual-method-for-research-analysis-a7e7d201105 (archived at https://perma.cc/WF2R-C2G9); C Fu. How a spreadsheet can make usability analysis faster and easier, User Research in Government Blog, 2019. userresearch.blog.gov.uk/2019/09/13/how-a-spreadsheet-can-make-usability-analysis-faster-and-easier/ (archived at https://perma.cc/SJR5-93DB)

12 R Miles. Managing research insights at a portfolio level, ResearchOps Community, 2020. medium.com/researchops-community/managing-research-insights-at-a-portfolio-level-45585c9594d8 (archived at https://perma.cc/DAE5-LKDJ)

13 R Miles. Managing research insights at a portfolio level, ResearchOps Community, 2020. medium.com/researchops-community/managing-research-insights-at-a-portfolio-level-45585c9594d8 (archived at https://perma.cc/DAE5-LKDJ)

14 R Miles. Managing research insights at a portfolio level, ResearchOps Community, 2020. medium.com/researchops-community/managing-research-insights-at-a-portfolio-level-45585c9594d8 (archived at https://perma.cc/DAE5-LKDJ)

PART TWO

People

One of the eight pillars of user research discussed in Chapter 1 is about environment, and that means people in the work environment. Anything we do, it's really all about people – the people creating and using the systems to support research and scale research. The support of discipline experts is needed in order for the right people to be recruited, and develop and grow within an organization. I believe this is true of user research, market research and research operations. It's important to enable different types of learning and adjust team structures, where they sit in an organization and identify new skills gaps as all practices mature within an organization and as business needs change.

We dive into all these facets in Part Two:

- how to recruit researchers
- how to recruit ReOps professionals
- and how to support sustainable, long-term learning and development, which for ReOps as a fledgling discipline we aren't at the stage of focusing on as yet

7

Recruiting researchers

I have done a lot of recruiting in my time. It is a real privilege to be able to offer someone a job (it's also hard when candidates aren't suitable or successful). I would say that researchers tend to make good recruiters, because of their interviewing skills, but equally the recruitment process has its own set of skills and being a good interviewee is also its own skill which not everyone has, even if they are very qualified for a job.

There is much support that can be provided if recruitment of team members is part of the remit of the ReOps team. Templates and guidance used to support most stages of the recruitment process include:

- jobs framework
- job descriptions
- advertising in the right places (for DEI)
- sifting CVs and candidate selection
- screener interview (done by recruitment/HR teams)
- interview and review
- practical interview and review
- offer

The first step in recruiting researchers is having a clear and well-scoped job description. If there is little infrastructure already set up to recruit researchers, you may need to first create a job framework appropriate to your organization before you can write an appropriate job description. This is because you must understand what level of experience you need to recruit to fill the skills gap you have identified. There may not be time to create a framework and then write the job description and then recruit someone, but a framework should be very close to the top of your priority list.

Job frameworks

Job frameworks set the expectation of the skills needed and at what level of experience a certain job level should have. There are broad areas that will be true of any research role, but there will also be nuances depending on your organization, industry and the focus of the research role itself. Table 7.1 breaks down the elements of a job framework. This framework was inspired by my time working in UK government and recruiting researchers based on an older version of the Government Digital and Data Profession Capability Framework (also known as the DDAT Framework, 1).

What the levels of experience mean:

- Awareness:
  o A person can describe the fundamentals of the skill.
  o And they can demonstrate basic knowledge of some of the skill's tools and techniques.
- Working:
  o A person can apply the skill with some support.
  o And they can adopt the most appropriate tools and techniques.
- Practitioner:
  o A person can apply the skill without support.
  o And determine and use the most appropriate tools and techniques.
  o And they can share knowledge and experience of the skill.
- Expert:
  o A person can lead and guide a team or organization in the skill's best practice.
  o And they can teach the skill's advanced tools and techniques.[1]

You may not entirely agree with my assessment of what skills are needed at each level, or it may not be quite appropriate to your organization: this is based broadly on 21 years of experience. It will also depend on the type of research job you need to recruit for to what level of experience candidates need in quantitative and qualitative research skills. For example, a senior market research analyst will be expected to have stronger quantitative research methodology skills compared with a senior user researcher, who is likely to do a lot more qualitative research. But I think it is fair to say that no one person has an equal level of expertise in each area of their job.

Table 7.1, as it stands, is too open to interpretation; what a 'working level of planning' means to me might differ in essential details to your expectations.

TABLE 7.1 Elements of a research job framework

	Junior	Midweight	Senior	Lead IC	Lead manager	Head
Planning	Aware	Working	Practitioner	Expert	Expert	Expert
Qualitative research		Working	Working-practitioner	Practitioner-expert	Practitioner-expert	
Quantitative research		Aware	Working	Practitioner		
Inclusive research					Practitioner	
Analysis and synthesis		Working	Practitioner	Expert	Practitioner-expert	
Communicating					Expert	
Implementation						
Data management						
Strategy		Aware	Working	Practitioner-expert		
Leadership	N/A	N/A	Aware			
People management	N/A	Aware	Working-practitioner	Aware		

The next step is to have a description about what it means to have expertise in communicating research, for example. Having a description of each skill area at each level of experience means that when you are working with colleagues to sift and interview candidates, there is an agreed expectation of each job role. This makes recruitment much fairer and consistent as the process is systematized and decreases the influence of personal opinions on candidates.

The following is a senior user researcher skills matrix, which contains descriptions of the expected skill levels of a senior user researcher at each phase of the research process.

SENIOR USER RESEARCHER

Phase: Planning
Level of experience: Practitioner

Description: A senior is able to independently:

- Scope a problem space and identify research objectives aligned with business objectives.
- Select the appropriate research method, sample size and participant criteria to answer the research questions.
- Prioritize research activities.
- Work with and support less experienced researchers.

Phase: Doing qualitative research
Level of experience: Practitioner

Description: Independently implement methods: in recruitment and data collection

- Usability testing, interviews, contextual inquiry, diary studies.
- Work with and support less experienced researchers.

Phase: Doing quantitative research
Level of experience: Working

Description: Can do with some support

- Implement methods for recruitment and data collection.
- Statistically significant surveys, card sorting, tree testing, usability benchmarking, UX metrics.

Phase: Doing inclusive research
Level of experience: Working

Description: A senior will:

- Have a broad understanding of access needs.
- Conduct research to be inclusive of a range of access needs.
- Practise diverse participant selection.

Phase: Analyse and synthesize
Level of experience: Working-practitioner

Description:

- Able to assess data quality, do data cleaning and processing.
- Analysis methods: content analysis, thematic analysis, affinity diagramming, severity assessment, persona creation.
- Analysis methods: choosing and implementing appropriately statistical tests, interpret similarity matrix and denograms.
- Triangulate with other data sources and secondary research.
- Create a strong narrative aligned to business objectives.

Phase: Communication
Level of experience: Practitioner

Description:

- Use audience-appropriate language and style.
- Adapt to different audiences with different priorities and levels of research literacy.

Phase: Implementation
Level of experience: Practitioner

Description: Work with a team to prioritize what needs to be actioned from the research and ground implementation of insights, such as sketching sessions grounded in data.

Phase: Data management
Level of experience: Practitioner

Description:

- Follow GDPR processes to ensure data privacy and security, support less experienced researchers.
- Data is collected and stored appropriately, data is deleted when required.

Phase: Strategy
Level of experience: Aware

Description:

- Be familiar with research strategy.
- Work to use research to influence strategy (for example, product roadmaps).

Phase: Leadership
Level of experience: Working

Description: Awareness and developing skills in stakeholder management, alignment with other teams, coordinating with other researchers working related areas.

Phase: People management
Level of experience: Working-practitioner

Description: Support recruitment of junior and midweight practitioners.

Support learning and development of less experienced practitioners.

The senior user research skills matrix is inspired by the work done in government and at Springer Nature in collaboration with colleagues.

I have not created a generic 'senior customer researcher' skills matrix. Rather, I have separated out user researcher and market researcher skills. There is a lot of overlap, but when it comes to recruitment and setting objectives and expectations for a person in a role, the nuance is important.

So, now let's look at a description of the expected skill levels of a senior market researcher.

SENIOR MARKET RESEARCHER

Phase: Planning
Level of experience: Practitioner

Description: A senior is able to independently:

- Scope a problem space and identify research objectives aligned with business objectives.
- Select the appropriate research method, sample size and participant criteria to answer the research questions.
- Prioritize research activities.

- Understand the marketing process and where research fits in it.
- Work with and support less experienced researchers.

Phase: Doing qualitative research
Level of experience: Working

Description: Qualitative research is done with support to implement methods:

- Recruit and data collection.
- Interviews, focus groups, ethnographic observation, secondary research.

Phase: Doing quantitative research
Level of experience: Practitioner

Description: Quantitative research is done independently.

- Implement methods: for recruitment and data collection.
- Statistically significant surveys, social media analysis.
- Work with and support less experienced researchers.

Phase: Doing inclusive research
Level of experience: Working

Description: A senior will:

- Have a broad understanding of access needs.
- Conduct research to be inclusive of a range of access needs.
- Practise diverse participant selection.

Phase: Analyse and synthesize
Level of experience: Working-practitioner

Description:

- Able to assess data quality, do data cleaning and processing.
- Analysis methods: thematic analysis, persona creation.
- Analysis methods: choosing and implementing appropriate statistical tests.
- Triangulate with other data sources and secondary research.
- Create a strong narrative aligned to business objectives.

Phase: Communication
Level of experience: Practitioner

Description:

- Use audience appropriate language and style.
- Adapt to different audiences with different priorities and levels of research literacy.

Phase: Implementation
Level of experience: Practitioner

Description: Work with teams and stakeholders, to ensure they are able to make evidence-based decisions based on understanding of market size and structure, use of and attitudes to products, customer satisfaction and loyalty, brand impact, pricing, market gap analysis, segmentation.

Phase: Data management
Level of experience: Practitioner

Description:

- Follow GDPR processes to ensure data privacy and security, support less experienced researchers.
- Data is collected and stored appropriately, data is deleted when required.

Phase: Strategy
Level of experience: Aware

Description: Be familiar with research strategy.

- Work to use research to influence strategy (for example, brand and marketing strategies).

Phase: Leadership
Level of experience: Working

Description: Awareness and developing skills in stakeholder management, alignment with other teams, coordinating with other researchers working in related areas.

Phase: People management
Level of experience: Working-practitioner

Description:

- Support recruitment of junior and midweight practitioners.
- Support learning and development of less experienced practitioners.

The senior market researcher skills matrix is inspired by the Market Research Society and P Hague.[2]

Now that expectations of roles have been agreed, it is time to create or iterate the job description that you need to recruit for.

Job descriptions and the types of roles we may need

Market research

Types of job available in the market research space:

- quantitative:
  - data analyst
  - data scientist
  - marketing forecaster
- quantitative and/or qualitative
  - market research analyst
  - insight executive
  - market researcher/research manager/research executive

Qualitative market research uses qualitative research methods such as focus groups, in-depth interviews and ethnographic observation; focusing on the how and why of the topic, focusing on attitudes and opinions, and common behaviours. Quantitative market research uses quantitative research methods focusing on numbers; big data, metrics, statistics that ask what, where and when. This type of research looks at the scale of problems or trends.[3]

Job descriptions will need to be in line with our organization's brand values and tone of voice.

The backbone of a job description

MARKET RESEARCH ANALYST/DATA ANALYST/INSIGHT EXECUTIVE

Summary
A data analyst collects, processes and analyses data to provide insights and support decision-making. They ensure data quality, select appropriate analytic techniques and assist in project set-up. Their work includes creating visualizations, reports and dashboards, and collaborating with stakeholders to meet business needs.

Skills

Technical and craft skills

They will have familiarity with:

- Research methodologies: surveys, customer feedback, research panels or internal databases, management of surveys, questionnaires and focus groups.
- Data quality – assessing quality [fit for purpose] (with support).
- Data cleaning.
- Statistical analysis techniques.
- Analysis tools Excel, SQL, Python, R.
- Triangulate data.
- Data visualization.
- Tracking trends.
- Producing regular reports.
- Critical thinking skills.
- Understanding the marketing process and where research fits in it.

Communication skills

Communicating about a project using language that audiences will understand.

Business skills

- Able to work in cross-functional teams.
- Align research with business needs; gathering data to help a company market its products or services. Understand consumer demographics, preferences, needs and buying habits.

Day-to-day responsibilities

Common day-to-day activities of juniors – leads with increasing size and complexity of project:

- Plan research studies.
- Explain data collection purposes and techniques to stakeholders with support.
- Run lawful data collection activities.

- Analyse and synthesize data, organize the results.
- Write survey reports.
- Monitor and forecast marketing and sales trends.
- Data management; store information securely.

Whether the roles require quantitative or qualitative, or mixed method data collection methodologies will depend on the role and the needs of the organization.

SENIOR: MARKET RESEARCH ANALYST/DATA ANALYST/INSIGHT EXECUTIVE

Summary

The role involves leading data analysis projects, cleaning and processing data, applying statistical modelling and predictive analytics. It includes collaborating with stakeholders, presenting insights, mentoring junior analysts and optimizing data processes to support strategic decision-making.

Skills

Technical and craft skills

Can work independently and lead projects of a particular size and complexity.

- Competent practitioner of a variety of research methodologies: surveys, customer feedback, research panels or internal databases, management of surveys, questionnaires and focus groups.
- Data quality – assessing quality [is data fit for purpose?].
- Data cleaning.
- Statistical analysis techniques.
- Analysis tools such as Excel, SQL, Python, R.
- Triangulate data.
- Data visualization.
- Monitor and forecast sales, government policies, market trends and developments.
- Produce regular reports.
- Critical thinking and problem-solving skills.

Communication skills

Have communication and presentation skills, with the ability to translate insights into actionable recommendations, project management, and the ability to influence and collaborate with stakeholders at various levels.

Business skills

- Provide insights to drive business growth and decision-making.
- Able to translate insights into actionable recommendations.
- Able to influence and collaborate with stakeholders at various levels.
- Lead and manage research projects from inception to completion.
- Collaborate with cross-functional teams.

Day-to-day responsibilities

- Supporting more junior colleagues.
- Communicating with clients and understanding their goals and objectives.
- Planning research studies, devising suitable research methodologies.
- Explaining data collection purposes and techniques to stakeholders with support.
- Running lawful data collection activities.
- Analysis and synthesis of data, organizing the results.
- Conducting in-depth secondary and primary research (including phone interviews, opinion polls, questionnaires and surveys for collecting data, as required).
- Conducting research on marketing strategies and consumer opinions.
- Writing survey reports.
- Monitoring and forecasting marketing and sales trends.
- Measuring the effectiveness of marketing programmes and strategies.
- Gathering and analysing data on consumers, competitors and market conditions.
- Converting complex data and findings into understandable tables, graphs and written reports.
- Collaborating with diverse research teams, marketing professionals, pollsters, statisticians and other professionals.
- Preparing reports and presenting results to clients and management.
- Data management; storing information securely.

Depending on the organization, seniors may also have people management responsibilities.

LEAD/PRINCIPAL DATA ANALYST

Summary
The role involves collaborating with project managers on data methods, setting up projects (e.g. randomizations, experimental design) and performing data cleaning, organization and basic statistical analysis. It includes advanced analytics (e.g. key drivers analysis, segmentation), researching new methods, and engaging with clients. Responsibilities also include selecting analytic techniques, ensuring data quality and managing data tools and infrastructure. Strong leadership, communication and stakeholder management skills are essential.

Skills

Technical and craft skills
Lead complex and large projects, coordinate across multiple projects.

- Expert practitioner of a variety of research methodologies: surveys, customer feedback, research panels or internal databases, manage surveys, questionnaires and focus groups.
- Support others to plan and deliver their projects using best practice including randomizations, experimental design, key drivers analysis, segmentation.
- Ensure data quality and cleansing across the team.
- Statistical analysis techniques using Excel, SQL, Python, R.
- Triangulate data.
- Data visualization.
- Monitor and forecast sales, government policies, market trends and developments.
- Produce regular reports.
- Critical thinking and problem-solving skills.
- In-depth understanding of data tools and data management, understanding of data governance frameworks and regulations, experience with data infrastructure, storage and architecture, data science.

Communication and business skills

- Leadership and people management, communication and presentation skills, stakeholder management, business acumen, influencing and negotiation.
- Client communications, e.g. immersion meetings or presentations, including providing prompt feedback to queries; senior client and stakeholder-facing role.

Day-to-day responsibilities

- Communicating with stakeholders and understanding their goals and objectives.
- Ensuring primary and secondary research are being conducted lawfully and to a high standard.
- Conducting more complex and high priority research.
- Collaborating with colleagues to align research with marketing strategies.
- Monitoring and forecasting sales, government policies, market trends and developments.
- Collaborating with diverse research teams, marketing professionals, pollsters, statisticians, and other professionals.
- Recruitment of research team members.
- Preparing market research reports and presenting research findings/results to the clients or stakeholders.
- Undertaking research into additional methods which may be useful in future research.
- Measuring the effectiveness of marketing programmes and strategies.

HEAD OF DATA/INSIGHT

Summary

The role involves developing data strategies, leading the data team, aligning projects with business goals, and overseeing data governance, quality and security. It promotes data-driven decision-making, manages relationships with external data vendors and ensures compliance. This is a senior leadership position responsible for the overall data strategy.

Skills

- Leadership and people management.
- Communication and presentation skills.
- Strategic thinking.
- Stakeholder management.
- Business acumen.
- Influencing and negotiation.
- Able to influence decision-making.
- Implement strategy.
- Foster a culture of data-driven decision-making.
- Deep expert understanding of data tools and collection and data management, understanding of data governance frameworks and regulations, experience with data infrastructure, security, storage and architecture.

Day-to-day responsibilities

- Provide strategic vision, setting the long-term strategic direction, driving innovation and influencing high-level decision-making within an organization.
- Leadership to the insight function.
- Ensure operational aspects of the work are following laws, regulations and support iteration and improvement.
- Engage directly with executive leadership and the board of directors.
- Such a role may have oversight of multiple teams or departments across insights and data.[4]

User research

There's a lot of overlap in the day-to-day responsibilities in market research and user research roles; it is the names of the roles and the focus areas that differ.

Types of job available in the user-centred design space:

- quantitative roles:
  - data analyst/performance analyst
  - data scientist
  - quantitative user researcher

- quantitative and/or qualitative roles:
  - user researcher
  - UX researcher
  - research manager

All roles need to understand (appropriate to their level of experience and expertise):

- the design process and where research fits in it
- the role of user research
- the role of a user researcher[5]

People in these roles will also need

- curiosity
- attention to detail[6]

All user research roles put user needs at the heart of decision-making. Common skills in such jobs at varying levels of expertise and experience:

- [persuasive storytelling]
- verbal communication
- written communication
- active listening
- analytical thinking
- problem solving
- proactive
- learning mindset
- organization

MID-WEIGHT USER RESEARCHER

Summary

The role may be embedded in a service or product team, or they may work agency style and be a part of a centralized research team, either way supporting teams to generate actionable, impactful findings and insights and work closely with teams to enable them to use the research insights to make decisions about the service or product. With support introduce user research practices into a team, establish a user-centred culture, and continually moni-tor and improve practices. Depending on the complexity and size of the project, a midweight may work independently or pair with a senior researcher.

Day-to-day responsibilities

- Organize qualitative research: Plan, schedule, set up and conduct user research sessions.
- Quantitative research: Design, execute and analyse quantitative surveys.
- Participant management: Identify appropriate segmentation and recruit participants using appropriate methodologies; be mindful of diversity and inclusion when recruiting.
- Use the appropriate tools: For data collection, processing and storage.
- Data management: Ensure data is collected, processed and stored in a compliant way.
- Research analysis and synthesis: Analyse data collected using established techniques, develop narratives based on the analysis.
- Collaboration: Collaborate with teams and stakeholders.
- Community contribution: Share insights with other researchers and contribute to discussions.

Skills and experience

- User research expertise: Demonstrable experience and passion for user-centred design practices in web, service or software development.
- UX principles and methodologies: A solid understanding of UX princi-ples and methodologies, with a strong grasp of various qualitative and quantitative research methods and their strengths and limitations.
- Understanding user needs: Proven experience in understanding user needs, or demonstrable transferable skills, for web content, tools, and transactional services, user journeys.
- Facilitation: Confident in facilitating user research sessions.
- Analysis: Confident in analysing data to identify user behavioural patterns, user tasks, motivation, needs and wants.
- Presentation skills: Able to present user research findings in various formats and contexts (catering to different audiences).

- Collaboration and teamwork: Be a team player with the ability to share ideas, gather feedback, and work effectively with designers, developers and product managers in an agile development environment.
- Organizational skills: Well-organized and self-motivated.[7]

SENIOR USER RESEARCHER

The next level of experience will focus on:

- Undertaking increasingly complex work.
- Being an independent worker.
- As they develop they can demonstrate increased ownership[8] of the end-to-end process in a research project as well as contributing to improving the research process and the maturing of the research practice.
- Working on programmes of research, rather than individual unconnected studies.

Summary

The senior UX researcher ensures digital products align with UX and UI goals, using discovery research, usability and contextual research and user feedback. They advocate for internal and external user needs, and collaborate with multidisciplinary teams. The role involves problem-solving and converting research into actionable insights, requiring strong communication skills and a deep understanding of user motivations and behaviours.

Day-to-day responsibilities

- Organize qualitative, quantitative and mixed method research: Plan, schedule, set up and conduct research to understand customer needs and behaviours.
- Participant management: Identify appropriate segmentation and recruit participants using appropriate methodologies, be mindful of diversity and inclusion when recruiting.
- Use the appropriate tools for data collection, processing and storage.
- Data management: Ensure data is collected, processed and stored in a compliant way.
- Research analysis and synthesis: Analyse data collected using established techniques, develop narratives based on the analysis.
- Research management: Identify and prioritize research needs, communicate findings effectively and manage research operations.

- Cross-functional collaboration: Work with various teams to ensure a user-centred product approach and align research with business goals.

- Contribute to managing a repository of research knowledge.

- Mentorship: Mentor researchers, develop research strategies and lead workshops to integrate user feedback.

- Community contribution: Share insights with other researchers and contribute to discussions. Contribute to building a community for testing and collaborate with analytical teams to measure product performance.

- Continuous improvement: Develop research strategies, foster team involvement and improve services through research.

Skills and experience

- Leadership: Lead research projects across teams.

- Methodology expertise in qualitative and quantitative UX research, and agile methodologies.

- Evangelizing: Strong communication skills for user advocacy, project management and user-centred design approach.

- Strategy: Experience in discovery and strategic research as well as iterative tactical research.

- Communication and persuasion: Strong communication skills for research insight storytelling for diverse audiences.

- Collaboration: Work effectively with stakeholders and cross-functional teams to integrate user insights into product development.

- Additional qualities: A growth mindset, curiosity and problem-solving skills.[9]

LEAD USER RESEARCHER

A lead practitioner's focus is on embedding user research into the company's strategic and product development processes to enhance the user experience. Such roles often have responsibility for establishing and leading a UX research practice.

The hardest transition to make is from senior to lead researcher (in my opinion). There is increased delivery responsibility, people management and strategic oversight and planning across multiple researchers/teams/programmes of work. Leads will also be responsible for managing (up to) increasingly senior stakeholders.

Sometimes lead practitioners can be either individual contributors or be a researcher and line manager at the same time. Some organizations will have lead research managers who focus on people management and learning and development frameworks across a team of researchers, and on prioritizing work.[10]

Summary

Lead user researchers develop a deep understanding of users to design efficient and cost-effective services. Lead user researchers guide research activities across teams, ensuring a user-centred, evidence-based approach. This involves mentoring researchers, collaborating with cross-functional teams, and using various research methods to inform service design and product development. Lead researchers are expected to set strategic direction, share knowledge and enhance user experience.

Day-to-day responsibilities

The role focuses on leading and conducting UX research, ensuring user-centred, evidence-based design and service delivery. Key responsibilities include:

- Consultancy: Providing user research expertise and consultancy in complex and high-profile projects.
- Mentoring: Mentoring researchers at many levels of experience and promoting best practices across the business area.
- Cross-functional collaboration: Collaborating with multidisciplinary teams across different departments that also provide insight or are impacted by the insight gained from user research.
- Alignment: Integrating research findings into agile workflows, and aligning research activities with organizational goals.
- Recruiting practitioners: Leading recruitment and ensuring recruitment practices and processes follow DEI and HR guidelines as well as being appropriate to the level being recruited.
- Skills capabilities: Leading development of user researchers, providing performance feedback and supporting development of learning and development frameworks.
- [If appropriate] Community contribution: Contributing to and leading research communities, and fostering a culture of user-centred design among practitioners.
- Senior stakeholder management: Fostering understanding and valuing of user-centred practices within the business area's leadership team.

Skills and experience

- In depth expertise in strategic and tactical research approaches, a range of research methodologies, taking a diverse and inclusive approach to user-centred design work. Have the ability to synthesize findings into actionable insights, with a focus on inclusive, user-centred design.

- Elevate research practice: Able to build a strong UX research culture, advocate for its value and develop impactful frameworks.

- Quality assurance: Support others to apply appropriate research methods, analysing data and advocating for inclusive practices.

- Leadership: Strong leadership in setting direction for research activities.

- Mentoring and advocacy: Mentor teams and provide expert advice on methodologies and ethical practices.

- Cross-disciplinary collaboration to ensure a holistic and multidisciplinary approach is taken in all initiatives.

- Critical thinking, especially when evaluating new tools, techniques and methodologies and how they might be applied.

- Prioritization: Prioritize work based on organization strategy and goals and the ability to synthesize findings into actionable insights, with a focus on inclusive, user-centred design.

- Experience in leading research initiatives and programmes of research.[11]

HEAD OF/DIRECTOR OF RESEARCH

This role ensures that strategic decision-making across research is happening. Most likely there will be a head of market research and a head of user research in large organizations, maybe with a director or VP of customer research or customer insight above them.

They are advocates and evangelists for research and evidence-based decision-making. Heads of research are often critical in getting budget for research to happen (whether that's personnel budget, incentives, tools and services, etc.). They make sure the right people see the research and understand it. They lead the development of the research practice they are overseeing.

The head of UX and head of user research roles involve strategic oversight and leadership in user experience and research, supporting their lead user researchers to ensure alignment with company goals and user needs.

Key responsibilities

- Research strategy: Aligning research and design strategies with company objectives and end-user needs, working closely with senior leadership.

- User research: Depending on the size and structure of the organization, they may be conducting and overseeing user research to inform design processes, ensuring products meet the needs of target audiences.

- Research standards: Developing and maintaining consistent research standards across products and services.

- Research leadership: Leading and mentoring UX teams, providing guidance, feedback and fostering professional growth.

- Research execution: Supporting leads to collaborate with product teams to ensure accurate implementation of design and maintaining desired user experience standards.

- Thought leadership: Capability building, and promoting innovative practices within the profession, ensuring the profession adds value and aligns with agile, user-centric approaches.

- Overall strategy: Such roles play a critical part in overall departmental or organization strategy, focusing on identifying user needs, including those of underserved groups, and translating them into actionable insights.

- Research operations: Heads of research may oversee the management of both strategic and operational aspects of user research, and integrating user research into the broader agile and user-centred design framework.[12]

Interview questions

Interview questions within the recruitment process should be designed for people to be able to demonstrate their capabilities, skills and experience, or their transferable skills in the areas that are important to the organization and role (see Table 7.1).

There are two different approaches to designing your interview questions:

- experience-based
- hypothetical-based

Experience-based questions are the most common, as this is the most direct way to understand a candidate's experience of doing a particular thing;

these are the 'Tell me about a time you…' questions. This allows candidates to tell a story using the STAR method, ideally (situation, task, action, result).

Hypothetical questions are more inclusive as candidates can demonstrate their understanding, critical thinking and transferable skills, even if they have not had direct experience in the particular area the interview question is focusing on. This is useful at any level (we can't all have experience in everything), but it is particularly useful for junior interviews and for career transitioners. The rest of this chapter gives a detailed list of the types of interview questions you might want to include and what areas of skills and capabilities they cover. We will need to prioritize what areas are most important to the role, as we only get to ask four or five questions in an hour-long interview, also giving time for the candidate to ask any questions themselves.

User and market research interview questions

QUESTION 1

- Level suitability: All.
- Question type: Warm-up.
- Questions and variations:
  - Can you tell us a bit about yourself and why you are interested in this role?
  - Can you tell us a bit more about your story? What led you to research?

QUESTION 2

- Level suitability: All.
- Question type: Learning mindset.
- Questions and variations:
  - How do you stay up to date with the field?
  - What's one skill you're currently improving?
  - How do you continue your professional development?
  - Tell us about a time that you learnt something new.

QUESTION 3

- Level suitability: Junior.
- Question type: Transferable skills and collaboration.

- Questions and variations:
  - Tell us about a time when you've worked with a team to produce a great outcome.

QUESTION 4

- Level suitability: Midweight/senior/lead.
- Question type: Research skills, implementation, [problem solving], [collaboration].
- Questions and variations:
  - Tell us about a time when you've worked with a team to produce a great research outcome.
  - Tell us about a time when you've worked with a team to produce a great research outcome using quantitative or mixed methods.
  - Can you tell me about a time when your research was used to inform a decision?

QUESTION 5

- Level suitability: Midweight.
- Question type: Learning and development.
- Questions and variations:
  - Tell us about a time when you used a new research method. How did you make sure you understood the method and applied it correctly?
  - How do you apply feedback to improve your research practice?

QUESTION 6

- Level suitability: Senior/lead.
- Question type: Supporting others, learning and development, people management.
- Questions and variations:
  - Tell us about a time when you introduced others to a research method they hadn't used before. How did you approach it and ensure the method was applied correctly?
  - How do you support and work with people that are less skilled than you in research?

QUESTION 7

- Level suitability: Junior.
- Question type: Communication and impact.
- Questions and variations:
  - Can you tell me about a time you had to get buy-in for a project or an idea?

QUESTION 8

- Level suitability: Midweight/senior.
- Question type: Communication and impact.
- Questions and variations:
  - Can you tell us about a time when you convinced a team to do something different to what they planned to do? Why was it needed and how did you get everyone on board?

QUESTION 9

- Level suitability: Senior/lead.
- Question type: Communication, strategy and leadership.
- Questions and variations:
  - How do you handle when stakeholders are sceptical of the value of your research?
  - How do you adapt your approach to work with low research literacy stakeholders?

QUESTION 10

- Level suitability: Midweight/senior/lead.
- Question type: Inclusive research, data management.
- Questions and variations:
  - Can you tell us about a product or service you worked on that had a diverse user population? How did you make sure your research was inclusive and sensitive?

QUESTION 11

- Level suitability: Junior.
- Question type: Planning, problem solving.
- Questions and variations:
  - Tell us about a time a piece of work didn't go to plan.

QUESTION 12

- Level suitability: Midweight/senior/lead.
- Question type: Analytical thinking, learning mindset, communication.
- Questions and variations:
  - Tell us about a time when some of your research has not gone to plan.
  - How do you manage situations in which your research findings and your team's wishes are misaligned?

QUESTION 13

- Level suitability: Junior.
- Question type: Communicating, implementation, [strategy].
- Questions and variations:
  - How do you approach sharing the outcomes of a piece of work?

QUESTION 14

- Level suitability: Midweight/senior/lead.
- Question type: Communication, implementation, [strategy].
- Questions and variations:
  - What is your approach to sharing insights with stakeholders?

QUESTION 15

- Level suitability: Senior/lead.
- Question type: Research skills.
- Questions and variations:
  - How do you account for bias in research?

QUESTION 16

- Level suitability: Lead.
- Question type: Planning, strategy, leadership.
- Questions and variations:
  - Can you tell us how you plan a programme of research (long-term plan with multiple research activities on same or different topics), people you work with, tools you'd use and the process?

QUESTION 17

- Level suitability: Lead.
- Question type: Planning, prioritization.
- Questions and variations:
  - Tell us about how you handle multiple pieces of work at the same time, managing your own work and supporting the work of junior colleagues.

QUESTION 18

- Level suitability: All.
- Question type: Wrap-up.
- Questions and variations:
  - What are the top challenges UX researchers face in the current environment?
  - What are the top challenges of doing UX research in an agile environment?
  - Why is market research essential to the success of a business?
  - Would you say market research is indispensable or optional for a start-up?[13]

Inspired by work I have done with colleagues including Lisa Koeman between 2018 and 2023.

Practical exercises

It is very common in a multi-step interview process to include a practical exercise. Often in user research, this is where the candidate is given a scenario of a research project and they are given a certain amount of time to create a research plan. The candidate will present their plan to the interview panel and talk through their reasons behind the plan.

Whatever relevant scenario the candidate is given, the things we need to look out for include:

- Their understanding of the scenario.
- How have they scoped the project?
- What assumptions they have made.
- Who they would include or collaborate with during the project.
- Their understanding of the research process and the tasks involved.
- Their reasoning for method and participant selection.
- Do they have a plan for implementing the research, or do they stop at the research being shared and then their work is done?
- Have they assumed a reasonable timescale?

As with interviews, there are two different ways to approach practical exercises:

1 In an hour session, share the scenario (10 minutes), give candidates 25 minutes to work on their plan and then 25 minutes for presentation, discussion and questions.

2 Give the candidate the scenario over email and three days to prepare for a session with the interview panel where the candidate will present, with discussion and questions (45 minutes).

There are benefits and drawbacks to both approaches:

1 Everyone has the same time to approach the exercise, and the candidate can ask clarifying questions before they start. But you are getting their first thoughts, and it's not particularly compatible with those candidates who don't work so well under pressure, especially during the recruitment process.

2 Giving people time to prepare means you can get greater insight into their understanding, experience and approach. However, the main drawback to this approach is not everyone has an equal amount of time to prepare. For example, if you have a full-time job and caring responsibilities, you will have little time to prepare compared to someone who currently doesn't have a job and doesn't have caring responsibilities.

Who to include on interview panels

I have found that two or three person interview panels work best. More than three and it's very intimidating for the interviewee, and interviews could last too long a time with everyone asking questions. Just one person doing all the interviews is not only a lot of work for one person, it introduces too much potential for that person's biases to influence the recruitment process, when we are aiming for diverse and inclusive recruitment. To have diverse and inclusive recruitment we need multiple perspectives on interview panels, in terms of discipline expertise, role experience and life experience.

If we are implementing a two- or three-stage interview process, then it is a good idea to have one or (maximum) two people consistent who will be in every stage of the process. These people should be research experts (for example a lead researcher or the head of research and a researcher of the same level being recruited). We may want to include people for the team or programme the role is for – the people the successful candidate will be working with, for example the product manager, the marketing manager, a designer, the research manager.

We should also actively work towards having balance and representation on interviews – so a mix of ethnicities, genders, access needs, etc. If a black woman or non-binary person has two interview panels of three white men, they may, understandably, be hesitant about whether it's the right place for them to work. Having a diverse group of people on the panel will also help to balance out people's inherent biases.

It is not just researcher roles that may include aspects of research. For other roles we may need to include customer research related questions in the interview process and research skill expectations, and therefore collaborate with our colleagues in other disciplines in the interview process:

- service designers
- UX designers
- content designers
- marketing performance and enablement managers

Roles we may want to have research awareness and literacy:

- product managers
- project managers and delivery managers
- operations roles
- business analysts

- marketing coordinators
- social media managers
- head of digital
- brand ambassador
- marketing manager
- director of marketing and sales
- head of business development and marketing
- director of communications/communications marketing
- digital marketing manager
- content marketing manager
- B2B or B2C marketing manager
- brand marketing manager
- marketing and communications manager
- internal communications lead

See Part Three where we'll reflect on the advantages and disadvantages of research democracy.

Conclusion

If a researcher is participating in the recruitment process, they already have a lot of the skills necessary for recruitment interviewing. Operations people and other roles may also be participating in the recruitment process; and interviewing is its own separate skillset. Many HR departments have training available and there is also a lot of independent training available to enable them to actively contribute to a fair, diverse and inclusive recruitment process. It is highly advisable – we may even want to make it a requirement – that people go through such training before they join in with recruiting new team members.

Notes

1 GOV.UK. How to use this framework, GOV.UK Government Digital and Data Profession Capability Framework, 2024. ddat-capability-framework.service.gov. uk/ (archived at https://perma.cc/TE3U-X63J) All text content is available under

the Open Government Licence v3.0 (www.nationalarchives.gov.uk/doc/open-government-licence/version/3/ (archived at https://perma.cc/5TFR-MZKL))

2   Market Research Society. Research career finder, Market Research Society, 2024. www.mrs.org.uk/yourcareer (archived at https://perma.cc/3CR5-UF3A); P Hague (2022) *Market Research in Practice: An introduction to gaining greater market insight*, 4th edn, Kogan Page, London; Intelligent People. Head of user experience job profile, Intelligent People, 2024. www.intelligentpeople.co.uk/head-of-user-experience/ (archived at https://perma.cc/N2YW-X3YU)

3   Bright Network. A career in market research, Bright Network, 2024. www.brightnetwork.co.uk/career-path-guides/marketing-pr/what-can-market-research-career-offer-you/ (archived at https://perma.cc/R3PJ-3KS5)

4   Market Research Society. Research career finder, Market Research Society, 2024. www.mrs.org.uk/yourcareer (archived at https://perma.cc/3CR5-UF3A); National Careers Service. Market researcher, National Careers Service, 2024. nationalcareers.service.gov.uk/job-profiles/market-researcher (archived at https://perma.cc/8XBQ-BDND) All text content is available under the Open Government Licence v3.0 (www.nationalarchives.gov.uk/doc/open-government-licence/version/3/ (archived at https://perma.cc/NS6C-B8W5)); GOV.UK. Data analyst, GOV.UK Government Digital and Data Profession Capability Framework, 2024. ddat-capability-framework.service.gov.uk/role/data-analyst (archived at https://perma.cc/KN22-9LY3) All text content is available under the Open Government Licence v3.0 (www.nationalarchives.gov.uk/doc/open-government-licence/version/3/ (archived at https://perma.cc/NYE8-4GKL)); RaiseMe. Market research analysts: Salary, career path, job outlook, education and more, RaiseMe Careers, 2024. www.raise.me/careers/business-and-financial/market-research-analysts/ (archived at https://perma.cc/Q7M4-PEA7); R Lokam. Thinking of a career in market research? Here's what you need to know! Blackridge Research and Consulting, 2024. www.blackridgeresearch.com/blog/thinking-of-a-job-career-in-market-research (archived at https://perma.cc/E2YL-R6L5)

5   S Bromley (2020) *Building User Research Teams*, Steve Bromley. ISBN: 9781670056849; GOV.UK. User researcher, GOV.UK Government Digital and Data Profession Capability Framework, 2024. ddat-capability-framework.service.gov.uk/role/user-researcher (archived at https://perma.cc/YDW7-TA8J) All text content is available under the Open Government Licence v3.0 (www.nationalarchives.gov.uk/doc/open-government-licence/version/3/ (archived at https://perma.cc/6FQ5-D675))

6   S Bromley (2020) *Building User Research Teams*, Steve Bromley. ISBN: 9781670056849; GOV.UK. User researcher, GOV.UK Government Digital and Data Profession Capability Framework, 2024. ddat-capability-framework.service.gov.uk/role/user-researcher (archived at https://perma.cc/YDW7-TA8J) All text content is available under the Open Government Licence v3.0 (www.nationalarchives.gov.uk/doc/open-government-licence/version/3/ (archived at https://perma.cc/6VYB-UWF7))

7   GOV.UK. User researcher, GOV.UK Government Digital and Data Profession
Capability Framework, 2024. ddat-capability-framework.service.gov.uk/role/
user-researcher (archived at https://perma.cc/YDW7-TA8J) All text content is
available under the Open Government Licence v3.0 (www.nationalarchives.
gov.uk/doc/open-government-licence/version/3/ (archived at https://perma.cc/
TE7U-W6D9)). National Careers Service. User researcher, National Careers
Service, 2024. nationalcareers.service.gov.uk/job-profiles/user-researcher
(archived at https://perma.cc/9QD8-8BR3) All text content is available under
the Open Government Licence v3.0 (www.nationalarchives.gov.uk/doc/
open-government-licence/version/3/ (archived at https://perma.cc/U5MK-
FX3Y)); L Burnaham

8   S Bromley (2020) *Building User Research Teams*, Steve Bromley. ISBN:
9781670056849

9   UCAS. Senior UX researcher job profile, UCAS, 2021. www.ucas.com/
file/419731/download?token=zH2Jrke5 (archived at https://perma.cc/3N6C-
MN3Q); Tesco Careers. Senior UX researcher Job Profile, Tesco, 2024. www.
tesco-careers.com/jobdetails/837968; Bently. Senior UX researcher job profile,
Bently, 2024. jobs.bentley.com/job/Dublin-2-Senior-UX-Researcher/1157264500/;
(archived at https://perma.cc/V5RM-L2LM) Admiral Jobs. Senior UX researcher
job profile, Admiral Jobs, 2024. www.admiraljobs.co.uk/job/senior-ux-researcher-
in-remote-jid-2278 (archived at https://perma.cc/YR82-XD8B)

10   S Bromley (2020) *Building User Research Teams*, Steve Bromley. ISBN:
9781670056849

11   Monzo Bank. Lead user researcher job profile, Monzo Bank, 2024. www.
escapethecity.org/opportunity/19452-lead-user-researcher-borrowing-at-
monzo-bank (archived at https://perma.cc/38QJ-NHTC); The National
Archives. Lead user researcher job profile, Manchester Digital, 2024. www.
manchesterdigital.com/job/cabinet-office-1/lead-user-researcher-the-national-
archives-g7 (archived at https://perma.cc/V9NM-MHDJ); Government Digital
Service. Lead user researcher job profile, Manchester Digital, 2024. www.
manchesterdigital.com/job/cabinet-office/lead-user-researcher (archived at
https://perma.cc/TX89-YDUE); Department for Education. Lead user
researcher job profile, DfE DDaT Job Description, 2024. https://ddat-
capability-framework.service.gov.uk/role/user-researcher#lead-user-researcher
(archived at https://perma.cc/PR5D-J7JF); Glassdoor LLC. What does a lead
user researcher do? Glassdoor, 2024. www.glassdoor.com/Career/lead-user-
researcher-career_KO0,20.htm (archived at https://perma.cc/YA9E-55Q3);
Ministry of Justice. Lead user researcher job profile, Justice Jobs, 2024. https://
justicejobs.tal.net/vx/mobile-0/appcentre-1/brand-2/candidate/so/pm/1/pl/3/
opp/14817-14817-Lead-User-Researcher/en-GB (archived at https://perma.cc/
H29B-EH6E); Tesco Careers. Lead UX researcher – product and supplier job
profile, Tesco, 2024. www.tesco-careers.com/jobdetails/777667 (archived at
https://perma.cc/TN2U-TAGU)

12   Government Digital Service. Head of user research job profile, Manchester
Digital, 2024. www.manchesterdigital.com/job/cabinet-office/head-of-user-
research (archived at https://perma.cc/N4CA-W23D); Ministry of Justice. Head
of user research job profile, Justice Jobs, 2024. https://justicejobs.tal.net/vx/
mobile-0/appcentre-1/brand-12/candidate/so/pm/1/pl/3/opp/66804-66804-
Head-of-User-Research/en-GB (archived at https://perma.cc/97ZS-65DQ);
Government Digital Service. Head of user research job profile, Manchester
Digital, 2024. www.manchesterdigital.com/job/cabinet-office/head-of-user-
research (archived at https://perma.cc/Y8S2-KR9E) All text content is available
under the Open Government Licence v3.0 (www.nationalarchives.gov.uk/doc/
open-government-licence/version/3/ (archived at https://perma.cc/JMM2-
HHDE))

13   L Burnam. Common UX research job interview questions and how to answer
them, User Interviews, 2022. www.userinterviews.com/blog/common-ux-
research-job-interview-questions-how-to-answer-them (archived at https://
perma.cc/YD8Q-GS9S)

8

Recruiting the research operations team

Note. Some of this content was inspired by a keynote conference talk I made at the Global ResearchOps Conference in 2023. reopsconference.com/#talkschedule

When to hire a ReOps person or team will vary from organization to organization. The best case scenario that I have seen is an Ops person being recruited once the organization had three researchers. There are still many organizations that do customer research without any Ops support, there are also organizations that may have one Ops person to every 50 or 100 people who do research. Everything in between probably exists. Unsurprisingly, my opinion is that as soon as more than one person is doing customer research, operations support is needed. User Interviews has done a lot of industry research that shows that when a team of researchers reaches 12 or more, this is the time that ReOps is bought in.[1] It is not necessarily the number of researchers that will influence the decision to hire ReOps people, but the number of people doing research.

Over the last few years UX design and research has been greatly impacted by waves of redundancies within the tech industry, but revenue generated by user experience work is also still increasing year on year.[2] Norman Nielsen Group suggests that even with the current redundancies, they predict the number of UX professionals will continue to grow.[3] The same is true of market research, where revenue generated continues to grow year on year, with the US and UK leading the way.[4] Whether the size of the research teams is large or small, the demand for customer research is high and increasing.

Operationalizing your research practices is equally important whether you have a small or large number of people doing the research.

The beauty of being an emerging field is that people come into it from diverse backgrounds, so it's important to think about skills we need to support high-quality, robust and impact research, rather than job titles, and think about transferable skills. There are well-established operations fields in other industries, for example those who work in customer services have a lot of relevant experience, librarians as well as researchers transitioning to ReOps roles, all have relevant and transferable skills. My current amazing team at Springer Nature is an excellent case study of diverse backgrounds, as demonstrated in Table 8.1.

Neither of my brilliant team members had a huge amount of experience in user research itself when they started working with me, but they had a keen interest in it, they were motivated to work in and learn the field and they had the direct and transferable skills we needed to support user research. We have been a team of three since May 2022, and we continue to learn from each other every day.

TABLE 8.1 Job history of Springer Nature Research Operations team as of 2025

Role	Background
Team lead	Researcher (junior, midweight, senior, lead, head)
	Head of digital
	UX manager
	UX lead
	PhD information science
	MSc geographic information science
	BSc environmental geoscience
ReOps senior	Customer service
	Account management
	Insurance policy administrator
	MSc in communication, culture and IT
	BSc sociology
UXR knowledge manager	Financial start-up knowledge manager
	Financial start-up trainer
	Business development executive
	Customer relations
	MSc management
	BSc management
	UX/UI bootcamp

There are a variety of skills that are needed for research operations roles, that aren't always mentioned in job descriptions. These include:

- service design
- service delivery
- user research
- change management
- engagement
- balancing strategic and tactical work

If you are in or know people in a customer research field, you most likely will have heard of those researchers talking about their craft. Research operations is also a craft. There are various types of operations jobs and therefore a wide variety of skillsets that could be needed, depending on the needs of the organization, just as there are different types of research job. Ops may be more diverse, especially as an emerging field. Because it's still a young, emerging field, we need to give greater consideration to transferable skills when recruiting. From my own experience of recruiting a small but well-formed ReOps team (neither of my teammates had worked in research operations before) critical factors in hiring them were transferable skills and a learning and growth mindset. Technically, when I was hired in this role, my first dedicated ReOps role, I hadn't had a directly relevant role either, although I had a lot of experience in doing many aspects of research operations.

As already stated, it will depend on what parts of the research process the Ops people/team will be taking on to what skills are needed. Table 8.2 is a non-exhaustive list of potential skills that are needed across the spectrum of ReOps jobs.

TABLE 8.2 ReOps craft, interpersonal and learning skills

Craft skills	Interpersonal and learning skills
Experimentation	Learning mindset
Deciphering data	Comfortable with ambiguity
Scoping work	Solo and collaborative work
User research	Active listening
Documentation writing	Critical thinking and problem definition
Design L&D frameworks	Stakeholder management

(continued)

TABLE 8.2 (Continued)

Craft skills	Interpersonal and learning skills
Deliver L&D frameworks	Storytelling and communication
Practitioner interviewing recruitment	Advocating, evangelizing, influencing
Procurement management	Supplier management
Budget management	Community management
Service design	
Service delivery	
Change management	
Administration	
Tool and infrastructure management	
Law and data protection	
Participant database management	
Participant recruitment	
Metrics implementation	
Metrics tracking	
Data and knowledge management	
Onboarding and offboarding	

Each skill deserves its own chapter, but that's a different book. We will look at these skills in Chapter 9 on learning and development. I do want to break down what I mean by administrative skills, which are numerous. I want to do this because unfortunately it is common for administrative jobs to be looked down on. ResearchOps is often considered 'just admin'. Administration is an important part of Ops and the research process cannot happen without it, but Ops is more than administration; but it's also not shameful to have an administrative or secretarial job. What is shameful is how people with such jobs are still treated as less than. This is why I want to talk about ReOps as a craft and the complexities of an Ops job. When I talk about complexities I mean that as a good thing, Ops jobs require talent and skill. This is very much to encourage people to think about moving into Ops jobs! Table 8.3 shows the administration skills that are critical for ReOps jobs.

TABLE 8.3 ReOps administrative skills

Organization	Organize, maintain data
Communication	Disseminate information in an understandable way
Collaboration	Build collaborative relationship with colleagues
Service provision	Dealing with complaints and problem resolution
Problem solving	Identify creative solutions to problems
Time management	Provide support when it's needed
Service delivery	Provide self-service options
Multi-tasking	Balance tactical and strategic work

The skills in Table 8.3 are generally skills that a user researcher needs too, but ReOps people are putting these skills to use in parts of the research process that researchers don't want to do or find it difficult to make the time to do, with everything else they are doing. Each skill under the category of administration can also be broken down further…

One of the key things about my team is that they are constantly practising a balancing act that involves both multi-tasking and context switching. On one hand they provide tactical reactive support that is needed to ensure the day-to-day research activities run as smoothly as possible for each person doing research at the same time within the current processes. On the other hand, they do long-term strategic work that will improve existing processes and infrastructure or build and implement new things to improve the experience of doing research for everyone. Thinking about it now, that's some kind of multi-tasking inception – supporting the needs of people at different stages of the research process right now as well as planning and delivering for supporting future research needs.

It's these kinds of things that we need to keep in mind when writing our research operations job descriptions and reviewing people's CVs when we are recruiting for research operations roles.

So what kinds of roles have transferable skills relevant to research operations? The good news is there are many!

- librarians
- information architects
- customer services
- administrators

- user researchers
- market researchers
- UX designers
- business analysts
- recruiters
- customer success managers

- project managers
- delivery managers
- service designers
- customer experience managers
- data analysts
- programme managers

What types of ReOps jobs do we need in our organization? There is a variety of potential roles that we can recruit for, depending on needs, skill gaps and resources available:

- research administrator
- participant recruiter
- data manager
- research manager

- research operations specialist
- knowledge manager/insight librarian
- research operations lead
- programme manager

Kate Towsey has talked about it being tricky to recruit ReOps people because of the lack of formal training and literature.[5] I'm sure it's the same for any emerging field that organizations are looking to bring in – there is little infrastructure and support to know who the right people are to recruit and scoping the roles we're recruiting for in the right way, and know what is realistic, especially when they haven't existed in the organization before. Often this leads to organizations looking for one unicorn to do the work for three unicorns (a unicorn being the mythical person who can do it all, in case that wasn't clear). Next we will look at ReOps job descriptions and interview guidance.

First we'll outline three versions of the midweight (or junior level) administrator job role. The three roles have different focuses: research administration, knowledge management administration and a role that combines both research and knowledge management administration. I think it's important to point out that the role which combines research and knowledge management has a selection of the responsibilities from the range that could be included in the roles that focus on one area. We are not asking a person to do two people's worth of work, which probably sounds like I'm stating the obvious, but it's worth highlighting as so often job descriptions are asking for more than any one person can do.

Table 8.4 shows the elements of a research operations job framework; these are the elements that go across all roles and the craft-specific skills that we'll look at in detail in the job descriptions that vary from role to role, depending on the focus. You may or may not agree with my current assessment (which may change in the future as the field evolves). The ReOps framework is a little more complicated to construct compared to the researcher framework as ReOps roles don't necessarily need to be research experts – ReOps practitioners will gain a lot of research-related knowledge over time, but there are different requirements to researchers themselves. It is hard to say just how much research expertise or operations expertise any one role should have, but this should be a useful guide.

Some of the following Ops role descriptions have been inspired by the work I have done at Springer Nature.

Research Administrator

Responsibilities

This role focuses on supporting and enabling researchers and people doing research to undertake and deliver high-quality research in a smooth, timely and expert manner.

Craft skills

PLANNING SKILLS
Expected level of skill: Working

- Support the scoping out of the problem space to understand the tactical activities that need to be done.
- Support planning for robust decision-making, know what type of data needs to be collected, plan for analysis and synthesis, and identify the constraints.
- With support from the lead or senior, prioritize individual and team activities, considering business priorities and problem spaces.
- Work to understand stakeholders' needs.

TABLE 8.4 Elements of a research operations job framework

	Junior	Midweight	Senior	Lead IC	Lead manager	Head
Planning	Aware	Working	Practitioner	Expert	Expert	Expert
Coordination and management	Aware	Working	Working-practitioner	Practitioner-expert	Practitioner-expert	Practitioner-expert
Participant recruitment	Aware	Working	Working-practitioner	Practitioner-expert	Practitioner-expert	Practitioner-expert
Stakeholder management	Aware	Aware	Working	Expert	Expert	Expert
Enable inclusive research	Aware	Working	Working-practitioner	Practitioner-expert	Practitioner-expert	Practitioner-expert
Internal research	Aware	Working	Working-practitioner	Working-practitioner	Working-practitioner	Working-practitioner
Communicating	Aware	Working	Working-practitioner	Expert	Expert	Expert
Implementation	Aware	Working	Working-practitioner	Expert	Expert	Expert
Strategy	N/A	Aware	Working	Practitioner-expert	Expert	Expert
Leadership	N/A	N/A	Aware	Aware	Expert	Expert
People management	N/A	Aware	Working-practitioner	Aware	Expert	Expert

COORDINATION AND MANAGEMENT
Expected level of skill: Working

- Offer accurate and timely support via assigned channels, redirecting requests to the right person where appropriate.
- Maintain and enable GDPR compliance during the research process.
- Lead participant recruitment and coordination.
- Lead on consent management.
- Lead on incentive payments.
- Provide access to specialist tools.
- Prioritize support requests.
- Project management; track the progression of multiple research and ReOps projects simultaneously.
- Research process management.
- Support improvement of the research practice.
- Collaborate on onboarding and offboarding of people doing research.

EXECUTE INTERNAL RESEARCH/CUSTOMER ENGAGEMENT
Expected level of skill: Awareness to working depending on existing skills

- Support ReOps team and participate in undertaking internal research or customer (the researchers) engagement to enable user-centred decision-making.
- Support or do secondary research.
- Observe/support moderated sessions and debriefing.
- Support analysis, synthesis and implementation.

STAKEHOLDER ENGAGEMENT (REOPS AS A TEAM SPORT)
Expected level of skill: Awareness to working

- Support the engagement of stakeholders and communication regarding planned, ongoing and implemented ReOps work.
- Support workshop facilitation.
- Support change management when process and guidance changes are required.

ENABLE INCLUSIVE RESEARCH
Expected level of skill: Awareness to working

- Awareness of inclusive research methodologies.

- Advocate of inclusive practices.

- Working knowledge of diverse participant selection (appropriate screeners to reach different audiences, etc.).

INTERPERSONAL AND LEARNING SKILLS

- Contribute to team culture.

- Able to reflect and improve.

- Have cultural awareness: understanding of how culture affects interactions and how to manage the differences.

- Learn how to maintain good relationships with colleagues and stakeholders.

- Manage own time effectively.

- Give and receive constructive feedback.

- Provide proactive and regular status updates.

- Confidently communicate technical information in an understandable way.

- Change communication style according to who you are sharing the work with and for what purpose.

Knowledge Management Administrator

Responsibilities

This role focuses on supporting and enabling researchers and people doing research to store, process, analyse, share and access data, information and knowledge to undertake and deliver high-quality research in a smooth, timely and expert manner.

Craft skills

PLANNING SKILLS
Expected level of skill: Working

- Support scoping out the problem space to understand the necessary tactical activities that need to be done.

- Support planning for robust decision-making, know what type of data needs to be collected, plan for the analysis and synthesis, and identify the constraints.
- With support from the lead or senior, prioritize individual and team activities, considering business priorities and problem spaces.
- Work to understand stakeholders' needs.

COORDINATION AND MANAGEMENT
Expected level of skill: Working

- Offer accurate and timely support via assigned channels, redirecting requests to the right person where appropriate.
- Maintain and enable GDPR compliance.
- Provide access to specialist knowledge management tools.
- Prioritize support requests.
- Project management; track the progression of multiple knowledge management projects simultaneously.
- Support improvement of knowledge management practices.
- Review and ensure that people are using appropriate file naming conventions, and work with them to embed this practice.
- Help colleagues find the research reports and insights they are looking for (respond to information requests).
- Package research on a particular topic in a digestible summary for stakeholders.
- Support work across domains and departments to remove barriers to content.
- Gather requests for training to help prioritize future training needs.
- Assist in knowledge management training by providing administrative support.
- Assist in maintaining knowledge management guidance and documentation.
- Assist in communication of new guidance and governance and iterated documentation.

EXECUTE INTERNAL RESEARCH/CUSTOMER ENGAGEMENT
Expected level of skill: Awareness to working depending on existing skills

- Assist in internal research by providing administrative support.

STAKEHOLDER ENGAGEMENT (REOPS AS A TEAM SPORT)
Expected level of skill: Awareness to working

- Support the engagement of stakeholders and communication regarding planned, ongoing and implemented knowledge management and ReOps work.
- Support workshop facilitation.
- Support change management when process and guidance changes are required.

INTERPERSONAL AND LEARNING SKILLS

- Contribute to team culture.
- Able to reflect and improve.
- Have cultural awareness: understanding of how culture affects interactions and how to manage the differences.
- Learn how to maintain good relationships with colleagues and stakeholders.
- Manage own time effectively.
- Give and receive constructive feedback.
- Provide proactive and regular status updates.
- Confidently communicate technical information in an understandable way.
- Change communication style according to who you are sharing the work with and for what purpose.

Customer Research and Knowledge Management Administrator

Responsibilities

This role focuses on supporting and enabling researchers and people doing research to undertake and deliver high-quality research in a smooth, timely and expert manner and store, process, analyse, share and access that research easily.

Craft skills

PLANNING SKILLS
Expected level of skill: Working

- Support scoping out the problem space to understand the necessary tactical activities that need to be done.
- Support planning for robust decision-making, know what type of data needs to be collected, plan for the analysis and synthesis, and identify the constraints.
- With support from the lead or senior, prioritize individual and team activities, considering business priorities and problem spaces.
- Work to understand stakeholders' needs.

COORDINATION AND MANAGEMENT
Expected level of skill: Working

- Offer accurate and timely support via assigned channels, redirecting requests to the right person where appropriate.
- Maintain and enable GDPR compliance.
- Provide access to specialist tools.
- Prioritize support requests.
- Project management; track the progression of research projects simultaneously.
- Review and ensure that people are using appropriate file naming conventions.
- Support people looking for past research.
- Lead participant recruitment and consent management.
- Lead on incentive payments.
- Provide access to specialist tools.
- Support improvement of the research practice by gathering feedback.
- Collaborate on onboarding and offboarding of people doing research.

EXECUTE INTERNAL RESEARCH/CUSTOMER ENGAGEMENT
Expected level of skill: Awareness to working depending on existing skills

- Assist in internal research by providing administrative support.

STAKEHOLDER ENGAGEMENT (REOPS AS A TEAM SPORT)
Expected level of skill: Awareness to working

- Support the engagement of stakeholders and communication regarding planned, ongoing and implemented knowledge management and ReOps work.

INTERPERSONAL AND LEARNING SKILLS

- Contribute to team culture.
- Able to reflect and improve.
- Have cultural awareness: understanding of how culture affects interactions and how to manage the differences.
- Learn how to maintain good relationships with colleagues and stakeholders.
- Manage own time effectively.
- Give and receive constructive feedback.
- Provide proactive and regular status updates.
- Confidently communicate technical information in an understandable way.
- Change communication style according to who you are sharing the work with and for what purpose.

Research Knowledge Manager (Senior)

Responsibilities

This role can work alongside different teams and across programmes. Their strategic function will help the organization to join up customer insights from different sources and facilitate alignment. This role also supports less experienced researchers in the knowledge management processes.

Craft skills

PLANNING SKILLS
Expected level of skill: Practitioner

- Scope out the problem space to understand the necessary tactical and strategic activities that need to be done.
- Plan for robust decision-making, know what type of data needs to be collected, plan for the analysis and synthesis, and identify the constraints.
- Prioritize individual and team activities, considering business priorities and problem spaces.
- Work to understand stakeholders' needs.

- Work alongside the lead (either knowledge management or ReOps lead, or both).
- Coach and train those less experienced in knowledge management to enable the development of good practices.

COORDINATION AND MANAGEMENT
Expected level of skill: Expert

- Maintain and enable GDPR compliance.
- Support researchers and designers to ensure data is well-managed.
- Work independently on management knowledge management tools and vendor relationships.
- Work across domains and departments to remove barriers to content.
- Gather requests for training to help prioritize future training needs.
- Collaborate with lead on knowledge management training.
- Lead on maintaining knowledge management guidance and documentation.
- Collaborate with lead in communication of new guidance and governance and iterated documentation.

EXECUTE INTERNAL RESEARCH
Expected level of skill: Working to practitioner depending on existing skills

- Support or lead the team and participate in undertaking internal research.
- Work with ReOps team to integrate research into the solution.
- Work with teams to measure success and make sure the solutions are meeting the expected user outcomes.

STAKEHOLDER ENGAGEMENT (REOPS AS A TEAM SPORT)
Expected level of skill: Expert

- Engage stakeholders and communicate regarding planned, ongoing and implemented ReOps work.
- Support/lead change management of both centralized and distributed ReOps and knowledge management processes.

ENABLE INCLUSIVE RESEARCH
Expected level of skill: Working to practitioner

- Working knowledge of inclusive research methodologies.
- Advocate of inclusive practices.

STRATEGIC DIRECTION
Expected level of skill: Practitioner

KNOWLEDGE MANAGEMENT TRAINING AND GOVERNANCE STRATEGY

- Partially responsible for developing, socializing and implementing knowledge management governance.
- Partially responsible for long-term knowledge management improvement strategy.
- Partially responsible for knowledge management best practice training.

INTERPERSONAL AND LEARNING SKILLS

- Contribute to team culture.
- Able to reflect and improve.
- Have cultural awareness: understanding of how culture affects interactions and how to manage the differences.
- Learn how to maintain good relationships with colleagues and stakeholders.
- Manage own time effectively.
- Able to undertake workshop facilitation.
- Evangelize research, and research operations and knowledge management.
- Skilled at maintaining good relationships with colleagues.
- Give and receive constructive feedback.
- Provide proactive and regular status updates.
- Confidently communicate technical information in an understandable way.
- Change communication style according to who you are sharing the work with and for what purpose.

Knowledge Management Lead

Responsibilities

This role can work across programmes and departments. Their strategic function will help the organization to join customer insights from different sources and facilitate alignment. This role works to increase awareness of knowledge management processes and practices.

PLANNING SKILLS
Expected level of skill: Expert

- Lead knowledge management for customer research strategy planning.
- Plan for fostering knowledge management innovation and growth.
- Support ongoing structural development of knowledge assets.
- Scope out the problem space to understand the necessary tactical activities that need to be done.
- Plan for robust decision-making, know what type of data needs to be collected, plan for the analysis and synthesis, and identify the constraints.
- Prioritize individual and team activities, considering business priorities and problem spaces.
- Work to understand stakeholders' needs.
- Coach and train those less experienced in knowledge management to enable the development of good practices.

COORDINATION AND MANAGEMENT
Expected level of skill: Expert

- Lead and coordinate the delivery of the customer research knowledge management strategy.
- Collaborate with ReOps lead to ensure that the overall ReOps strategy and the knowledge management strategy align.
- Design and facilitate a programme of knowledge management training on best practices and effective knowledge management tool use.
- Support enablement of GDPR compliance.
- Support selection of appropriate knowledge management tools.
- Support team to work across domains and departments to remove barriers to content.

- Collaborate with senior knowledge management training.
- Support senior on maintaining knowledge management guidance and documentation.
- Collaborate with the senior in communication of new guidance and governance and iterated documentation (if applicable).

EXECUTE INTERNAL RESEARCH
Expected level of skill: Working to practitioner depending on existing skill

- Support or lead the team and participate in undertaking internal research.
- Work with team to integrate research into the solution.
- Work with teams to measure success and make sure the solutions are meeting the expected user outcomes.

STAKEHOLDER ENGAGEMENT (REOPS AS A TEAM SPORT)
Expected level of skill: Expert

- Lead stakeholders' engagement and communication of planned, ongoing and implemented knowledge management work.
- Lead change management of both centralized and distributed ReOps and knowledge management processes.
- Identify and train knowledge management champions across the community; to help socialize governance and best practice.
- Share knowledge management work done regularly inside and outside of the community.

ENABLE INCLUSIVE RESEARCH
Expected level of skill: Working to practitioner

- Working knowledge of inclusive research methodologies.
- Advocate of inclusive practices.

STRATEGIC DIRECTION
Expected level of skill: Expert

Knowledge management training and governance strategy

- Responsible for developing, socializing and implementing knowledge management governance.
- Responsible for long-term knowledge management improvement strategy.

- Conduct knowledge audits and analyse to identify gaps and opportunities for improvement.
- Evaluate the effectiveness and impact of knowledge management activities and initiatives, and provide feedback and recommendations for improvement.
- Knowledge management best practice training.
- Ensure knowledge assets are accurate, relevant and up to date, and comply with quality standards and best practices.
- Enable disseminating and communicating knowledge across the business.
- Set up a regular cadence for knowledge auditing and maintenance, and data gardening to support the embedding of good knowledge management practices.
- Influence senior leaders to ensure commitment and advocacy for knowledge management.
- Collaborate with other knowledge management experts across the organization.

PEOPLE MANAGEMENT
Management and support of knowledge management specialists

- Manage knowledge management people in the Ops Team.
- Support people reacting to knowledge management support requests when they need to be escalated.
- Support knowledge management people's learning and development and career.

INTERPERSONAL AND LEARNING SKILLS

- Lead on team culture.
- Able to reflect and improve.
- Have cultural awareness: understanding of how culture affects interactions and how to manage the differences.
- Learn how to maintain good relationships with colleagues and stakeholders.
- Manage own time effectively.
- Able to undertake workshop facilitation.

- Evangelize research, and research operations and knowledge management.
- Skilled at maintaining good relationships with colleagues.
- Give and receive constructive feedback.
- Provide proactive and regular status updates.
- Confidently communicate technical information in an understandable way.
- Change communication style according to who you are sharing the work with and for what purpose.

LINE MANAGEMENT

- Be aware of differences in administration and policies for different countries.
- Performance.
- Career paths.
- Objectives.
- Coaching (power skill development).
- Cascading information from leadership.

Research Operations Senior

Responsibilities

This role can be responsible for managing strategy and implementation of research operations processes, both centralized and distributed, collaborating with all team members to support their research needs and problems. This role balances the delivery and progression of strategic and tactical operations work and support, and provides tactical and strategic support to the team experiencing difficulties during the research process (larger, more complex projects), collaborating on problem resolution. For complex non-critical problems, demonstrate a solution-focused mindset and ability to resolve issues independently.

It will depend on the make-up of the team what the senior does. The following job description assumes that an administrator is within the team. However, if an administrator is not on the team, the ReOps senior role will need to be reshaped to include appropriate administrative tasks for what the organization needs.

Craft skills

PLANNING SKILLS
Expected level of skill: Practitioner

- Scope out the problem space to understand the necessary tactical activities that need to be done.
- Plan for robust decision-making, know what type of data needs to be collected, plan for the analysis and synthesis, and identify the constraints.
- Prioritize individual and team activities, considering business priorities and problem spaces.
- Work to understand stakeholders' needs.
- Work alongside the lead and administrator.

COORDINATION AND MANAGEMENT
Expected level of skill: Practitioner

- Maintain and enable GDPR compliance.
- Support researchers and designers to ensure data is well-managed.
- Incentive budget management.
- Lead on tool and vendor relationship management for participant recruitment.
- Lead on participant database management and strategy.
- Monitor tool usage.
- Responsible for identifying gaps and opportunities on distributed tasks, tool management and participant recruitment.

Depending on team size and structure

- Support or lead: research tool management.
- Support or lead: participant recruiting and coordination.
- Support or lead: consent management.
- Support or lead: incentive payments.
- Collaborate or lead on onboarding and offboarding of people doing customer research.

EXECUTE INTERNAL RESEARCH

Expected level of skill: Working to practitioner depending on existing skills

- Support or lead the team and participate in undertaking internal research.
- Work with the ReOps team to integrate research into the solution.
- Work with teams to measure success and make sure the solutions are meeting the expected user outcomes.

STAKEHOLDER ENGAGEMENT (REOPS AS A TEAM SPORT)

Expected level of skill: Practitioner

- Support the engagement of stakeholders and communication regarding planned, ongoing and implemented ReOps work.
- Support/lead change management of both centralized and distributed ReOps processes.

ENABLE INCLUSIVE RESEARCH

Expected level of skill: Practitioner

- Working knowledge of inclusive research methodologies.
- Advocate of inclusive practices.
- Practitioner of, or expert in, diverse participant selection (appropriate screeners to reach different audiences).

STRATEGIC DIRECTION

Expected level of skill: Expert

Participant recruitment and engagement strategy

- Responsible for recruitment and incentive governance.
- Long-term recruitment activities.
- Recruitment best practice training.
- Engagement: participant communication.

INTERPERSONAL AND LEARNING SKILLS

- Contribute to team culture.
- Able to reflect and improve.
- Have cultural awareness: understanding of how culture affects interactions and how to manage the differences.

- Learn how to maintain good relationships with colleagues and stakeholders.
- Manage own time effectively.
- Able to undertake workshop facilitation.
- Evangelize research, and research operations and knowledge management.
- Skilled at maintaining good relationships with colleagues.
- Give and receive constructive feedback.
- Provide proactive and regular status updates.
- Confidently communicate technical information in an understandable way.
- Change communication style according to who you are sharing the work with and for what purpose.

Research Operations Lead/Research Manager (with research expertise)

Responsibilities

This role can work across programmes and departments. Their strategic function will help the organization to join up customer insights from different sources and facilitate alignment. They are able to help domain plan research that is proactive about improving the user experience. They are able to bring others on the journey and skill up others. This role manages others in the ReOps Team.

Craft skills

PLANNING SKILLS
Expected level of skill: Expert

- Lead research operations for customer research strategy planning.
- Plan for fostering research operations innovation and growth.
- Support ongoing structural development of the research process.
- Collaborate with knowledge management lead to ensure that the overall ReOps strategy and the knowledge management strategy align.

- Scope out the problem space to understand the necessary tactical activities that need to be done.
- Plan for robust decision-making, know what type of data needs to be collected, plan for the analysis and synthesis, and identify the constraints.
- Prioritize individual and team activities, considering business priorities and problem spaces.
- Work to understand stakeholders' needs.

COORDINATION AND MANAGEMENT
Expected level of skill: Expert

- Lead strategy to ensure GDPR compliance.
- Tools and services budget management.
- Lead tools and service strategy.
- Manage research tools and vendor relationships.
- Support senior on tool and vendor relationship management for participant recruitment.
- Support senior on participant database management and strategy.
- Work with senior to identify gaps and opportunities on distributed tasks, tool management and participant recruitment.
- Work alongside the ReOps team and collaborate with DesignOps and research leads where appropriate.
- Coach and train those less experienced in research practices to enable learning and development.

EXECUTE INTERNAL RESEARCH
Expected level of skill: Expert

- Lead the ReOps team in internal research to make user-centric, evidence-based decisions. Where appropriate, support the team's learning and development of research skills.
- Work with team to integrate research into the solution.
- Work with team to measure success and make sure the solutions are meeting the expected user outcomes.

STAKEHOLDER ENGAGEMENT (REOPS AND RESEARCH AS A TEAM SPORT)
Expected level of skill: Expert

- Lead the engagement of stakeholders and communication regarding planned, ongoing and implemented ReOps work.
- Lead change management when process and guidance changes are required for centralized and distributed Ops processes.
- Collaborate with research leads on upskilling people doing research.
- Provide research consultancy to those doing research to ensure high-quality research is done.

ENABLE INCLUSIVE RESEARCH
Expected level of skill: Practitioner to expert

- Practitioner of inclusive research methodologies.
- Advocate of inclusive practices.
- Practitioner of diverse participant selection (appropriate screeners to reach different audiences).
- Support others' learning and development of inclusive research.

STRATEGIC DIRECTION
Expected level of skill: Expert

Overall research operations strategy

- Responsible for developing, socializing and implementing high-level research operations governance.
- Responsible for a long-term improvement strategy.
- Deliver GDPR compliance training.
- Coordinate all aspects of the research operations strategy.

INTERPERSONAL AND LEARNING SKILLS

- Lead on team culture.
- Able to reflect and improve.
- Have cultural awareness: understanding of how culture affects interactions and how to manage the differences.
- Learn how to maintain good relationships with colleagues and stakeholders.
- Manage own time effectively.
- Able to undertake workshop facilitation.

- Evangelize research, and research operations and knowledge management.
- Skilled at maintaining good relationships with colleagues.
- Give and receive constructive feedback.
- Provide proactive and regular status updates.
- Confidently communicate technical information in an understandable way.
- Change communication style according to who you are sharing the work with and for what purpose.

LINE MANAGEMENT

- Be aware of differences in administration and policies for different countries.
- Performance.
- Career paths.
- Objectives.
- Coaching (power skill development).
- Cascading information from leadership.

Research Operations Lead (limited research expertise)

The main difference between a lead with and without research expertise is supporting or not researcher training and providing consultancy, and they won't lead on internal research to inform ReOps work. If the ReOps lead is dedicating some of their time to evolving the research practice in terms of craft skills, then other roles in the team will need to take on some of the responsibilities that the lead won't have time for. What these responsibilities are and how they are distributed will depend on what the organization needs, who is in the team and what their skills and capabilities are. If there isn't research expertise within the ReOps team to undertake internal research and analysis of feedback, the team will need to collaborate with willing research colleagues to do this work and start to build some of this capability within ReOps team members. It really isn't one size fits all.

In the next part of this chapter we are going to look at interview questions for recruiting the roles outlined above.

Interview questions

Interview questions within the recruitment process should be designed for people to be able to demonstrate their capabilities, skills and experience, or their transferable skills in the areas that are important to the organization and role (see Table 8.4).

There are two different approaches to designing your interview questions:

- experience-based
- hypothetical-based

Experience-based questions are the most common, as this is the most direct way to understand a candidate's experience of doing a particular thing; these are the 'tell me about a time you…' questions. This allows candidates to tell a story using the STAR method, ideally (situation, task, action, result).

Hypothetical questions are more inclusive as candidates can demonstrate their understanding, critical thinking and transferable skills, even if they have not had direct experience in the particular area the interview question is focusing on. This is useful at any level – we can't all have experience in everything, but it is particularly useful for junior interviews and for career transitioners. The rest of this chapter gives a detailed list of the types of interview questions you might want to include and what areas of skills and capabilities they cover. We will need to prioritize what areas are most important to the role, as we only get to ask four or five questions in an hour-long interview, also giving time for the candidate to ask any questions themselves.

QUESTION 1

- Level suitability: All.
- Question type: Warm-up.
- Questions and variations:
  - Can you tell us a bit about yourself and why you are interested in this role?
  - Can you tell us a bit more about your story? What led you to [research operations/knowledge management]?

QUESTION 2

- Level suitability: All.
- Question type: Learning mindset.

- Questions and variations:
  - How do you stay up to date with the field?
  - What's one skill you're currently improving?
  - How do you continue your professional development?
  - Tell us about a time that you learnt something new.

QUESTION 3

- Level suitability: Junior/midweight/senior/lead.
- Question type: Implementation, problem solving, collaboration.
- Questions and variations:
  - Tell us about a time when you've worked with a team to produce a great outcome.

QUESTION 4

- Level suitability: Midweight/senior.
- Question type: Learning and development.
- Questions and variations:
  - Tell us about a time when you used a new participant recruitment method. How did you make sure it was suitable and that you implemented it appropriately?
  - Tell us about a time when you used a new knowledge management method. How did you make sure it was suitable and that you implemented it appropriately?
  - Tell us about a time when you used a process or method in your work. How did you make sure it was suitable and that you implemented it appropriately?
  - How [do you/would you] apply feedback to improve your practice?

QUESTION 5

- Level suitability: Senior/lead.
- Question type: Supporting others' learning and development, people management.
- Questions and variations:
  - Tell us about a time when you introduced others to a new process. How did you approach it and ensure the method was embedded correctly?

o How do you support and work with people to ensure processes are followed?

QUESTION 6

- Level suitability: Junior/midweight/senior.
- Question type: Communication and impact.
- Questions and variations:
  - o Can you tell us about a time you had to get buy-in for a project or an idea?

QUESTION 7

- Level suitability: Midweight/senior.
- Question type: Communication and impact.
- Questions and variations:
  - o Can you tell us about a time when you convinced a team to do something different to what they planned to do? Why was it needed and how did you get everyone on board?

QUESTION 8

- Level suitability: Senior/lead.
- Question type: Communication, strategy and leadership.
- Questions and variations:
  - o How do you handle when stakeholders are sceptical of the value of research operations?
  - o How do you adapt your approach to work when people think research processes are slowing down the delivery of research?

QUESTION 9

- Level suitability: Midweight/senior/lead.
- Question type: Inclusive research, data management.
- Questions and variations:
  - o How would you approach ensuring diversity of participant recruitment, and ensure inclusion of those with access needs?

QUESTION 10

- Level suitability: Junior.
- Question type: Planning, problem solving.
- Questions and variations:
  - Tell us about a time a piece of work didn't go to plan.

QUESTION 11

- Level suitability: Midweight/senior/lead.
- Question type: Analytical thinking, learning mindset, communication.
- Questions and variations:
  - Tell us about a time a piece of work didn't go to plan.
  - How do you manage situations when legal and ethical requirements for the research process and researchers' wishes are misaligned?

QUESTION 12

- Level suitability: Junior.
- Question type: Communicating, implementation, [strategy].
- Questions and variations:
  - How do you approach sharing the outcomes of a piece of work?

QUESTION 13

- Level suitability: Midweight/senior/lead.
- Question type: Communication, implementation, [strategy].
- Questions and variations:
  - What is your approach to sharing new governance to be implemented with colleagues and stakeholders?

QUESTION 14

- Level suitability: Junior/midweight.
- Question type: Transferable skills.
- Questions and variations:
  - Tell us about your experience working in administration, communicating information, customer service, operations [and other relevant roles].

QUESTION 15

- Level suitability: Senior/lead.
- Question type: Planning, strategy, leadership, prioritization.
- Questions and variations:
  - Tell us about how you approach balancing tactical and strategic work.

QUESTION 16

- Level suitability: Lead.
- Question type: Planning, prioritization.
- Questions and variations:
  - Tell us about how you handle multiple pieces of work at the same time – managing your own work and supporting the work of junior colleagues.

QUESTION 17

- Level suitability: All.
- Question type: Planning, implementation, [strategy].
- Questions and variations:
  - When do you think your work has been most effective and why?

QUESTION 18

- Level suitability: Midweight/senior.
- Question type: Planning, implementation, [strategy].
- Questions and variations:
  - Describe your current recruitment process, incentives and panel management. And how do you approach improving the process?
  - Describe how you would approach managing a recruitment process including incentives and panel management. And how would you approach improving the process over time?

QUESTION 19

- Level suitability: Senior/lead.
- Question type: Planning, implementation, strategy, communication.

- Questions and variations:
  - How do you go about socializing a [research operations/knowledge management] strategy?
  - How do you go about creating a [research operations/knowledge management] strategy?
  - How do you measure and share the impact of your work?

QUESTION 20

- Level suitability: All.
- Question type: Wrap-up.
- Questions and variations:
  - What are the top challenges operations people face in the current environment?
  - What are the top challenges of doing research operations in an agile environment?
  - Why is research operations essential to the success of a business?
  - Would you say research operations are indispensable or optional for a start-up?

Practical interview scenarios

The multi-step interview process is common in research. I'm not aware if it is very common in recruiting operations people, but if we want a rounded interview process, including a practical exercise is an option. As with research, this is where the candidate is given a scenario of a project or an operations scenario and is given a certain amount of time to create a plan on what they would do within the scenario. The candidate will present their plan to the interview panel and talk through their reasons behind the plan.

Whatever relevant scenario the candidate is given, the things we need to look out for include:

- their understanding of the scenario
- how they have scoped the project
- what assumptions they have made
- who they would include or collaborate with during the project
- their understanding of the process and the tasks involved

- their reasoning behind their approach
- whether they assumed a reasonable timescale

As with interviews, there are two different ways to approach practical exercises:

1 In an hour session, share the scenario (10 minutes), give candidates 25 minutes to work on their plan and then 25 minutes for presentation, discussion and questions.

2 Give the candidate the scenario over email and three days to prepare for a session with the interview panel, where the candidate will present, with discussion and questions (45 minutes).

There are benefits and drawbacks to both approaches:

1 Everyone has the same time to approach the exercise, and the candidate can ask clarifying questions before they start. But you are getting their first thoughts, and it's not particularly compatible with those candidates who don't work so well under pressure, especially during the recruitment process.

2 Giving people time to prepare means you can get greater insight into their understanding, experience and approach. However, the main drawback to this approach is not everyone has an equal amount of time to prepare. For example, if you have a full-time job and caring responsibilities, you will have little time to prepare compared to someone who currently doesn't have a job and doesn't have caring responsibilities.

The types of scenarios we can set for operations role practical interviews include:

- Set up a participant recruitment process, where nothing is yet established, giving context of the relevant customer groups and other organizational constraints.
- Give an overview of a less-than-ideal operations or knowledge management process and ask the candidate to draft a plan of how they would go about iteratively improving the process.
- Stakeholders are struggling to find past research to use to inform decisions. How would they approach such a problem?
- Stakeholders are struggling to understand the insights shared based on customer research. How would they approach such a problem?

Who to include on interview panels

I have found that two or three person interview panels work best. More than three and it's very intimidating for the interviewee, and interviews could last too long a time, with everyone asking questions. Just one person doing all the interviews is not only a lot of work for one person, it introduces too much potential for that person's biases to influence the recruitment process, when we are aiming for diverse and inclusive recruitment. To have diverse and inclusive recruitment we need multiple perspectives on interview panels, in terms of discipline expertise, role experience and life experience.

If we are implementing a two- or three-stage interview process, then it is a good idea to have one or (maximum) two people consistent who will be in every stage of the process. These people should be research experts and operations experts. We may want to include the people the successful candidate will be working with, which aren't necessarily all going to be research and operations experts.

We should also actively work towards having balance and representation on interview panels – so a mix of ethnicities, genders, access needs, etc. If a black woman or non-binary person has two interview panels of three white men, they may, understandably, be hesitant about whether it's the right place for them to work. Having a diverse group of people on the panel will also help to balance out people's inherent biases.

Notes

1   N Lioudis. What's included in a research operations job description? A ReOps hiring guide (and template), User Interviews, 2024. www.userinterviews.com/blog/research-operations-job-description-examples-template (archived at https://perma.cc/8DV8-R9UL)

2   Fortune Business Insights. UX services market size and share, by service type (UX research, UX design, UX audit, UX training, and UX strategy and consulting), by enterprise type (large enterprises and SMEs), and regional forecast, 2023–2030, Fortune Business Insights, 2024. www.fortunebusinessinsights.com/ux-services-market-108780 (archived at https://perma.cc/C2NJ-GB79)

3   J Nielsen. A 100-year view of user experience, Nielsen Norman Group, 2017. https://www.nngroup.com/articles/100-years-ux/ (archived at https://perma.cc/V2TQ-K9BK)

4   Statista Research Department. Revenue of the market research industry worldwide from 2008 to 2023 with a forecast for 2024, Statista, 2024. www.statista.com/statistics/242477/global-revenue-of-market-research-companies/ (archived at https://perma.cc/V7UK-X3SU)

5   K Towsey. How to hire for ResearchOps: Skills, experience and potential, ResearchOps Life Medium Blog, 2020. medium.com/researchopslife/how-to-hire-for-researchops-skills-experience-and-potential-406881202011 (archived at https://perma.cc/H54V-7PBR)

9

Supporting research and operations learning and development to deliver effectively

Kate Towsey stated in 2020 that there was little formal ResearchOps training available, and this is still true in 2024.[1] She also stated that there is little literature. Although there is more now, ReOps literature often focuses on the recruitment of people rather than the development of people within ReOps roles. I think this will change over time; the longer the field exists, we will build up that literature. This kind of literature can be found for researchers – as we saw in Chapter 1, market research and user research have both been around for a long time.

There are obviously specific skills to develop depending on our role, whether that is market research, user research or research operations. These are the craft skills specific to a practice. There are also a number of skills to develop that are relevant to any research or operations role, particularly when it comes to interpersonal skills. We are going to look at what skills can be included in research and operations learning and development frameworks, and how to support and track a person's development.

If we are working in an established research or operations team, with established roles, skills development frameworks should be directly in line with job descriptions and expected skills and responsibilities roles within a particular discipline. If we are in a position to create research and operations teams from the ground up, or we have a research team but not operations roles, the place to start is with a skills gap analysis. To enable us to do skills-based planning we must understand what skills we already have, and what skills we need to achieve the business strategy.[2]

Understanding the skills we have and the skills we need will help us to plan and organize to deliver what the organization needs. Do we have the skills available already and do we need a redistribution, a reorganization of talent? Perhaps we have the majority of skills needed and our people can be supported in intentional learning and development to fill the skill gaps identified. Or perhaps the gaps are such that new talent needs to be recruited. One option is to develop a skills roadmap with a timeline that can be incorporated into performance frameworks and objective setting.[3]

We will focus on the learning and development (L&D) of the people we already have in this chapter. How L&D (or upskilling) happens, how it needs to be supported and what those much needed skills might be will depend on where the team sits within the organization, the type of organization that we're in, and the mix of people in the team(s).[4] There will be a certain amount of consistency in terms of skills needed in research and operations people, but there is nuance depending on the organization's situation and focus. We can also look beyond the organization, and do some horizon scanning of the job market for skills we may need in the near future by looking at what competitor employers are asking for when recruiting new people.[5]

Before we get into the skills themselves, let's have a quick look at how to do a skills gap analysis. This is the process of identifying the gap between the skills we have in the organization, the level of proficiency of those skills and the skills we need to succeed.[6] We are focusing on skills gap analysis to enable learning and development for individuals, using it to uncover new L&D goals for a person's current job or move into another job within the organization (at the same level), improve productivity and identify skills they might need for a future promotion.[7]

At a high level, there are three steps in the process of undertaking a skills gap analysis:

1 Plan and identify critical skills.

2 Collect and analyse data.

3 Take action.

Depending on the need, we can do the analysis on multiple levels:

• individual

• team

• department

• organization[8]

To be most effective, this isn't a one-time exercise, but can be used for ongoing tracking on capabilities and needs in the team/department/organization.

Step 1: Plan

- Scope: What level of analysis is needed? Individual, team, department, organization?
- Essential skills: What skills are critical and what levels of competency are needed to achieve the current goals? What is likely to be automated? What market trends are likely to require new skills?
- Create matrix: Skills and competencies matrix required to do the work needed.
- Inventory: Audit current job descriptions.

Step 2: Data collection and analysis

- Complete skills assessment with the relevant individuals with identified critical skills.
- Identify gaps for individuals, team, department, organization.
- Review current position descriptions: Do they match identified critical skills and required levels of competencies? What's missing in terms of future needs? Are adaptations needed?
- Identify constraints to building out the skills needed.

Assessments should be undertaken using 360 feedback techniques, with individual self-assessment, manager assessment and feedback from multiple teammates and stakeholders at varying levels of seniority.

Step 3: Take action

- Update current job descriptions to match current and future needs.
- Create new job descriptions, if needed, to fill gaps.
- Work with individuals to design learning and development plans where appropriate.
- Work with individuals to design pathway plans to transition to new roles.[9]

What is needed to successfully achieve goals is a combination of skills, knowledge and behaviours. Chapters 7 and 8 detailed the craft skills and many interpersonal skills needed in the various types of research and operations roles available. The other aspect a well-rounded team member will need to build the most effective and successful team or community is knowledge of the sector we're working in, what are the intricacies of the industry, and knowledge of adjacent disciplines.[10] Adjacent disciplines will very much depend on organizational structure; are we working in a tech, product or engineering focused way? Are we working most closely with design people or marketing people? As ReOps, are we embedded in research or operations (we'll look at this closely later)?

So if we're a researcher or Ops person working within the marketing department, we need to develop a deep understanding of marketing processes. If we're a researcher or Ops person within the design or product department, then we need to develop a deep understanding of these development processes.

In terms of recruitment, choosing people who have the craft and interpersonal skills needed is the priority. Industry and process knowledge can be developed on the job.

Research operations skills development

There are a plethora of skills that any one ReOps role requires, depending on the needs of the team, department and organization and the skills already present in other Ops people and the researchers themselves. The following is a description of various skills that are essential and/or beneficial to Ops roles and should be on the learning and development menu; which courses people take (pun intended) will depend on the role and the individual.

Budget management

ReOps roles may be required to manage research related expenses, and responsible for organizing and allocating funds in specific areas. This could include all or some of:

- people-related (salary etc.)
- tools and services
- incentives
- training
- hardware
- facilities, e.g. labs

In my experience, budget management is something that is learnt on the job. However, I and most ReOps people would jump at the chance to have formal budget management and best practice training. It always surprises me that such monetary responsibilities don't come with training. This would definitely be a differentiator to an organization's offering if they provided such training.

Procurement management

This encompasses the evaluation, selection and creation of formal contractual agreements as well as managing the company's ongoing supplier relationships.[11] There are independent courses to learn procurement management, and although a full course may not be required internal training should definitely be provided to ensure that ReOps are following the right processes when procuring specialist research tools.

Change management

I would say all ReOps roles require the ability to manage change to some extent. Implementing changes and improvement to operations and research processes requires careful planning, excellent communication and sensitive delivery to be effective, to minimize disruption and issues while research work continues as things change. There are specific change management techniques that we'll look at in Part Three, but change management in essence is made up of skills that are definitely transferable. As already mentioned, planning and communication, as well as administrative skills, organizational skills, engagement and advocacy are important, as no one really likes change.

Service design

Service design encompasses the activities of planning and organizing a business's resources to improve the employee's experience, and subsequently the customer's experience. I think it is useful for ReOps people to have an understanding of service design and customer support skills. ReOps people are creating work processes, providing services and support to specialists to enable them to do their jobs. We can learn a lot from the service design discipline for the approaches we can take in ReOps.

Customer support and customer service

Zendesk differentiate between customer support and customer service; customer support is the how, troubleshooting a problem; customer service is the why – why it's recommended to set up your research in a certain way to avoid future issues.[12] ReOps is often called upon to do both. This means that ReOps people will need to have a deep understanding of specialist research tools being used and how they fit into the wider technological ecosystem of the organization. Central IT and tech support teams, in my experience, don't tend to get involved too much with the management of specialist tools. ReOps must also provide customer service in the sense that we need those using our processes, guidance and tools to have a good experience and continue to be willing to collaborate to ensure things are done in the right way.

Technical writing/content design

Many ReOps roles will be creating guidance, governance and various kinds of documentation to enable research to happen smoothly. Thus, it makes sense to have a good understanding of clear writing and plain language, and how to make the content we produce as useful and understandable as possible.

Research skills

Depending on how many researchers and operations people there are in the organization, and how many are needed, Ops people may need a certain amount of research skills. This isn't necessarily an essential requirement, but it is beneficial for understanding the work of the people we're supporting and also to take a user-centred approach to ReOps and conduct internal research. In terms of research methodologies to be aware of, the two or three key methods for ReOps people to know would be interviewing, surveys and, if working with UX research people, usability research.

Skills that both ReOps and researchers need

There are overlapping skill needs for ReOps and research people, although these skills could be employed for different purposes in different ways.

Training skills

More experienced researchers and ReOps people may need to provide internal training to others. This will depend on how much budget is available for training for learning and development, what upskilling needs to happen (how niche is the need?) and the scale of upskilling required.

For ReOps people you may be providing training in the form of onboarding new researchers in the research processes, GDPR practices, etc. People in the Ops team are likely to need to provide knowledge management practice training if that is within the remit of the team.

Researchers may need to provide training and coaching to less experienced teammates and colleagues across the range of research skills needed, as shown by the ResearchOps Community: www.researchskills.net/skills. Effective approaches to training are useful to have in the research and ReOps toolkit.

STAKEHOLDER MANAGEMENT

Stakeholder management is about the ability to keep all parties informed, providing the right level of information,[13] sharing the right thing at the right time, depending on the parties' level of responsibility or accountability and their level of knowledge about the project. Communication skills and getting the cadence right are key.[14]

STORYTELLING AND COMMUNICATION

Obviously outputs and outcomes will be different for research and operations, but the skills required to build and deliver a compelling narrative are the same. Presentation and storytelling encapsulates a wide range of activities and skills; all of these have the ultimate aim to convey evidence in a clear and compelling manner that will drive impact tailored to the audience.[15]

PROJECT MANAGEMENT

It's often not directly stated within a research or ReOps role that project management skills are required, but such skills are integral nonetheless. Especially if we are the person leading a project. And if we are supporting rather than leading, we should have enough awareness of project management to be an effective member of the team.[16]

RESEARCH ETHICS

There is little interactive training out there with respect to research ethics. I myself have run several research ethics workshops at international conferences as well as internally at Springer Nature (with a colleague) because of such a gap. These skills and awareness are developed through reading and internal training, if there are people to provide it. However people are getting this training, everyone involved in the research process needs to understand the moral and ethical responsibilities that come with it.

LEADERSHIP AND PEOPLE MANAGEMENT

Leadership and management are often used interchangeably. There is some overlap between the work done for leadership and management; with often one person doing both jobs, there are also significant differences.[17]

Leadership is the ability to create positive non-incremental change such as vision and strategies to drive and empower change.[18] Management is the ability to organize and prioritize to get things done through regular tasks.

These skills are outside of the craft skills we need to be researchers and operations people, and can be the hardest skills to gain. There is a huge variety of training available for both, so it's important to understand which aspects of leadership and/or management we need to develop.

AI SKILLS

AI is becoming a foundational skill. This is the first time in the 10 years that I have been a manager and thinking about individuals' learning and development, and the eight years I have been thinking about teams and communities' learning and development that I now think it is of the benefit of everyone to understand how to use AI in their roles. For me, training for research and operations people should be the fundamentals of prompt engineering and the assessment of AI output to understand their accuracy and quality. Understanding where and when to use AI in the research process is also needed (see Chapter 10).

DEI employee recruitment

For those involved in recruiting team members, there is useful training that can be done to ensure the best outcome and that candidates have a good and consistent experience participating in the recruitment process. Outside of what the organization's recruitment process and policies are, we can undertake training on unconscious bias and inclusive recruitment to improve how we approach our recruitment processes.

Sustainable and consistent learning and development

Skills development won't be a linear and even process. Depending on the type of research that the organization tends to do, for example, they might get quite experienced and confident in planning, conducting and analysing surveys, but will need a lot more assistance in moderating focus groups, which is a different skill entirely and perhaps done less frequently. Thus, it is important to keep track of their progress, so when you are looking for opportunities for them to grow you know where to focus. Tables 9.1, 9.2 and 9.3 are different variations of skills mapping and tracking frameworks I have used in the past.

Table 9.1 is a more universal approach, not specifying the skills themselves, but it provides a structure for assessing and tracking progress for an individual and their manager. In this framework the learning stage can be considered the first couple of stages of mastery – novice and advanced beginner. The transition to the thriving stage is the competence level of mastery and then thriving is proficient and expert. Even when we are experts in a particular skill there is always room for further development as the organization, industry or discipline changes and evolves.

Table 9.2 provides a framework of enabling a person to first self-assess and then reassess with their manager. Rather than using the mastery levels (novice, competent, etc.) more descriptive terms are used:

- Can do with guidance.
- Can do independently.
- Could teach others.
- I can't do this yet.
- I need to get feedback.

Another benefit of this particular framework is that it requires examples to be given to show how the assessment was arrived at.

(Based on work I have done with colleagues at Springer Nature.)

Table 9.3 focuses on how to progress through mastering a new skill and to demonstrate to a manager or lead what point we are at with each skill that we are trying to master. Are we shadowing, collaborating or leading on using a particular skill, and what are our questions at each stage (as well as examples of work)?

We must empower people to do learning and development. We need to do this through providing a budget for learning and development, and supporting people to invest time in their own learning and development. It is a common complaint that people don't have enough time in their day jobs for L&D.[19] Without the culture for taking time out for learning and

TABLE 9.1 Record your UX research learning and development

Role/experience	What is going well	What could be improved	Actions to take	What change do you want to see?	How will the action help you achieve the outcome?	How can you measure success?
Responsibilities						
Core skills at thriving stage						
Core skills at learning stage						
Interpersonal skills						

TABLE 9.2 Skills assessment and progress framework

Research phase	Skill	Can do with guidance	Can do independently	Could teach others	Can't do this yet	Need to get feedback	How long have you been at this level?	Examples of how skill has been applied	What could be improved?
Planning									
Execute research									
Analysis and synthesis									
Sharing									
Implementation									
Data management									

TABLE 9.3 Recording how progress is made

Research phase	Skills	Shadow	Collaborate	Lead	Outstanding questions	Examples of work
Planning	Surfacing and identifying assumptions and hypothesis					
	Identify research questions					
	Select research method					
	Write usability session guide					
	Write interview session guide					
Doing	Interviews					
	Focus groups					
	Surveys					
	Workshops					
	Diary studies					
Analysis and synthesis	Compile and clean data					
	Thematic analysis					
	Statistical analysis					
	Document actionable findings and insights					
Sharing	Communicate based on audience needs					
Implementation	Work with team to implement recommendations					

development and identifying opportunities for L&D, people find it very difficult to evolve and we then risk stagnation, demotivation and attrition.

There are many approaches to providing the right support for different styles of learning and development, and how to keep people motivated, as progression isn't always easy or linear. One approach I recommend looking into is the SLII approach taught in Blanchard's leadership training programmes.[20]

People have different preferred styles of learning; this is something we need to try to accommodate whether it be:

- reading books, blogs and articles on theory
- reading books, blogs and articles on case studies
- watching videos
- attending training courses
- learning through practical experience (shadow, collaborate, lead)
- reflecting on feedback through coaching and mentoring
- group training (organized training in groups)
- individual learning
- informal social learning (peer to peer in pairs or groups)

What can be provided will depend on the resources and support available for L&D. Each type of learning has pros and cons and costs associated with them. We need to understand what we can do within the organizational constraints, but we need to do something, as learning and development are essential.

How to support learning and development

There are various research specific and general templates for tracking skills development progress. There isn't a one size fits all approach to undertaking and tracking the progress of learning and development. Therefore, I want to provide a few options for others to take and develop their own, according to what works for the person, team, department or organization.

One example that I have previously taken inspiration from in developing skills frameworks is the Research Skills Framework developed by the ResearchOps Community:

www.researchskills.net

www.researchskills.net/tool/skill-map

www.researchskills.net/tool/skills-and-themes-inventory

www.researchskills.net/tool/career-trajectory-map

www.researchskills.net/insights/report

Learning and development can be about the aim to improve within a role, but it can also be about career progression 'upwards'. In terms of career trajectory, a traditional journey up the career ladder could be:

1 Junior/associate [role].

2 [Midweight] role.

3 Senior [role] or [role] specialist.

4 Associate director/lead/principal [role].

5 Director/head of [role].

An example for insight roles:

1 Junior insight executive.

2 Insight executive.

3 Senior insight executive.

4 Associate director of insight.

5 Director of insight.

Research operations career paths and structuring ReOps teams

There aren't the same established career paths for ReOps people currently, although this will change over time, so most will be career transitioning into a ReOps role. When Gibson and Friedman were writing about ReOps career pathways, they stated that only 9 per cent of ReOps people had been in their role for more than three years, with 17 per cent transitioning from a research background (UX research and market research) and 19 per cent coming from project or programme management.[21] And unsurprisingly ReOps people come from a wide variety of fields (HR, customer support, etc.). Opportunities to progress within research operations will partly depend on how ReOps is viewed – function vs discipline and generalist vs specialist – and craft and interpersonal skills and levels will vary.[22] Because the field is still a fledgling one, most writing we find about ResearchOps career paths are about moving into a role and not so much how to progress once we're there. Not that progression up the career ladder is required, but it is often desired. But research operations are starting to be recognized as a strategic function with a totally distinct set of skills from research and design. It's about strategically enabling research to operate efficiently and impactfully in organizations.[23]

As Lamb stated, navigating a career in an emerging field like research operations often feels like charting unexplored territory.[24] With few play-books to draw upon, practitioners are essentially writing them along the way. Similarly, advancing a career in this space is a journey of reflection and self-discovery, where we must define our own successes as we go. Many organizations unfortunately require people to become managers if they want to move to the next level up. This is unfortunate because, just because you are good at the craft skills, doesn't mean you are the right person to be a manager or may not want to be a manager. ReOps within organizations are at risk of falling into this trap as well. As Lamb points out, professional growth isn't only about climbing the ladder, it can be about expanding breadth and depth of skills within a role.[25] So one thing within the many things to consider when reflecting on long-term professional growth is the options:

- individual contributor
- manager[26]

In fields such as software development it is very common to have dev manager roles that focus on the people management of developers. From my experience it is less common in research fields such as UX and marketing. In all the managing roles that I have had, and all the managers that I have had, they have all been contributing managers. As the field continues to mature the type of roles available will expand and diversify, though it won't be linear (taking into account economic factors of expansion and contraction).

Because we are at the point in the field where we are still writing our own job specs and career paths in ReOps, I have laid out a few potential varia-tions in terms of career paths and structuring ReOps teams (depending on organizational needs). If we are considering a ReOps generalists career path it may look something like this:

1 Administrator (midweight).

2 Coordinator (senior).

3 Lead.

4 Director.

Career progression and team structure are obviously not the same thing, but they are closely related. If staying within one organization, we progress within the established structure or we build a new structure. Now we are going to imagine an established research operations team and structure and consider what the career pathway might be through different structures. But, if we are a ReOps team of one, career progression is likely to be increasing both the depth and breadth of skills and knowledge, rather than changing positions and job titles, or it could be both.

Additional factors that will affect career progression and team structure are how ReOps work is distributed and whether there are opportunities to specialize or if all ReOps roles are generalist; one isn't better than the other, both are needed but it will affect what opportunities we have within one organization.

Common ReOps tasks structures (as visualized in Figure 9.1):

- Solitary: One person is doing it all.
- Centralized: All ReOps tasks are done by a dedicated team.
- Decentralized: There are ReOps people embedded within specific teams or programmes of work.
- Distributed: There are no dedicated ReOps people but it's done by people in addition to their day job.
- Hybrid: This is where some ReOps is centralized and some is distributed.

FIGURE 9.1 Modes of distribution

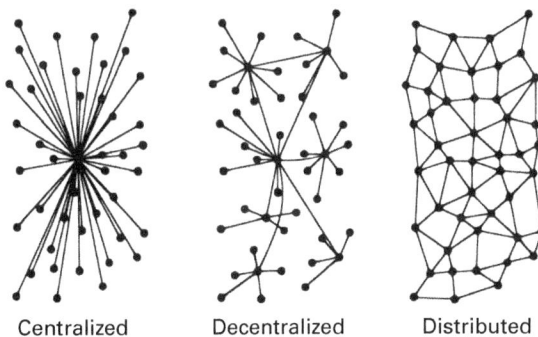

Centralized   Decentralized   Distributed

SOURCE R Dangi. Why do we need decentralized social media platforms? Medium, 2018. medium.com/hapramp/decentralized-blockchain-social-media-hapramp-7161d6ce7041 (Original source: J F Grissom. Who controls crypto currencies? Steemit, 2017. https://steemit.com/crypto/@jfgrissom/who-controls-crypto-currencies

How people are distributed will affect what responsibilities they have and whether generalists or specialists are required; what kind of specialists are needed is also very context-dependent.

Figure 9.2 visualizes potential ReOps job titles available at different levels of seniority, focusing solely on ReOps. Later in the chapter, we'll look at what other roles might sit in a wider team.

An organization won't necessarily have all these roles within a ReOps team and a team wouldn't necessarily have one of each if they are all present. It very much depends on the needs of the organization. But, let's imagine all the roles are present, in terms of career pathways they aren't necessarily linear like the ReOps generalist career path we looked at earlier. Depending on the skills and interests of the people in the team and the needs of and opportunities available in the organization, there are a multitude of ways through the roles.

We don't necessarily need to 'go up the ladder' through a specialist track either, such as:

1 Knowledge management administrator.

2 Knowledge management senior.

3 Knowledge management lead.

4 Director of insight.

FIGURE 9.2 Examples of ReOps roles at different levels of seniority

Midweight	Senior	Lead	Director
Participant recruiter	ReOps senior	ReOps lead	Director ReOps or UXOps or CXOps
Research administrator	Storyteller	KM lead	
KM administrator	KM senior	Inclusion research lead	
	Inclusion research manager		

KM = Knowledge management

Depending on skills, interests and opportunities available, we can go between generalist and specialist roles, such as the pathway shown in Figure 9.3. We may also go from specialist to generalist or generalist to specialist within one seniority level, as shown in a different pathway in Figure 9.4.

FIGURE 9.3 Example of ReOps roles career pathway 1

KM = Knowledge management

FIGURE 9.4 Example of ReOps roles career pathway 2

KM = Knowledge management

Where should the ReOps team live
within the organization's wider structure?

The following has been inspired by or reflects directly a discussion I had on a ReOps podcast.[27]

It has long been debated in user research, where is the best structure for research teams and who should they report to? As always, the answer is 'It depends', and the same is true of ReOps. And it may change over time as the practice scales and matures.

If we are building UX research operations specific capability, initially it makes sense to embed the operations person/people in the research team. Working closely with and reporting to the people we are directly supporting establishes the necessary synergy to embed and mature UX research and operations together. Understanding the research process nuances and how researchers need to be supported or iterated upon has the least barriers when embedded in the team.

It also depends what the remit and scope of the Ops team are. That may suggest where the best place for the operations team lives. It is important, particularly with more junior appointments, to have support from people that are familiar with what ReOps is trying to achieve and tasks they need to do. That may be the research team, or it may be the DesignOps team, etc.

If a midweight participant recruiter is the only ReOps person in the organization, it probably makes most sense for them to be embedded in the research team. But it isn't necessarily so simple, if the majority of research isn't being done by researchers themselves but by product people or marketers. Once again, it is very context dependent.

In the past, as a researcher, I have been through organization restructuring where the research community had been reporting into the director of UX and was moved to report into the director of product. The ultimate outcome was that another restructure was needed, it did not work for research to report into product in this case, although it is currently very common to do so, as shown in the User Interviews state of user research report.[28]

It is my opinion that in this case it did not work for research to report into product for a couple of reasons; user researchers often have the burden to deliver news that product managers don't want to hear. Perhaps whatever the team is working on, or an aspect of it, is not meeting users' needs and the team will need to pivot or go back to the drawing board. Depending on the product manager, it can put researchers into a difficult position if they are telling their line manager (who is also their product manager) what the team is doing isn't working. Some product managers will be open to the evidence and strive to meet user needs and are measured on the value delivered to the customer; others are measured on the delivery speed and just want to check the validation box using confirmation bias. Another reason that it didn't work, as it depends on how organizations work, is the product managers, no matter how supportive of research they are, mostly do not have the skills and experience to support a researcher's development and career progression. If in the organization line managers are responsible for a direct report's learning and development, and figuring out their career progression, the line manager, in my opinion, needs to be knowledgeable about the discipline both are working in. That means user researchers managing user researchers.

For ReOps, depending on how many ReOps people there are, ReOps may report into Ops or into research. When going through the same thought process we need to balance what is best for the ReOps individuals and where they should structurally sit to be the most impactful. As discussed during the podcast, ReOps has been around in some organizations long enough now that where this team sits has had to be reconsidered.[29] As discussed earlier, when we are first building a ReOps team, it makes sense for ReOps to be embedded in and reporting directly to research. However, as both research and ReOps mature as disciplines within an organization, it can make sense for ReOps to move out of research, and into a centralized operations team for customer experience, for example. There are multiple benefits to this happening:

- If the research team has stable, mature ReOps processes and research has been democratized within the organization, there could be a lot more non-researchers doing research, so it makes sense for ReOps to pivot their focus to the wider organization doing research.

- For ReOps to continue to mature, the support of other Ops specialists could beneficial, through gaining different perspectives for designing and delivering things.

Where ReOps sits also depends who the ReOps team is supporting: market research, user research or both (customer experience?). It is a rare thing, as far as I'm aware, to have a ReOps team that sits across MR and UXR if they're in different departments. It is more likely that there will be separate Ops teams (or persons), or one practice will have an Ops team and the other practice will not have dedicated Ops support. Market research professionals have been within organizations for longer than UX researchers, and MR teams usually sit within the marketing department. And marketing departments have usually been around longer than the department that UX research tends to sit in. Where a user research team sits is more 'flexible' or less consistent (if we're being honest). Which could affect where the ReOps team sits. UX research could sit in one of the following:

- user-centred design
- design
- customer experience
- technology
- digital
- marketing
- communications
- product

So the research operation team could sit in any of these and won't necessarily sit in the department where the people they support sit; it could be within a centralized function such as:

- IT
- DesignOps
- operations
- UXOps
- CXOps
- insight department

DesignOps has also been around longer than ReOps, so it's common for ReOps to report into DesignOps. However, ultimately (in my opinion) DesignOps and ReOps are peers, and should both report equally into a broader Ops director/head, such as customer experience operations.

On the podcast we discussed that ReOps, who are all professional problem solvers and people connectors, will get the work done and collaborate with whoever they need, regardless of where they sit in the organization. In this way it doesn't matter who we are reporting into. Where it can have an impact is on budgets, resources and priorities. We need to ask ourselves as the team matures, who do we need to align our priorities with to be the most effective and impactful team we can be? It may seem counterintuitive at first from the outside that it's not always going to be research. And if that's the case, then we need new reporting lines and new peers. If the ReOps team does move to report into a different function, it is important to maintain those initially critical relationships; after all, we will still be supporting the research team through our Ops work. So another question we will need to ask ourselves is how do we maintain those relationships? If we attended the rituals of every team we support, we wouldn't have time to do anything else, so we need to find other ways.

More visibility means, when democratizing of research is happening, we can avoid people reinventing the wheel in an area that isn't their specialism – like every product manager creating their own research process. If there is visibility they can move into that space and say 'Hey use mine', which means reporting to something other than research, which often doesn't have the most visibility.

Based on the podcast discussion, I came to the conclusion that the title of the person that ReOps is reporting into doesn't matter; what is important is that they trust us and they get what we're trying to achieve, even if they aren't a specialist themselves. This is because as much as we are problem solvers and enablers, we are also disruptors. As ReOps works to improve processes for research, there will inevitably be periods of disruption as research needs to continue to happen as changes occur. Therefore, we need coverage and support from above to do this work that has short-term pain for long-term gain.

Notes

1   K Towsey. How to hire for ResearchOps: Skills, experience and potential, ResearchOps Life Medium Blog, 2020. medium.com/researchopslife/how-to-hire-for-researchops-skills-experience-and-potential-406881202011 (archived at https://perma.cc/2SL5-GG5X)

2   O Shaw. Understand your workforce skills gaps before you rush in to bring in AI, Orgvue, 2023. www.orgvue.com/resources/articles/understand-your-workforce-skills-gaps-before-you-rush-to-bring-in-ai/ (archived at https://perma.cc/2SL5-zzzz)

3   J Williams. Unlocking potential: Training to transform research teams, Great Research Conference, 2024. www.youtube.com/watch?v=1xf33Gm0BQE (archived at https://perma.cc/7WRE-4USZ) Timestamp: 2:10:00 – 2:34:41

4   J Williams. Unlocking potential: Training to transform research teams, Great Research Conference, 2024. www.youtube.com/watch?v=1xf33Gm0BQE (archived at https://perma.cc/7WRE-4USZ) Timestamp: 2:10:00 – 2:34:41

5 J Williams. Unlocking potential: Training to transform research teams, Great Research Conference, 2024. www.youtube.com/watch?v=1xf33Gm0BQE (archived at https://perma.cc/7WRE-4USZ) Timestamp: 2:10:00 – 2:34:41

6 N Bika. How to conduct a skills gap analysis, Resources For Employers, 2023. resources.workable.com/tutorial/skills-gap-analysis (archived at https://perma.cc/XG5F-AU5M); S E Personio and K G Co. What is a skills gap analysis and how to effectively conduct one. Personio.com, 2024. www.personio.com/hr-lexicon/skills-gap-analysis/ (archived at https://perma.cc/BCK4-6ZHJ)

7 N Bika. How to conduct a skills gap analysis, Resources For Employers, 2023. resources.workable.com/tutorial/skills-gap-analysis (archived at https://perma.cc/XG5F-AU5M); S E Personio and K G Co. What is a skills gap analysis and how to effectively conduct one. Personio.com, 2024. www.personio.com/hr-lexicon/skills-gap-analysis/ (archived at https://perma.cc/BCK4-6ZHJ)

8 N Bika. How to conduct a skills gap analysis, Resources For Employers, 2023. resources.workable.com/tutorial/skills-gap-analysis (archived at https://perma.cc/XG5F-AU5M); S E Personio and K G Co. What is a skills gap analysis and how to effectively conduct one. Personio.com, 2024. www.personio.com/hr-lexicon/skills-gap-analysis/ (archived at https://perma.cc/BCK4-6ZHJ)

9 N Bika. How to conduct a skills gap analysis, Resources For Employers, 2023. resources.workable.com/tutorial/skills-gap-analysis (archived at https://perma.cc/XG5F-AU5M); S E Personio and K G Co. Skills matrix how-to guide: Template, examples and tips, Personio.com, 2024. www.personio.com/hr-lexicon/skills-matrix/ (archived at https://perma.cc/BCK4-6ZHJ); N Verlinden. Skills gap analysis: All you need to know, Academy To Innovate HR, 2024. www.aihr.com/blog/skills-gap-analysis/ (archived at https://perma.cc/3CKP-9BYZ)

10 J Williams. Unlocking potential: Training to transform research teams, Great Research Conference, 2024. www.youtube.com/watch?v=1xf33Gm0BQE (archived at https://perma.cc/2XN4-QD56) Timestamp: 2:10:00 – 2:34:41

11 Oracle. What is procurement management? Oracle, 2024. www.oracle.com/uk/erp/procurement/what-is-procurement/ (archived at https://perma.cc/K8X3-5RR8)

12 T Ramroop. How customer support and customer service work hand in hand, Zendesk, 2021. www.zendesk.co.uk/blog/customer-support-vs-customer-service/ (archived at https://perma.cc/R82Z-PFPC)

13 ResearchOps Community. Stakeholder management/communication, Research Skills Framework, 2020. www.researchskills.net/human-skill/stakeholder-management-communication (archived at https://perma.cc/E4EP-42ZU)

14 ResearchOps Community. Stakeholder management/communication, Research Skills Framework, 2020. www.researchskills.net/human-skill/stakeholder-management-communication (archived at https://perma.cc/E4EP-42ZU)

15   ResearchOps Community. Presentation and storytelling, Research Skills Framework, 2020. www.researchskills.net/human-skill/presentation-storytelling (archived at https://perma.cc/W3TU-T7E3)

16   ResearchOps Community. Project management/ownership, Research Skills Framework, 2020. www.researchskills.net/human-skill/project-management-ownership (archived at https://perma.cc/H6HF-363L)

17   M Gavin. Leadership vs management: What's the difference? Harvard Business School Online, 2019. online.hbs.edu/blog/post/leadership-vs-management (archived at https://perma.cc/2QFK-F4XY)

18   M Gavin. Leadership vs management: What's the difference? Harvard Business School Online, 2019. online.hbs.edu/blog/post/leadership-vs-management (archived at https://perma.cc/2QFK-F4XY)

19   J Williams. Unlocking potential: Training to transform research teams, Great Research Conference, 2024. www.youtube.com/watch?v=1xf33Gm0BQE (archived at https://perma.cc/3Z4S-U2N3) Timestamp: 2:10:00 – 2:34:41

20   Blanchard. SLII: Powering inspired leaders, Blanchard, 2024. www.blanchard.com/our-content/programs/slii (archived at https://perma.cc/87JM-9MUC)

21   L Gibson and O Friedman. The many pathways into Research Ops, Rally, 2022. www.rallyuxr.com/post/pathways-into-research-ops (archived at https://perma.cc/6VCC-VQJY)

22   A Martin. Careers in ResearchOps – all roads lead to Rome, ResearchOps Community, 2023. medium.com/researchops-community/careers-in-researchops-all-roads-lead-to-rome-928273cc1d07 (archived at https://perma.cc/T4FW-AXFQ)

23   J Wolstenholm. Research operations: Processes, strategies and tools for 2024, Great Question, 2023. greatquestion.co/blog/ux-research-operations-101 (archived at https://perma.cc/P7VY-EZRQ)

24   N Lamb. Advancing your career in research operations, Great Question, 2024. greatquestion.co/blog/advancing-your-research-ops-career (archived at https://perma.cc/BX8R-BGSV)

25   N Lamb. Advancing your career in research operations, Great Question, 2024. greatquestion.co/blog/advancing-your-research-ops-career (archived at https://perma.cc/BX8R-BGSV)

26   N Lamb. Advancing your career in research operations, Great Question, 2024. greatquestion.co/blog/advancing-your-research-ops-career (archived at https://perma.cc/BX8R-BGSV)

27   K Towsey, S Osborne, E Lyon and S Marsh. What are the pros and cons of ResearchOps reporting into research versus other operational roles, ProductOps or DesignOps, That's a Great ResearchOps Question Podcast, 2024. https://podcasts.apple.com/gb/podcast/what-are-the-pros-and-cons-of-researchops/id1756436113?i=1000668242977 (archived at https://perma.cc/92K9-M3MB)

28 User Interviews. The state of user research: 2024 report, User Interviews, 2024. www.userinterviews.com/state-of-user-research-report (archived at https://perma.cc/2G4P-PP7K)

29 K Towsey, S Osborne, E Lyon and S Marsh. What are the pros and cons of ResearchOps reporting into research versus other operational roles, ProductOps or DesignOps, That's a Great ResearchOps Question Podcast, 2024. https://podcasts.apple.com/gb/podcast/what-are-the-pros-and-cons-of-researchops/id1756436113?i=1000668242977 (archived at https://perma.cc/92K9-M3MB)

PART THREE

Advanced operations

I struggled with what to call this part, because these three chapters also cover important aspects of research operations, which is why I have written about them. I settled on advanced operations, not only because they are highly sophisticated things to do, but also taking into consideration what things will be prioritized if we are just starting out in creating a research operations practice to support and enable the customer research practice.

The nuance is that these things shouldn't necessarily be left to do last, but in reality we can't build and deliver everything at once and there are likely to be other things that need to happen first, before these more advanced things – such foundational things as recruiting or identifying internally the right people to work in research operations, and then ensuring the basic research processes are functioning and broadly legally compliant.

I have included the use of AI in customer research and research operations in this section on advanced operations as it's a relatively new thing to consider within research and it's becoming increasingly prevalent very quickly. It is my conviction that in order to understand how best to use AI, and when to avoid it in our work, we need a solid foundation in both customer research and research operations first.

It can be difficult to identify the right metrics to track to demonstrate the value of both research and research operations, depending on the type of field/industry and organization we are working in. To me, identifying, implementing, tracking and communicating the valuable metrics is also a sophisticated thing that we need to do. It is especially complex when we need to implement and track metrics as we are setting up and establishing teams, which we need to prove the worth of.

And last but certainly not least, we look at change management. This again has the paradox of something we may not focus on how to do immediately (unless we have a background in organizational change) but it is something we are likely doing from the very beginning, especially if we are building a new practice. But if we are coming to support an existing research process, then the first thing we need to do is learn about the as-is process and support in progress research, ensuring things don't break while we work out what the hell is going on. And then we can think about sustainable and effective change management, and being able to adapt customer research and research operations to the changing needs of the people and the business.

10

How to use AI as part of the research process

Artificial intelligence is an inaccurate description of what it actually is. A more accurate description would be applied statistics.[1]

Automation is about using technology to minimize or eliminate human effort or intervention in common and repetitive tasks. Some task automation involves AI, but not all task automation includes an AI component; automation is often about integration.

The User Interviews 'State of user research: 2024 report' found that 56 per cent of researchers are using AI to support their work in some way.[2] In 2023, they reported that 20 per cent of researchers were using AI to support their work.[3] This is a significant increase in one year, and just one indicator that we need to pay attention to AI and think critically about how to use it in our work.

What do we need to know about AI?

There are many considerations in this newly prominent topic. It is important to stress that a grounding in the practices of market and user research are required to know how to properly use AI to aid and improve our research and maintain high quality and robustness at the same time. And we need an understanding of AI and how it works to know when it is or isn't appropriate to use within research operations work, especially when considering data protection and data privacy.

Table 10.1 provides a few definitions of terms that are commonly used when we're talking about AI.

TABLE 10.1 What is AI?

Artificial intelligence (AI)	Field of computer science for creating systems that perform tasks that usually require human intelligence.
Machine learning (ML)	A sub-field of AI where algorithms are developed that enable computers to learn from data and make predictions and decisions based on it.
Generative AI (GenAI)	GenAI are AI systems that can create new content by learning from existing data, meaning that the output is similar to the training data. GenAI uses generative models.
Large language model (LLM)	LLMs use AI models to learn from and produce human-like text. Trained on textual data specifically and perform language related tasks. All LLMs are GenAI but not all GenAI are LLMs.

SOURCE S Tracy, A Sen, Milieu Insight. Applications of generative AI in market research (and the risks you need to know), UX Quant Con, 2024. www.quantuxcon.org/quant-ux-con/past-conferences

AI hallucinations

AI hallucinations are instances where a large language model (LLM) perceives patterns and objects that don't exist or are not perceptible to humans and the output either doesn't make sense or doesn't exist.[4] A common example from the field of academics is AI models (such as ChatGPT) creating citations for books and journal papers that do not exist.

We need to be AI literate

In order to use AI robustly and confidently, we need to be AI literate. AI literacy encompasses varied skills required to understand, analyse and evaluate the uses and impacts of AI technologies. Ethical AI thought leaders agree that these skills should not be developed through a solely technical lens; instead AI literacy programmes must also consider the social implications of such technologies.[5]

AI isn't going to save us, or even level the playing field

In Chapter 4, we looked at digital inclusion through the lens of participant recruitment. AI is changing what inclusion means in today's digital society and economy. Not having a device, and/or connectivity, and/or digital skills and confidence makes life harder – especially for disadvantaged groups and in areas of multiple deprivation. AI is increasing the digital divide and has profound consequences on everything from individual wellbeing to multibillion pound implications for a country's productivity, economic growth, public health, levelling up, education. The UK, for example, lags behind its peers with regards to developing and implementing AI literacy frameworks and interventions. In the absence of government or civil society literacy programmes, tech companies fill this market gap, and their market dominance maintains the perspective of AI as unambiguously positive. The tech industry's ability to wield this power on the narrative around AI in turn influences government policy, at the same time limiting public input.[6]

AI is not neutral

In 2024 Jakob Nielsen, one of the pioneers of the field of user experience, wrote an article on his Substack that accessibility had failed and we need to look to AI to save us, that AI will make computers more accessible.[7]

I completely disagree. While I will say that it is very disappointing how long it has taken organizations to be more accessible, it is happening, it has been happening for a long time and it will continue to do so. It hasn't failed. Yes we do live in an ableist society where people who don't fit the 'norm' are marginalized. It is important that we enable those with the greatest needs to live their lives, but we all have access needs (as described by Microsoft in 2016[8]). There is more and more legislation coming into force around the world that requires the private as well as the public sector to be accessible to citizens, including the European Accessibility Act coming into force in June 2025.

I also disagree with Nielsen that making existing systems accessible produces substandard user experiences. Making things accessible makes things better for everyone, there are many studies demonstrating this. A simple example is everyone prefers plain language, whatever your literacy level. Plain language benefits both a person with low literacy, the harassed and overworked lawyer and the person who is working in their third language.

Nielsen's example of a poor experience is using alt text to describe images. This is an extremely flippant example – it is an established practice that if an image is purely decorative, you don't need to describe it at length with alt text. Going back to writing plainly for everyone's benefit means not relying on AI to write your alt text; LLMs don't have the context to produce what you need.

Nielsen suggests that the future is generative user interfaces (UIs) – using AI to automatically generate UI design for disabled users. But he wilfully ignores the inherent bias of AI models. LLMs are trained on data produced by people, so the data we feed into LLMs will focus on what people in society focus on and that is WEIRD – western, educated, industrialized, rich and democratic, as well as cis-gendered, heteronormative, able-bodied, neurotypical, white, male. We can't assume that AI models are going to provide us with what we need if we aren't one of these people.

Digitally excluded people have a lower digital footprint. Their invisibility in datasets used to train large language models and other AI tools raises red flags about reliability and robustness. Where AI is used to inform policies and decisions, then the policies and decisions will be flawed, possibly in different ways to a human making a decision. The dangers to social justice are highest where policies and decisions impact people who need public and health services most, and who are more likely to be digitally excluded because of old age, low income or fear and distrust of digital. When we create tools that are using unrepresentative, biased data, we are replicating harms that are happening at a structural level.[9]

There is an acute need to focus on data as foundational to AI. Many (most, or even all) AI systems are built on biased or incomplete data, with digitally excluded people's perspectives missing altogether, leading to flawed policy and decision-making, and outright discrimination. To shift AI narratives to serve public interest, we need not only more comprehensive data, but also AI skills and literacy programmes, connecting AI tools to people's everyday realities and providing safe spaces for experimentation.[10]

There are three main stages of AI where bias can become part of your research without your knowledge:

- Pre-processing: Bias can exist in the data without us being aware of what we're feeding into the algorithm.

- In-processing: Algorithms are trained, but how they are trained to assess, prioritize and ignore data can also incorporate bias.

- Post-processing: Delivers the output to us, and however the AI selects what to show us in the end can also include bias, including common forms of discrimination.

The sad truth is that most founders of AI tools, as well as most other businesses, are male, white, middle-class, educated, and so on. That leaves a lot of bias to be accounted for in AI processes.[11]

One of the biggest challenges is the time, resources and level of support it takes to create these equitable datasets. There are many challenges to obtaining reliably annotated datasets for AI models, which can involve time-consuming and resource-intensive experimentation and simulations, further perpetuating bias in the use of AI and thus exclusion.[12]

What can be automated and augmented in research and Ops?

We need to consider the difference between two types of AI tools commonly used for customer research that is important for GDPR considerations:

- tools that use the data you input to train models, e.g. ChatGPT
- tools that don't use the data you input to train models, e.g. AI functionality in tools such as Dovetail and Miro, rather using pre-trained LLMs

For our participants, and our duty of care towards them, we need to think about our consent forms for research – do they need to include how AI tools are being used when processing, etc., data collected from research?

For our internal processes, we also need to think about other implications of using AI in customer research. In the *It's a Great ResearchOps Question!* podcast, Towsey et al discussed the additional dimension for evaluating tool and services suppliers;[13] we need to understand how data is used in our tools with AI features, before we can make an informed selection, and AI features are increasing prices for these tools, even if we aren't going to make use of the AI functionality. And it can make it harder to get approval to procure tools, where we are making use of AI functionality – we need to demonstrate their usefulness and that they are secure, etc.

Another important thing to do when identifying opportunities for automation and AI assistance is to map research and ReOps workflows, to identify the necessary triggers, actions, conditions and desired outcomes, and the main tools we use that have integrations with each other and enable other automations.[14]

AI isn't going to replace customer researchers or data scientists, but it will change, and is changing, the way we work, augmenting human intelligence, because machines are good at answering complex questions, parsing huge amounts of complex data to arrive at a conclusion, but it is humans that prioritize the questions to ask, are able to discern which questions it's worth putting effort into asking and which it is not.

In order to use AI robustly, we need to learn how to work with AI. This means learning prompt engineering and understanding the question models that can be utilized to use an LLM effectively. But we, either ourselves or through collaboration, also need the expertise to be able to assess the outputs provided by the LLM to understand whether they are accurate and relevant, and how they can potentially be refined through further use of prompts.[15]

Table 10.2 summarizes when and how to use AI in customer research and the things we need to consider if we are using AI or automation at a particular research stage.

Let's look at some examples in detail.

Generating research hypotheses with AI

Generating hypotheses is a task that typically requires a creative spark to ask interesting and important questions. AI can help scientists ideate blind spots. This is where AI might prove most useful, in a similar way to spotting themes during analysis, for example exploring vast spaces of candidate hypotheses to form theories, and generating hypotheses and estimating their uncertainty to suggest relevant experiments. By parsing large amounts of data, potential hypotheses can be generated. In science, experimentation and hypothesis generation often form an iterative cycle: a researcher asks a question, collects data and adjusts the question or asks a fresh one. The same approach should be taken with AI as the data being parsed will include the same biases we've already discussed.[17] Humans know which hypotheses are worth pursuing; this isn't an assessment that AI models are sophisticated enough to identify as yet.

Using AI to conduct secondary research

AI can be used to support secondary research that in turn informs primary research. Using an example of a market research survey that is focusing on what product features are most desirable, we can use something like generative AI (GenAI) to generate a feature list as inspiration to draft our survey. I imagine it will draw upon features in products similar to that which we have or we are building, we could specify in the prompt itself which competitors we want to pull from, or identify our competitors for competitor analysis inspiration by identifying common issues in a product type or service type. It could also be used as inspiration about potential personas, using publicly

TABLE 10.2 When and how to use AI in customer research[16]

Research phase	Research task	Augmentation, inspiration or automation, none?	Constraints and considerations
Planning	Desk/secondary research	For publicly available research AI can be used for inspiration and augmentation, gathering together and summarizing research. For internal organization research AI can be used for both automation and augmentation, utilizing smart searches (chat based and semantic) and auto-summaries in insight libraries and repositories.	We need to be aware of hallucinations when using AI rather than search engines to find publicly available research. It is well known that tools such as ChatGPT make up citations, for example. For internal tools with smart searches we need to consider how good the summary is, and it will depend on how well our prompt is formulated.
	Hypothesis generation	Inspiration and augmentation: Can be useful to identify hypotheses humans would overlook but needs an iterative approach.	Human intelligence is needed to prioritize which hypotheses are worth pursuing.
	Writing research questions	If a hypothesis is a problem statement, the next step is to create research questions. Inspiration: It can help us identify types of questions that we may not have considered. Augmentation: It can be used to summarize a long list of questions identified from stakeholder workshops.	We need to have a grounding in what a good research question is to assess the quality of the output. We need to have a clear understanding of what is in scope and out of scope for the research to assess the relevance of the output.
Set up	Recruitment	None. We should not rely on AI tools to recruit participants for our research. The potential for bias is too great and data protection risks are high. There may be tools that can be integrated into our existing processes to automate part of the process to increase efficiency.	In a tool like User Interviews, where we can manage our participant panel, we can set up rules that automatically approve participants who meet certain criteria speeding up the process from invitation to scheduled session but this isn't AI.

(continued)

TABLE 10.2 (Continued)

Set up	Writing survey/interview/focus group questions	**Augmentation:** AI can support the rephrasing of questions and fluency in language used. Many tools have smart templates to suggest questions based on the type of research we want to set up.	Again we need to have a grounding in what makes a good question to avoid bias, lead, compound questions, etc. AI lacks the context of our study scope and nuances to be able to use a smart template without any intervention.
	Creating scenarios for usability tasks	**Augmentation:** A lot of research tools have smart templates that suggest scenarios and tasks based on a small amount of input. For some this is automation, but I prefer an augmentation approach.	AI lacks context, so we need to carefully assess the auto-generated scenarios and tasks for relevancy and robustness. Are they going to help us learn what we need to, to answer our questions?
	Content generation	**Augmentation:** Can be used to support the creation of prototypes, visuals, content for user interfaces. Humans need to add emotional intelligence into the content.	We need to consider whether there are going to be any copyright-related issues. Currently such tools are generally only capable of generic layouts.
Conducting research	Active data collection	**None.** There are a lot of people who will enthusiastically disagree with me. But, until we have enough academic studies or large-scale robust commercial studies comparing the output of AI data collection and human data collection in market and user research, the topic will be hotly debated and for me the risks of synthetic users and synthetic moderators are just too high.	Unless our target customer group are rich, educated white men in the west trying to buy things, I would avoid using synthetic users. There is too much risk in the output providing poor data to ask an AI tool to simulate people and data collection with imaginary people. Currently experiments suggest that synthetic participants can't replace human participants, due to the lack of emotional intelligence and nuance in AI models.

Data processing	Note taking	**Augmentation:** Automated note taking can be useful when there is no human support in research sessions and meetings.	Output will need to be reviewed for accuracy. Semantic summaries of sessions could be useful, but again won't know what the most important things are to the research purpose/objectives.
	Transforming data	**Automation (with some augmentation):** Automated generation of transcripts from video and audio recordings is a great time-saver.	The accuracy of the transcript will depend on what data the tool has been trained on. Many tools have difficulty with particular accents (i.e. all accents that aren't from an English as a first language country and non-European accents).
			A lot of such models are often trained on e-commerce related data, because it is the most widely available. If we work in a field or industry more niche than e-commerce then there will be terminology that the model won't recognize. We need to factor in time for correcting inaccuracies in transcripts.
	Cleaning data	**Automation and augmentation:** Identify outliers and anomalies in our data, including bot answers in survey data.	Output will need to be reviewed for accuracy.
Analysis and synthesis	Persona and user journey generation	**Augmentation:** There are currently a few tools that will generate personas and user journeys using demographic and user behaviour prompts; generating user goals, needs, motivations, barriers, tasks.	QoQo (AI persona generation tool) themselves say that it is not a replacement for research and analysis but as support for our work. The AI is trained on data from the 'internet across the work' using OpenAI; it will have the biases that all AI training data has, it also does not include context or EQ which is always essential in persona generation.
		This would be a place to start; as with other types of analysis it will need refinement.	

(continued)

TABLE 10.2 (Continued)

Analysis and synthesis	Qualitative analysis	**Augmentation and inspiration:** AI can support initial analysis, such as clustering and thematic analysis, and inspire thinking about connections and themes within the data. But with current functionality, this will always need human intervention and refinement; it is just a starting place.	If using open source tools like ChatGPT, we need to consider whether the dataset contains personally identifiable information and/or commercially sensitive information. If so this will need to be removed first. Many qualitative analysis tools have AI functions to support clustering etc. that don't use our data to train their models (so can include personal data), such as Dovetail and Miro.

Equally, AI may identify patterns and themes in the data not immediately apparent to the human researcher. This should be used as inspiration to go back to the data and investigate further. Any analysis done will be based purely on text input, missing microinteractions, facial expressions and body language, which are all a part of the story. We need to review outputs critical to evaluation if a product or concept has been misunderstood or misinterpreted. |
| | Quantitative analysis | **Automation and augmentation:** AI tools can be used for statistical analysis of quantitative data; such as trend analysis, regressions etc. | GDPR is a key consideration again here.

We need to know how to interpret the output that is produced. And without expertise we won't know if mistakes are being made or if the right statistical test has been chosen. |

available demographic data associated with particular consumer behaviours, for example. However, they will need to be common and broad consumer types and behaviours and should be used as inspiration and validated through research, and it will very much depend on the industry we work in as to how reliable this will be.[18]

Using AI in research set-up

Depending on the type of research we are doing, research set-up can be fairly formulaic, especially for usability testing and other structured research. Many research tools have standardized templates and AI/smart templates for structured research, which is a good enough starting point for setting up a study. Sullivan experimented with AI tools and said they haven't seen a test structure that they completely disagreed with.[19] It's a place to start, as with many AI assisted tasks, which will need modification but it can still save us significant time. However, AI tools aren't able to be creative about research plans that involve more than best practice when it comes to more novel and complex research needs.[20] We can also use AI to support the rephrasing of questions and fluency in language used.[21]

Using AI to analyse qualitative data

SURVEY USING AI CASE STUDY[22]

Analysing and synthesizing the qualitative/open-ended (subjective) data collected from surveys is very time-consuming. This is often where researchers run into difficulty with their teams, especially when working in agile environments. In fast-paced, lean, agile workplaces researchers rarely get the time they need to fully analyse a qualitative dataset in the depth that they want to. AI can help speed up the process, but what we need to avoid is thinking that AI can do the analysis for us, without input or intervention from those with expertise. That way leads to bias, inaccurate results and poor decisions made because of it.

Dedicated analysis tools are often expensive and open source tools often require coding skills, such as R or Python in the case of many open sourced statistical analysis tools. This makes using GenAI and LLMs very attractive.

Milieu Insight presented a case study in UX Quant Con 2024 where they ran an experiment on open-ended data coding from a large-scale market research survey using various GenAI models and a person to do a human coded version.[23]

They had 1,500 open-ended responses, using thematic analysis with inductive coding (no predefined codes and categories) on this data. A human did multiple rounds of coding, to ensure familiarity with the data.

Coding was repeated with GenAI models; they started using a simple prompt:

> <Prompt: thematic analysis of opened responses with list of themes and percentage score against them>

As we will see below, throughout the experiment the researchers iterated the prompt. The final prompt (see the 'Real-world example' below) is much longer and more detailed, but it's useful to point out at the beginning that one of their key findings was that the quality of the initial prompt still matters. It matters how the role for the LLM is specified, how the input data is defined, how the task is described. All these elements can help achieve better outputs.

With a prompt like this it is easy to get an output. However, after initial assessment, the output didn't seem to be of a high quality (based on expert evaluation) compared to the human coded output.

The results were interrogated with further prompts, requiring the output to include codes used and verbatim examples to assess the robustness of the output. This allowed the researchers to understand whether the whole dataset had been used; based on the researchers' findings, it appeared probable that only 20 responses were used to generate the codes and quotes. This demonstrates the need to improve the quality of the prompt used to generate higher quality responses and results.

The prompts were improved by making use of persona prompts; the GenAI is asked to act as an expert market research analyst. The researchers also gave more detailed context, defined input and output and provided clear instructions within the prompt to use all data and how many themes were the upper limit.

They found that the same prompt in different sessions in the same tool won't necessarily give out the exact same answer, so if we are doing something similar we may want to run it a few times and then review the major themes. This means human input is still needed to synthesize the results. The same prompt and data were used in different tools, which unsurprisingly gave different results. The same human-synthesis process should be used to identify whether there is high overlap in major themes, but we should expect there to be variability in smaller scale themes.

The most powerful and reliable interaction of humans and AI is when AI is supporting an expert to enable them to do their job. In this experiment, high-frequency codes in the GenAI output were missing from human coding. This is because humans are also biased; human interpretation also identifies patterns that we want to see, or think should be there. This is why the most robust analysis is done by more than one researcher who uses a combination of independent and comparative rounds of coding.[24] The models may be able to process data a lot faster than humans, but in the end AI models and humans aren't that different, because, well, humans made the AI models.

REAL-WORLD EXAMPLE
Final prompt: Forget all prior instructions and information

You are an expert survey research analyst. You excel in analysing qualitative, open-ended data.

I ran a survey with N = 1500 respondents. One of the questions asked in the survey was an open-ended question and there were N = 1500 answers to this question.

I will upload a document that consists of all the responses. In the file, each row represents a unique respondent (identified by unique participant_ID).

Please do a thematic analysis of the answers and categorize them into relevant topics (up to 20 topics). For each topic provide the number of samples and a percentage count. While coming up with the codes and themes, please review ALL the responses.

Please organize the output into a table format. The first column is the name of the theme, the second column being descriptions of the themes, the third column is frequency, the fourth being the percentage of respondents, and the fifth column includes some verbatim quotes that belong to this theme.

This example clearly demonstrates that:

- Like any research, you need a clear and well defined process to get the highest quality and most robust results from AI.
- Human coding is not perfect.
- AI coding is also not perfect.
- You need to ask the AI tool for proof of how it got to its results – in the same way as a maths exam paper will ask you to show your working out.
- You still need to be familiar with the data in order to identify hallucinations.

There is an ever-increasing number of academic research papers that are experimenting with if and how AI can be used in the scientific research process. An example of a sub-set of papers test whether AI can replace or augment humans in qualitative analysis.[25]

Hitch applied AI thematic analysis to semi-structured interviews and other long form source data using reflexive thematic analysis, which incorporates the researchers' routine reflection on assumptions, expectations, choices, actions, values and politics throughout the analysis process. Hitch experimented with this in healthcare data and academic research, highlighting:

- The importance of cleaning data and ensuring it is a machine readable format (which can be labour intensive), but it is still possible to have a 75 per cent reduction in time needed for thematic analysis of qualitative data.

- Data privacy: If using a tool like ChatGPT it is vital to anonymize the data being analysed, which is not only time-consuming, we need to consider whether anonymizing the data changes the meaning of the data.

- Ethical issues: Most AI models focus on the English language, and have poor understanding of other languages, greatly skewing the data and perspectives that can be analysed and processed using AI.

- AI can augment but not replace the human in reflexive thematic analysis.

- Researchers still need to immerse themselves in the data – AI isn't a short-cut to skipping this step. Reliance on AI as the sole source of analysis prevents a deep understanding of the data.

- We need to be aware of character limits when uploading data to an AI tool – is the whole dataset being used?

- They observed that AI developed themes are more 'literal' in comparison to the reflexive thematic approach taken by the researcher applying expertise in the field and emotional intelligence to inform the coding.

- Themes identified by AI that were missed by the researchers were not taken at face value but used as inspiration for further analysis.

- AI augmented human work was done to confirm the coherence of themes and ensure they were robustly grounded in the data, including identifying illustrative verbatim quotes.

- Critical analysis must be applied to all output generated.

- It is not possible to confidently say that AI increases objectivity in qualitative analysis as humans built these AI models.

Last but not least, an important component that researchers and ReOps people will need to keep an eye on, to see how things develop in the future, is using AI to support analysis of data in longitudinal studies. The question we need to ask of AI analysis is how do the models deal with the combination of old and new data, and how do we engineer our prompts to analyse the data in the way we need it done? For example:

- Do we want old data to be reanalysed in light of the new data, generating new themes and patterns?

- Do we want the old data to remain untouched, with only the new data being analysed each time and compared with the older data to benchmark changes?

- How do we maintain categorization across all new and old data, with the tendency for AI models to re-categorize previous data?

AI is not emotionally intelligent

In October 2024 I and my colleague Susana Vilaça spoke at the Market Research Society's User Research Conference in London, about using AI in user research. Through watching a presentation by the user research team at Santander UK about their work supporting vulnerable users, I gained a powerful perspective in terms of the complexity of language we use in sensitive and difficult situations, which AI models aren't necessarily trained to identify. We have a wide range of words, phrases and idioms to talk about death, because it can be hard to face it directly. As a human doing analysis, we have the emotional intelligence and the context to understand that different words and phrases are being used to talk about the same topic. AI is not emotionally intelligent, so it won't be able to make connections in this way.

Researchers, or research trained people will have a trained scepticism and unease about relying on AI tools without a clear understanding of how it generated its responses.[26] However, in the age of research democracy not all the people doing the customer research are necessarily research trained. I don't mean to pick on product managers, but I am going to use them as an example here.

The busy product manager, who is leading a team, making decisions, prioritizing the work the team does, that also has to do their own customer research, will understandably be grateful if AI can reduce the time and effort required to conduct a piece of research. But if you are under pressure to deliver and you are not research trained or particularly research literate, you may be inclined to take the AI research output at face value and use it as fact and truth, before moving on to the next of many tasks that you need to do. It's understandable, but it doesn't mean that it's right. When we don't assess and interrogate research outputs from AI, we greatly increase the risk of making decisions based on bad data and bad insight. The other possibility is that our fictional beleaguered product manager is research literate (hooray!) but they don't have a robust understanding of prompt design – which means they may not get as robust results, even though they seem decent, because they have used sub-optimal prompts. If the PM is not literate in prompt engineering results, even search, then we're all crying about the insight that they've based their decisions on. It sounds rather doomsday, but with the increase in researcher layoffs and research democracy it's not a fantasy to think this is happening in all sorts of organizations to some degree.

Zhang et al improved junior researchers' understanding of ChatGPT's capabilities in qualitative analysis by providing a structured approach to prompt design that emphasizes context, methodology, data organization and transparency, a framework that helps less experienced researchers develop a deeper understanding of qualitative research methods and best practices.[27]

In a vision paper, Gerosa et al pose the possibility of combining approaches between real human participants and synthetic participants, where AI has a supportive role.[28] With strategic prompting, a foundation model can simulate a particular demographic profile, mimicking human generated content – using detailed personas and corresponding prompts. However, currently, there are no foundational models that can replicate the nuanced spectrum of human behaviour within a given software engineering environment. Prompts will need clear context and persona specification; accurately simulating a diverse population would require the model to be trained on a carefully selected, intentionally diverse dataset with representation across age, region, gender, experience, education, ethnicity, neurodiversity, a spectrum of different abilities physical and mental, etc., otherwise we risk perpetuating the bias that AI models already have towards rich, educated, neurotypical, able bodied, white, western men.

USING AI FOR SYNTHESIS

Tools like Dovetail have AI functionality to automate synthesis, grouping tagged (coded) data into themes. This is useful as a first draft of an affinity diagram, a place to start and a source of inspiration especially when analysing and synthesizing very large qualitative datasets. From experience, this cannot be relied upon, as our synthesis of the data and should only be used as a place to start, to reduce the initial overwhelm. Such tools are not yet sophisticated enough to be reliable without human intervention.

One of the reasons that such tools are not yet sophisticated enough is that AIs aren't yet able to make connections between examples of different terms being used to describe the same thing (as discussed above), so AI models and tools will currently group related things separately.[29]

Using AI to generate research narratives

Potentially we can leverage GenAI to craft compelling narratives. This can be done by incorporating GenAI in writing tools. AI can improve content generation efficiency by analysing large data volumes and finding new patterns, and outputting content at a much faster rate than humans can do alone. This isn't a copy-and-paste exercise on a large scale, but a recombination or reinterpretation of information. But we also need to consider the ethical implications and transparency to our users, thus we need to be transparent about what is human-generated and what is machine-generated content.[30]

As AI cannot revolutionarily and sophisticatedly understand all nuances of human emotions, culture, society and its values, it is important that at some stage while using AI content, humans are brought in to take a call or weigh in with their opinion, so as to make the content accurate and understandable.[31] But, in theory, AI could be used to aid customized storytelling: AI could tailor narratives to suit specific audiences, tweaking the presentation deck, language, examples, cultural references, and even the delivery type.[32]

Features in specialist tools greatly support building impactful narratives, for example, Dovetail automatically creates clips from transcript text you've highlighted and tagged; this does take a lot of manual labour (time and effort) out of synthesis and building our narrative – it is well known that showing the participants using their own words is impactful for getting stakeholders on board with our insights.

AI or integration for automation

What we really want from AI is automation – making tasks quicker and easier to help manage our heavy workloads. But not all automation is going to come from AI, sometimes it comes from integration.

To illustrate what I mean, here is an example taking inspiration from my previous experience...

In order to save money I was utilizing tools that were already being used within the organization, meaning no additional costs were involved:

- To gain consent for moderated research I used DocuSign for consent forms.
- A spreadsheet was used to manage the participant database, segment and screen participants to invite to research using filters.
- I used Calendly for managing participant invites.
- Outlook was used for correspondence with participants.
- Zoom was used for moderated research sessions.
- And I used Tremendous for incentives.

This is a cost-saving process in terms of spending the budget. However, it is not cost-saving in terms of time and effort required to make the process work seamlessly, because of the number of tools involved, which requires extra steps in the process (with additional administration and tool management). Much time and effort can be saved through tool integrations; for example I have experience of using User Interviews and their integrations:

- Using integrated document signing in User Interviews for consent.
- Using User Interviews for the usual (segmenting, screening, inviting and corresponding with participants).
- Using Tremendous integrations in User Interviews for incentives.
- Use Zoom for moderated sessions.

The process is much less labour-intensive than it previously was with everything integrated, but there are costs for tools and extra integrations. This is just to say, we should look for efficiencies in the process, whether or not it is AI related. Task scheduling can be automated to help with project management.[33] Another example is setting up email triggers when identified customers complete a customer satisfaction or NPS survey with a negative score. We can set up rules to automatically delete research data after a certain period of time, for example three years, to support GDPR compliance. One final example is effective notifications for Ops to do a thing, for researchers to do a thing, which is essential when coping with heavy workloads and juggling multiple projects and tasks.[34]

Conclusion

AI is on CX practitioners' minds, in terms of how it is changing their roles, as an enabler and perhaps generating a certain amount of fear, and organizations are investing in automation as a priority to increase business efficiency and effectiveness.

AI isn't going to steal our customer research jobs, but we do need to master it to stay relevant in the job market and to use it robustly in our roles.[35]

Changing skillset needs seems to be increasingly fast, especially with AI changing the nature of the work we do. A good example here is how reporting in banking has largely been automated, yet employment in the sector has grown fivefold. Interestingly, recent research has found that a combination of AI and human skills working in collaboration produces consistently better work outcomes and an average 40 per cent improvement in productivity.[36] Analysing tasks and activities will reveal where work is being done productively, whether it's fragmented or being duplicated, and whether it could be automated, consolidated or centralized.

I will finish this chapter with one last reflection, that isn't being talked about or considered as much as it should be in the excitement of using AI tools. In the *It's a Great ResearchOps Question!* podcast, Towsey et al discussed the environmental impact of data processing greatly increasing with the amount of processing required for AI tools to be effective.[37] For me, this means we are morally obliged to consider whether or not we need an AI tool or function to do a particular kind of task for us and we should include sustainability when we are undertaking cost-benefit analysis for such things.

Notes

1 M Murgia (2024) *Code Dependent: Living in the Shadow of AI*, Pan Macmillan, Picador, London

2 User Interviews. The state of user research: 2024 report, User Interviews, 2024. www.userinterviews.com/state-of-user-research-report (archived at https://perma.cc/JK97-4CWL)

3 User Interviews. The state of user research: 2023 report, User Interviews, 2023. www.userinterviews.com/state-of-user-research-2023-report (archived at https://perma.cc/XH8P-6HC5)

4 IBM. What are AI Hallucinations? IBM, 2024. www.ibm.com/topics/ai-hallucinations (archived at https://perma.cc/5Y7Y-APJQ)

5 T Durate and I K Garcia. We must act on AI literacy to protect public power, Joseph Rowntree Foundation, 2024. www.jrf.org.uk/ai-for-public-good/we-must-act-on-ai-literacy-to-protect-public-power (archived at https://perma.cc/Y6EK-Q9F5)

6 Y Ibison. AI and the power of narratives, Joseph Rowntree Foundation, 2024. www.jrf.org.uk/ai-for-public-good/ai-and-the-power-of-narrative; E Stone. AI shifts the goalposts of digital inclusion, Joseph Rowntree Foundation, 2024. www.jrf.org.uk/ai-for-public-good/ai-shifts-the-goalposts-of-digital-inclusion (archived at https://perma.cc/Y96J-M3B4)

7 J Nielsen. Accessibility has failed: Try generative UI = individualised UX, Jakob Nielsen on UX, 2024. jakobnielsenphd.substack.com/p/accessibility-generative-ui (archived at https://perma.cc/U2HS-9227)

8 Microsoft. Microsoft Inclusive Design, Microsoft, 2016.inclusive.microsoft. design/ (archived at https://perma.cc/HX97-CUUZ)

9 Y Ibison. AI and the power of narratives, Joseph Rowntree Foundation, 2024. www.jrf.org.uk/ai-for-public-good/ai-and-the-power-of-narratives (archived at https://perma.cc/H7BC-9SAY)

10 Y Ibison. AI and the power of narratives, Joseph Rowntree Foundation, 2024. www.jrf.org.uk/ai-for-public-good/ai-and-the-power-of-narratives (archived at https://perma.cc/U35W-RZ45)

11 C Sullivan. The UX research tasks you can let AI help with, Great Question, 2024. greatquestion.co/blog/ux-research-tasks-you-can-let-ai-help-with (archived at https://perma.cc/Y582-X5VF)

12 H Wang, T Fu, Y Du, et al. Scientific discovery in the age of artificial intelligence, *Nature*, 2023, 620, 47–60. doi.org/10.1038/s41586-023-06221-2 (archived at https://perma.cc/T4RC-UTNQ)

13 K Towsey, J Lewes, J Forney and T Toy. What are the challenges and opportunities of AI for ResearchOps? *It's a Great ResearchOps Question!* podcast, 2024. https://podcasts.apple.com/gb/podcast/what-are-the-challenges-and-opportunities-of/id1756436113?i=1000661732587 (archived at https://perma.cc/YXY6-ED57)

14 R Dalcin. Increasing ResearchOps impact through automation, ResearchOps Community, 2022. medium.com/researchops-community/increasing-researchops-impact-through-automation-183a0fd8e121 (archived at https://perma.cc/FC8J-JWQM)

15 S Tracy, A Sen, Milieu Insight. Applications of generative AI in market research (and the risks you need to know), UX Quant Con, 2024. www.quantuxcon. org/quant-ux-con/past-conferences (archived at https://perma.cc/E5PG-HVNH)

16 S Tracy, A Sen, Milieu Insight. Applications of generative AI in market research (and the risks you need to know), UX Quant Con, 2024. www.quantuxcon.org/quant-ux-con/past-conferences (archived at https://perma.cc/D9NU-6N6P); T Raj. 14 Chat-GPT prompts for faster UX research, Looppanel, 2024. www.looppanel.com/blog/14-chat-gpt-prompts-to-use-for-ux-research (archived at https://perma.cc/8KZ4-ZMUL); Y Keshtcher. AI advancements in UX research, UX Writing Hub, 2023. uxwritinghub.com/ai-advancements-in-ux-research/ (archived at https://perma.cc/98GT-236U); I Oladigbolu and A Fard. AI-powered UX research: Ultimate guide to future trends, Adam Fard, 2024. adamfard.com/blog/ai-ux-research-trend (archived at https://perma.cc/GRL7-5978); E Stevens. The top 5 AI-powered tools for user research (and how to use them), UX Design Institute, 2024. www.uxdesigninstitute.com/blog/top-ai-tools-for-user-research/ (archived at https://perma.cc/G8LJ-EVVW); C Sponheim and M Brown. AI UX-design tools are not ready for primetime: Status update, Nielsen Norman Group, 2024. www.nngroup.com/articles/ai-design-tools-not-ready/ (archived at https://perma.cc/NS7M-9PAL); F Liu and K Moran. AI-powered tools for UX research: Issues and limitations, Nielsen Norman Group, 2023. www.nngroup.com/articles/ai-powered-tools-limitations/ (archived at https://perma.cc/C9X6-LDB7); E Webber. 8 AI tools to transform your user research process, In the Loop, Maze, 2023. maze.co/blog/AI-tools-user-research/ (archived at https://perma.cc/G2SR-9BNJ); R Lee. 20+ powerful AI-based tools for UX research toolkits in 2023, User Interviews, 2023. www.userinterviews.com/blog/ai-ux-research-tools (archived at https://perma.cc/SJE5-88HN); L Principe. Is it worth the hype? Synthetic respondents vs human insight, CivicCom Marketing Research Services, 2024. www.civicommrs.com/is-it-worth-the-hype-synthetic-respondents-vs-human-insight/ (archived at https://perma.cc/24FT-WMX9); J Ostler and A Kalidas. What is synthetic sample – and is it all it's cracked up to be? And can GenAI be used off-the-shelf to create one? Kantar, 2023. www.kantar.com/inspiration/analytics/what-is-synthetic-sample-and-is-it-all-its-cracked-up-to-be (archived at https://perma.cc/7N7D-NXF2); M Hannan and A Dhareshwar. A comparative analysis: Real vs synthetic responses in B2B research, Emporia, 2023. www.emporiaresearch.com/case-studies/real-insights-or-robotic-responses-a-comparative-analysis-of-real-vs-synthetic-responses-in-b2b-research (archived at https://perma.cc/6LEV-JFUC); M Rosala and K Moran. Synthetic users: If, when, and how to use AI-generated 'research', Nielsen Norman Group, 2024. www.nngroup.com/articles/synthetic-users/ (archived at https://perma.cc/DWD4-8SJR); Wishbyte Pty Ltd. Userdoc Features, Userdoc, 2024. userdoc.fyi/#features (archived at https://perma.cc/3F87-SW8M); V Pegon, T Okail, A Okail and Y Karkhachev. QoQo Use Cases, QoQo, 2024. qoqo.ai/index.html#useCases (archived at https://perma.cc/WL4K-5HLB); K Arora. 8 best AI note-taking apps: Your shortcut to smarter UX research, Hey Marvin Blog, 2023. heymarvin.com/resources/ai-note-takers/ (archived at https://perma.cc/GTL9-B5VT)

17 H Wang, T Fu, Y Du, et al. Scientific discovery in the age of artificial intelligence, *Nature*, 2023, 620, 47–60. doi.org/10.1038/s41586-023-06221-2 (archived at https://perma.cc/Y96M-6TFF); M Hutson. Hypotheses devised by AI could find 'blind spots' in research, Nature Index, Nature, 2023. www.nature.com/articles/d41586-023-03596-0 (archived at https://perma.cc/ETS4-6MGU)

18 A Sachdeva. How to use ChatGPT for market research. GapScout, 2023. gapscout.com/blog/how-to-use-chatgpt-for-market-research/ (archived at https://perma.cc/Q37A-7LBS); N Babich. Using ChatGPT for user research, UX Planet, 2023. uxplanet.org/using-chatgpt-for-user-research-5c3bdf7e26af (archived at https://perma.cc/FGD4-B5RJ); S Tracy. 4 ways you can use ChatGPT for market research, Analythical, 2024. analythical.com/blog/using-chatgpt-for-market-research (archived at https://perma.cc/YQ4Y-96WR)

19 C Sullivan. The UX research tasks you can let AI help with, Great Question, 2024. greatquestion.co/blog/ux-research-tasks-you-can-let-ai-help-with (archived at https://perma.cc/P5XX-WQ4L)

20 C Sullivan. The UX research tasks you can let AI help with, Great Question, 2024. greatquestion.co/blog/ux-research-tasks-you-can-let-ai-help-with (archived at https://perma.cc/5A6F-KKW7)

21 K Towsey, J Lewes, J Forney and T Toy. What are the challenges and opportunities of AI for ResearchOps? It's a Great ResearchOps Question Podcast, 2024. https://podcasts.apple.com/gb/podcast/what-are-the-challenges-and-opportunities-of/id1756436113?i=1000661732587 (archived at https://perma.cc/4ZT4-GV5W)

22 S Tracy, A Sen, Milieu Insight. Applications of generative AI in market research (and the risks you need to know), UX Quant Con, 2024. www.quantuxcon.org/quant-ux-con/past-conferences (archived at https://perma.cc/YUH7-FQTF)

23 S Tracy, A Sen, Milieu Insight. Applications of generative AI in market research (and the risks you need to know), UX Quant Con, 2024. www.quantuxcon.org/quant-ux-con/past-conferences (archived at https://perma.cc/6UJA-JLS4)

24 D Hitch. Artificial intelligence augmented qualitative analysis: The way of the future? *Qualitative Health Research*, 2024, 34 (7), 595–606. journals.sagepub.com/doi/full/10.1177/10497323231217392 (archived at https://perma.cc/YS99-YXNZ)

25 D Hitch. Artificial intelligence augmented qualitative analysis: The way of the future? *Qualitative Health Research*, 2024, 34 (7), 595–606. journals.sagepub.com/doi/full/10.1177/10497323231217392 (archived at https://perma.cc/YS99-YXNZ)

26 H Zhang, C Wu, J Xie, Y Lyu, J Cai and J Carroll. Redefining qualitative analysis in the AI era: Utilising ChatGPT for efficient thematic analysis, Human Computer Interaction (cs.HC) Preprint, 2023. arxiv.org/pdf/2309.10771 (archived at https://perma.cc/E75C-9FHR)

27 H Zhang, C Wu, J Xie, Y Lyu, J Cai and J Carroll. Redefining qualitative analysis in the AI era: Utilising ChatGPT for efficient thematic analysis, Human Computer Interaction (cs.HC) Preprint, 2023. arxiv.org/pdf/2309.10771 (archived at https://perma.cc/B9N9-CX9N)

28 M Gerosa, B Trinkenreich, I Steinmacher and A Sarma. Can AI serve as a substitute for human subjects in software engineering research? Automated

Software Engineering, 2024, 31, 13. doi.org/10.1007/s10515-023-00409-6 (archived at https://perma.cc/M5BW-HECG)

29 C Sullivan. The UX research tasks you can let AI help with, Great Question, 2024. greatquestion.co/blog/ux-research-tasks-you-can-let-ai-help-with (archived at https://perma.cc/Q67D-2NEZ)

30 A Chand, G Debankur, N Senthil, R Gupta and H Singh. Generative AI and storytelling: Crafting narratives with AI, PwC, 2024. www.pwc.in/assets/pdfs/ generative-ai-and-storytelling-crafting-narratives-with-ai.pdf (archived at https://perma.cc/5YXT-F2WF)

31 A Chand, G Debankur, N Senthil, R Gupta and H Singh. Generative AI and storytelling: Crafting narratives with AI, PwC, 2024. www.pwc.in/assets/pdfs/ generative-ai-and-storytelling-crafting-narratives-with-ai.pdf (archived at https://perma.cc/5BRW-XCEK)

32 R Reitsma. Crafting compelling narratives from AI-generated insights, Research World, 2023. researchworld.com/articles/crafting-compelling-narratives-from- ai-generated-insights (archived at https://perma.cc/T3YC-7Y6X)

33 E Webber. 8 AI tools to transform your user research process, In the Loop, Maze, 2023. maze.co/blog/AI-tools-user-research/ (archived at https://perma. cc/33UP-U585); R Lee. 20+ powerful AI-based tools for UX research toolkits in 2023, User Interviews, 2023. www.userinterviews.com/blog/ai-ux-research-tools (archived at https://perma.cc/L99S-PF2D); J Vagadiya. Here's how you can automate repetitive tasks and save time as a UX researcher using technology, LinkedIn, 2024. www.linkedin.com/advice/0/heres-how-you-can-automate- repetitive-tasks-save-ssp2f (archived at https://perma.cc/8RWF-R6TT)

34 R Dalcin. Increasing ResearchOps impact through automation, ResearchOps Community, 2022. medium.com/researchops-community/increasing-researchops- impact-through-automation-183a0fd8e121 (archived at https://perma.cc/ Z493-PWWS)

35 CX Network. The global state of CX 2024: How generative AI, data and customer demands are shaping CX in 2024, CX Network Research Report, 2024. eco-cdn.iqpc.com/eco/files/channel_content/posts/cxn-globalstatereport- 2024talkdesk07ZicFib9CzLs62Se5kMG6qMZxF5npnRktedrDAPPb.pdf (archived at https://perma.cc/D3FB-4D8F)

36 O Shaw. Understand your workforce skills gaps before you rush to bring in AI, Orgvue, 2023. www.orgvue.com/resources/articles/understand-your-workforce- skills-gaps-before-you-rush-to-bring-in-ai/ (archived at https://perma.cc/ HV4W-XL9Z)

37 K Towsey, J Lewes, J Forney and T Toy. What are the challenges and opportu- nities of AI for ResearchOps? It's a Great ResearchOps Question Podcast, 2024. https://podcasts.apple.com/gb/podcast/what-are-the-challenges-and- opportunities-of/id1756436113?i=1000661732587 (archived at https://perma. cc/R8Q8-YHNZ)

11

Metrics for research and research operations

There are a couple of reasons to track metrics for research and ReOps. It is common that a newly formed team such as a ReOps team (or research team) will be required to track their work from the start to demonstrate their value, to support their continued existence. However, we're collecting data not just to demonstrate value, but also to enable data-driven user-centric iterative improvement of research and operations practices. It is a very common conundrum... How do you measure whether you are moving the needle with all the work that's being done? How do we know whether that work is delivering value?[1]

I have included metrics for both research and ReOps, as it is a possibility that the ReOps team will be the one(s) tracking the impact of the research findings and insights. As always, it really depends on the size and capabilities within the ReOps team and the research team as to who will track research impact. I'm going to assume the ReOps will be tracking the metrics for ReOps itself.

In this chapter, I'm going to give the TL;DR version or the two takeaways upfront... the main two to know when working on metrics is:

1 Track what's valuable, not what is easy.
2 Combine quantitative and qualitative data for impactful narratives.[2]

Demonstrating value is something that many research and possibly operations teams struggle with, but it's important in terms of getting a seat at the table to influence strategy, etc., or to protect ourselves from multiple rounds of redundancies (lay-offs) as much as we can. So it's important to arm ourselves with data on usage, experience, trends and spending.[3]

Figure 11.1 demonstrates the importance of combining different types of data. If we are thinking about efficiency and effectiveness, for example, we need to be able to zoom in and out. Look at the bigger picture as well as the detail and go back-and-forth to create that holistic view of what's going on. So the macro might be understanding the landscape – the context our users are living and working in, the context in which they're using products and services or processes and documentation, and what their needs are, what their goals are; what is helping them and what the barriers are to achieving their goals. The micro can zoom right down to do the interaction on this component in this step of the digital service work. Is it accessible? Do people understand it? Can they use it? And we need to iteratively go back and forth to make sure you are doing the right thing and you are doing the thing right. We use qualitative research and numbers to help us understand why something is happening and how people feel about it. Quantitative research and metrics can tell us the scale of a problem or a trend, or whether something works better compared to another thing, etc.

The reason stakeholders like numbers is that they can help us to understand at what scale something is happening. Scale is a suggestion of importance whether it is positive or negative (see Figure 11.2), as is frequency. Numbers help us to draw people's attention; to show they need to pay attention to a thing because of its scale and the frequency of its occurrence. Combining this with stories of the impact on the human experience is a consistently influential way to tell the stories we need to tell, to demonstrate the value of customer research and ReOps.

How to track the impact of research operations

Before we think about what those metrics we are tracking might be, one of the many reasons to prioritize tracking the most valuable things is because of the amount of work required to set up and track metrics. This is the kind of thing that is ideally done by an analyst but this is often not the case.[4] Some metrics can be automated; some of the tools we use within research

FIGURE 11.1 Creating holistic evidence-based narratives

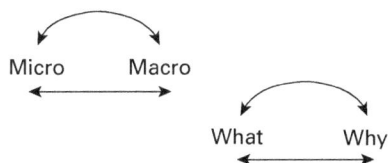

FIGURE 11.2 Visualization of frequency

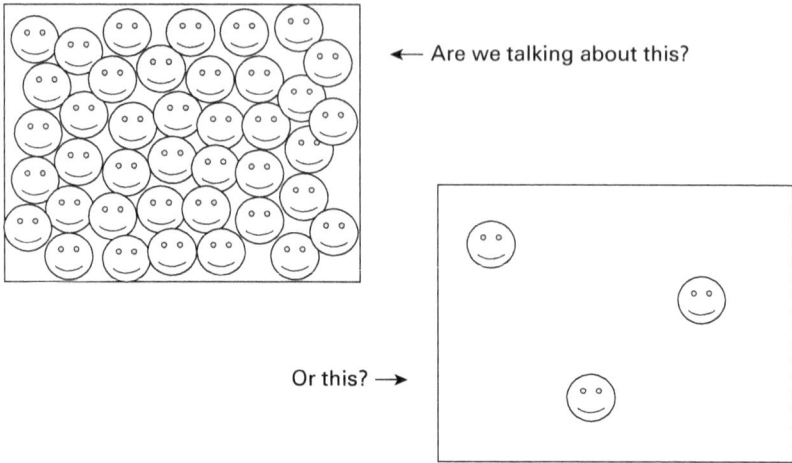

and operations will have metrics available, so we may want to make it part of our tool procurement to ask about what analytics are available for administrators.[5] If we need to manually collect data then we need to make peace that it is time-consuming and not as accurate as we want it to be. Our data will come from multiple sources, so we will also need to consider how to consolidate it and curate it into a digestible and actionable format.[6]

WHAT METRICS SHOULD WE BE TRACKING?

As with UX metrics we can combine usage data, experience data and support data to tell a holistic story of the value we have delivered.[7] Usage data does not tell us the experience that users had while using the thing; if someone already has an excellent experience with the design you've offered, why change it? If they're having a poor experience, you'll need to make it better for them.[8] People can still successfully complete a task while having a terrible experience, if they are motivated enough. This is true of external products and services and internal support and documentation, for example.

GETTING AN EXPERIENCE BASELINE

Benchmarking is a powerful way to track change over time, to be able to demonstrate that work we have delivered has contributed to change that can be seen both quantitatively and qualitatively.

It may take some time to figure out which are the right things to track. Once we have established a consistent and stable thing or suite of things to track, then it's time to create a template that can be reused and will allow reliable comparison each time a benchmark is done.[9] The other thing to figure out is a cadence at which the benchmark happens. It could be annually, quarterly or whenever a major change happens – it really depends on the context. It is important to have a cadence that allows us to take action based on the insight gained from experience benchmarking.[10] There is no point doing regular benchmarking if we can't take action on what we have learnt.

Benchmarking can be used to track the impact and value of both ReOps and customer research.

UX metrics for research operations

What we track in terms of research operations really depends on what the remit of the team is. We need to start somewhere, even if it's not clear where to start. We can see below a potential place to start. I have adapted the system usability scale (SUS) to be relevant to research operations. We could start here and then learn as we go what metrics will be valuable for us.

SUS for ReOps

Please rate your agreement or disagreement with the following statements on a 1 to 7 scale, with 1 being completely disagree to 7 completely agree:

1 I think that I will use these systems and processes frequently.
2 I found the systems and processes unnecessarily complex.
3 I thought the systems and processes were easy to use.
4 I think that I would need the support of a technical person to be able to do research.
5 I found the systems and processes were well integrated into the research process.
6 I thought there was too much inconsistency in these systems and processes.
7 I would imagine that most people would learn to use these systems and processes very quickly.
8 I found the systems and processes very cumbersome to use.
9 I felt very confident using the systems and processes.
10 I needed to learn a lot of things before I could get going with these systems and processes.

Thomas at Usability Geek describes the SUS approach and how to apply it in more detail.[11] This SUS for ReOps, in the same way the original scale does, asks the respondent to rate the level of agreement with 10 statements about ReOps support, processes and documentation, as a general overview of 'how ReOps are doing'.

UX-lite for ReOps

Alternatively, I have adapted the UX-lite metric to ReOps. The original metric was developed and iterated by Lewis and Sauro:[12]

1 The ReOps capabilities meet my requirements.

2 The provided tools' functionality meets my needs.

3 The ReOps processes meet my needs.

4 The ReOps documentation meets my needs.

5 ReOps does what I need it to do.

UX-lite for ReOps has the same intentions as SUS, but it is simpler and shorter, making it easier to deploy and complete quickly.

NASA Task Load Index for ReOps

One more adaptation I want to look at is the NASA Task Load Index. I think that the NASA Task Load Index is a very useful set of metrics to make use of when trying to understand how ReOps is supporting the people doing research. If it's good enough for NASA, it's good enough for me, and it has been around for a long, long time, having been first used in the mid 1980s:[13]

1 How mentally demanding was the task?

2 How hurried or rushed was the pace of the task?

3 How successful were you in accomplishing what you were asked to do?

4 How hard did you have to work to accomplish your level of performance?

5 How insecure, discouraged, irritated, stressed and annoyed were you?

We can use a seven-point scale again to collect the respondent's ratings. This scale focuses on the respondent's cognitive load and can be used to demonstrate how ReOps makes doing research easier. This is a good place to pause and consider the importance of also collecting qualitative data on the topic. Because we need to consider the context in which the ReOps team is supporting people. For example, the researcher may be very irritated and stressed, but that is nothing to do with the support that Ops has given. We, through our support, may have in fact eased the stress and irritation, but it still remains, so it's important to understand the context in which the questions were answered.

There are other elements we can track that can be useful to demonstrate both the impact and value of ReOps and also identify where we need to focus our attention to improve ReOps processes and documentation, etc. Table 11.1 includes metrics related to processes and documentation and why such tracking might be useful.

TABLE 11.1 Additional metrics to consider for Ops process and documentations tracking[14]

Metrics	Why track this
It was easy to find the documentation	Part of the usefulness and usability of the documentation provided by ReOps to enable self-service (for example) it needs to be quick and easy to find
I trust the accuracy of the documentation (correct and up to date)	It is critical to ReOps success that what we provide is trusted. Documentation provided needs to be accurate and up to date and needs to be perceived that way
I know where to store my research data and artefacts	This measurement is important for GDPR compliance and findability of research and also demonstrates the ReOps communication is effective
Number of times documentation is accessed vs documentation delivered	This is a usage metric that can be supported by many tools; demonstrating that what ReOps provides is being used
Keyword tracking in documentation tools	This can help us understand if naming conventions are right, if things are stored in the right tool and identify potential unmet needs of the people doing research
No results searches – what documentation is missing	This is another very useful indication of potential unmet needs of the people doing research
Click/open rate after documentation announcements	This is a way to track if ReOps internal communications are working. It can also be used with participant recruitment related work to demonstrate effectiveness, or lack of

A more complicated thing that would be useful to track is whether research operations tasks are seamlessly embedded in the research process. It's more complicated as there are many factors that will contribute to this metric such as:

- actual implementation of processes
- perception of implementation (which can be different)
- when changes/processes were implemented

These are all influencing factors as ReOps processes can be seen as a barrier to speedy research, because, for example, these processes are ensuring GDPR compliance. ReOps can and does support lean research processes without compromising compliance and quality, but sometimes people cut corners to make processes lean in a way that will compromise compliance and quality. Even with well-implemented newly integrated processes, it takes time for people to adjust, especially if there was no established process previously, with everyone doing their own thing. This is most likely going to negatively affect people's perception of ReOps for a while, even if it's subconscious.

Table 11.2 includes metrics related to overall ReOps support and why such tracking might be useful. Table 11.3 shows useful internal metrics for both ReOps and customer research, broken down by stages of the research process.

And now we will look at customer research metrics specifically.

TABLE 11.2 Additional overall metrics to consider for Ops support tracking[15]

Metrics	Why track this
GDPR issues identified and resolved (and timescale)	Tracking GDPR issues will hopefully demonstrate a decrease over time with ReOps support, it is useful for understanding where to focus documentation, guidance and training with regards to GDPR
Issues raised and resolved [questions asked and answered]	This more broadly demonstrates the support ReOps is providing and is also a resource for future work
Number of support requests and turnaround time	Show process adoption rates

(continued)

TABLE 11.2 (Continued)

Metrics	Why track this
Research project completion time	This can be a contentious metric, because the length of time a project takes isn't always the sole responsibility of those doing the research and ReOps
Health and confidence check	Does the support provided enable positive change? Are the people doing research more confident and more easily completing research?
Quality of support	The support provided is perceived as high quality; this helps us understand if we are doing the right thing or where we can make improvements
Level of trust (people, data, etc.)	Do people we are providing the support to trust us? This is key to effective ReOps and research collaboration
Training attendance	Are people attending the training provided? This is another type of adoption rate
Money saved	If there is a dedicated ReOps team, this obviously costs money, so it can be very useful to demonstrate money saved. This isn't necessarily easy to track, if we are considering, for example, the reduction in duplicated research; it is easier if we are, for example, streamlining the tools used (potentially saving money)
Number of projects supported	This is another type of adoption rate and the scale of the work being done
Number of people onboarded and offboarded	This is another type of adoption rate and the scale of the work being done
ReOps pain points and positives	This is very explicitly about what is and isn't working in ReOps to demonstrate value, impact and areas of future improvement

TABLE 11.3 Research process specific metrics to consider at each stage for research and Ops impact tracking

Scope and plan research	Recruitment	Doing the research	Analysis and synthesis	Sharing and implementation
Number of research requests	Number participants invited	Tools used	Tools used	Views of insights and reports
	Number of participants scheduled	Number of consent forms signed		What findings and insights people are using in their work and what they find useful and not useful
	Number of participants, drop-outs and replacements	Amount of incentives sent		What top three characteristics make UX research findings and insights useful for your work
	Recruitment methods and tools used	Diversity of methods used		What challenges people face using findings and insights
	Diversity of participants recruited			Preferred formats for insights
	Participant quality rating			Frequency research reports are accessed
	The participants recruited matched the selection criteria			

SOURCE User Interviews. The state of user research: 2024 report, User Interviews, 2024. www.userinterviews.com/state-of-user-research-report

External and internal metrics for customer research

There are two ways we can track the impact and value of customer research: how it is used internally, and what change it contributes to externally.

Internal metrics

When it is difficult to tie research delivered directly to profit or improvement in usage (external metrics), etc., there is internal tracking that we can turn to, to start to accumulate evidence of the impact and value of customer research.

An example of direct tracking would be as easy as 1, 2, 3:

1 Research demonstrates issue with website shopping basket.

2 Shopping basket improvement is implemented.

3 Conversion rate increases after change is launched.

Things are often more complicated than this. So an alternative place to start is shown in Table 11.4.

Definitions of how research is used:

- **Decisions:** Research is directly used to make decisions about design, content, marketing, etc.

- **Influence:** Research influences strategy and vision, e.g. product strategy, marketing strategy, etc.

- **Citations:** Research is cited and shared in presentations, blog posts, etc.

There are more complicated ways to track these things, for example evaluate the type of decision being made; is it at the product, programme,

TABLE 11.4 Tracking internal impact of customer research

How research was used	Description	Teams involved	Point of contact	When did this happen
Decision				
Influence				
Citations				

SOURCE Inspired by work done with Rita R Silva at Springer Nature and collaborations with Susana Vilaça, Ola Tyrek, Tania Ramos, Angela Collins Rees and other colleagues.

departmental or organizational level? And so on. But, I think it's best to start small and simple in general, as this will need to be tracked manually either by the researchers or by ReOps. I say in general, as it is easier to track some types of research than others. For example, if measuring the impact of usability research, it will probably be relatively easy to track the insights used to make product improvements. If doing large-scale exploratory research on a potential new area of business, it can take a long time to become clear what the impact of the research was.

External metrics

There are several types of metrics that research can contribute to in terms of business goals and experience metrics.

Business KPIs:

- growth
- acquisition
- retention
- support calls
- lifetime value
- cost per acquisition
- cost per lead
- leads generated
- conversion
- return on investment (ROI)

Attitudinal metrics:

- customer satisfaction (CSAT)
- NPS
- ease of use
- loyalty
- trust
- desirability
- brand awareness
- reputation
- confidence

Behavioural and experience metrics:

- task success
- perceived task success
- time on task/time on page
- click-through rates
- engagement rates
- bounce rate
- error rate
- views/visitors/likes/shares/mentions/sign-ups
- subjective mental effort questionnaire (SMEQ)
- standardized user experience percentile rank questionnaire (SUPR-Q)
- NASA Task Load Index (NASA-TLX)
- effective
- efficiency
- comprehension
- SUS
- usability magnitude estimation (UME)
- usability metric for user experience (UMUX)
- UMUX-lite
- UX-lite
- Google Heart Framework
- experience benchmarking
- user testing quality experience (QX) score (proprietary metric that combines: task success average, attitudes on appearance, ease of use, trust, NPS)[16]

Each potential metric has strengths and weaknesses. Self-reported metrics (attitudinal metrics in particular) can be inaccurate because people tend to inflate or overrate feedback.[17] And single measures such as NPS or CSAT are easy to collect and use, but they are very broad; to make them more useful we need to be able to tie them to different journeys and experiences, and consider different customer groups, to be accurate. Such metrics do not tell us the 'why', and they don't reflect multifaceted experiences.[18] To measure the quality of experience we need to have an emotional component that is combined with behavioural measures. It is important, as we have discussed before, to have both self-reported and observed metrics, as what people say and what people do are not always the same and tasks might have been performed successfully but the user did not have a good experience.[19]

Conclusion

Whether we are tracking ReOps or customer research, we want metrics to be user-centric, but these are generally hard to measure and often need multiple metrics,[20] which is why it's important to focus on those that are most valuable. And it's important to remember that measurement is not the target. It's not what we're aiming for, but it's a reflection of where we are at. And whatever metrics we choose, we want them to be across all relevant channels, not just digital,[21] to be as inclusive as possible.

Notes

1   C Vize and A Muir. How human insight can elevate UX measurements and help you make more informed decisions, CX Network and User Testing Webinar, 2024. www.cxnetwork.com/customer-insights/webinars/elevate-ux-measurement (archived at https://perma.cc/V852-JWNX)

2   K Towsey (2024) *Research That Scales: The research operations handbook*, Rosenfeld Media, New York; J M Spool. Combining our UX metrics with compelling, emotional stories, Jared M Spool Medium Blog, 2020. jmspool. medium.com/combining-our-ux-metrics-with-compelling-emotional-stories-ead9198f117d (archived at https://perma.cc/5QT3-886L)

3   K Towsey (2024) *Research That Scales: The research operations handbook*, Rosenfeld Media, New York

4   K Towsey (2024) *Research That Scales: The research operations handbook*, Rosenfeld Media, New York

5   K Towsey (2024) *Research That Scales: The research operations handbook*, Rosenfeld Media, New York

6   K Towsey (2024) *Research That Scales: The research operations handbook*, Rosenfeld Media, New York

7   J M Spool. Combining our UX metrics with compelling, emotional stories, Jared M Spool Medium Blog, 2020. jmspool.medium.com/combining-our-ux-metrics-with-compelling-emotional-stories-ead9198f117d (archived at https://perma. cc/5QT3-886L); J M Spool. Measuring experiences, not product use, UX Collective Medium Blog, 2024. uxdesign.cc/measuring-experiences-not-product-use-83b052c78211 (archived at https://perma.cc/88G3-4J2F)

8   J M Spool. Combining our UX metrics with compelling, emotional stories, Jared M Spool Medium Blog, 2020. jmspool.medium.com/combining-our-ux-metrics-with-compelling-emotional-stories-ead9198f117d (archived at https://perma.cc/5QT3-886L); J M Spool. Measuring experiences, not product use, UX Collective Medium Blog, 2024. uxdesign.cc/measuring-experiences-not-product-use-83b052c78211 (archived at https://perma.cc/88G3-4J2F)

9   T Awodiya. Benchmarking research operations, ResearchOps Community Medium Blog, 2022. medium.com/researchops-community/benchmarking-research-operations-58ddfe11d8d8 (archived at https://perma.cc/5M8C-Q4PQ)

10   T Awodiya. Benchmarking research operations, ResearchOps Community Medium Blog, 2022. medium.com/researchops-community/benchmarking-research-operations-58ddfe11d8d8 (archived at https://perma.cc/5M8C-Q4PQ)

11   N Thomas. How to use the System Usability Scale (SUS) to evaluate the usability of your website, Usability Geek, 2024. usabilitygeek.com/how-to-use-the-system-usability-scale-sus-to-evaluate-the-usability-of-your-website/ (archived at https://perma.cc/L59G-W349)

12   J Lewis and J Sauro. Evolution of the UX-Lite, Measuring U, 2021. measuringu.com/evolution-of-the-ux-lite/ (archived at https://perma.cc/M22T-BPCP)

13   NASA Human Systems Integration Division. Figure 8.6 Hart and Staveland's NASA Task Load Index, NASA, 2024. humansystems.arc.nasa.gov/groups/TLX/downloads/TLXScale.pdf (archived at https://perma.cc/QM3F-T6FU); S G Hart. NASA-Task Load Index (NASA-TLX): 20 years later, NASA-AMes Research Center, 2006. human-factors.arc.nasa.gov/groups/TLX/downloads/HFES_2006_Paper.pdf (archived at https://perma.cc/ZM42-HK5X)

14   Inspired by work done with Rita R Silva and Susana Vilaça and by: T Awodiya. Benchmarking research operations, ResearchOps Community Medium Blog, 2022. medium.com/researchops-community/benchmarking-research-operations-58ddfe11d8d8 (archived at https://perma.cc/5M8C-Q4PQ); M Mishek. How to create UX research benchmarks for your org, Great Question, 2024. greatquestion.co/blog/ux-research-benchmarking (archived at https://perma.cc/QUR7-5A6X); C Hyland. Lessons from setting up a user research operations function, User Research in Government Blog, 2023. userresearch.blog.gov.uk/2023/11/02/lessons-from-setting-up-a-user-research-operations-function/ (archived at https://perma.cc/R9A3-KB2F); M Herman. 10 metrics and KPIs for internal communications, Lumapps, 2024. www.lumapps.com/internal-communication/metrics-kpis-for-internal-communications/; Papirfly. 12 corporate communication metrics you should be tracking, Papirfly Corporate Communications, 2023. www.papirfly.com/blog/corporate-communications/12-corporate-communication-metrics-you-should-be-tracking-2/ (archived at https://perma.cc/J7QC-TQ79)

15   Inspired by work done with Rita R Silva and Susana Vilaça and by: K Towsey (2024) *Research That Scales: The research operations handbook*, Rosenfeld Media, New York; T Awodiya. Benchmarking research operations, ResearchOps Community Medium Blog, 2022. medium.com/researchops-community/benchmarking-research-operations-58ddfe11d8d8 (archived at https://perma.cc/5M8C-Q4PQ); M Mishek. How to create UX research benchmarks for your org, Great Question, 2024. greatquestion.co/blog/ux-research-benchmarking (archived at https://perma.cc/QUR7-5A6X); and C Hyland. Lessons from setting up a user research operations function, User Research in Government Blog, 2023. userresearch.blog.gov.uk/2023/11/02/lessons-from-setting-up-a-user-research-operations-function/ (archived at https://perma.cc/R9A3-KB2F)

16   C Vize and A Muir. How human insight can elevate UX measurements and help you make more informed decisions, CX Network and User Testing Webinar, 2024. www.cxnetwork.com/customer-insights/webinars/elevate-ux-measurement (archived at https://perma.cc/V852-JWNX); J Lewis and J Sauro. Evolution of the UX-Lite, Measuring U, 2021. measuringu.com/evolution-of-the-ux-lite/ (archived at https://perma.cc/M22T-BPCP); A Ferreira. Market Research Society conference: Combining customer experience, user experience and market research – making it count: Developing a custom digital metric framework that works, Alberto Ferreira for Vodafone, 2021

17   A Ferreira. Market Research Society conference: Combining customer experience, user experience and market research – making it count: Developing a custom digital metric framework that works, Alberto Ferreira for Vodafone, 2021

18   A Ferreira. Market Research Society conference: Combining customer experience, user experience and market research – making it count: Developing a custom digital metric framework that works, Alberto Ferreira for Vodafone, 2021

19   C Vize and A Muir. How human insight can elevate UX measurements and help you make more informed decisions, CX Network and User Testing Webinar, 2024. www.cxnetwork.com/customer-insights/webinars/elevate-ux-measurement (archived at https://perma.cc/V852-JWNX)

20   A Ferreira. Market Research Society conference: Combining customer experience, user experience and market research – making it count: Developing a custom digital metric framework that works, Alberto Ferreira for Vodafone, 2021

21   A Ferreira. Market Research Society conference: Combining customer experience, user experience and market research – making it count: Developing a custom digital metric framework that works, Alberto Ferreira for Vodafone, 2021

12

How to adapt to changing needs and requirements

The final chapter will cover the importance of adapting research operations to the changing needs of:

- business
- researchers
- participants
- tools/techniques/method evolutions

The role of managing change in ReOps:

- migration
- changing research processes, based on feedback
- offboarding tools
- onboarding tools
- when legal requirements change
- onboarding new people
- implementing new processes, e.g. assurance processes

The TL;DR version of keeping up with needs is to listen to your users and stakeholders; do check-ins and internal research. Keep up to date with the latest changes with horizon scanning. It's also important to be aware of any organizational changes that are upcoming to figure out if it's going to impact us. We aren't always the instigators of the changes happening, but ReOps always needs to be proactive in understanding the impact of changes, how to prepare and implement them with minimal disruption, what support is needed and how long for, despite feeling a loss of power when we haven't chosen the change. Where you are creating new processes and practices or improving existing ones, change management is an integral part of how you will create and embed or iterate, while ensuring that whatever research is being undertaken continues to happen as smoothly as possible.

Change management can be a huge part of the ReOps remit (depending on the scope of the role/team). It's not always specifically called out on job descriptions, but it will almost always be there in the day-to-day work. A lot of what we have covered in the preceding chapters have touched upon change, so let's look into what it is to manage change. If you don't have a lot of experience with change management, this is definitely something that is worth investing your training budget in.

Doing change management

When we are talking about change management, we are talking about the management of organizational changes, both large and small. This may include culture, internal processes, underlying technology or infrastructure and all sorts of other things.[1]

Changes can be either adaptive (small, gradual, iterative) or transformational (large in scale and scope). Both kinds of change need to be managed.[2] As people who manage change, we need to ensure those impacted can navigate the transition smoothly. The aim is to make sure everyone is prepared, everyone has a shared understanding, the environment is safe and conducive to change and people are working towards the same common goal. The key to change management is preparedness and communication.

Step 1: Identify or understand the need for change

As we previously touched on, sometimes we are the instigators of a change and sometimes not. How the change is instigated will affect the way we manage the change. Regardless, we need to understand why change is needed.

IDENTIFYING A NEED

Through our work in ReOps we will often see the need for various changes. Before we start a change project we need to understand what needs to change and why it needs to change.

If change is being instigated by another part of the business or it's coming from leadership, we still need to first understand what and why.

Step 2: Assess needs and impacts

Once the initial need has been identified, we need to understand the scope, scale and impact of the potential change:

- What is the business goal or user need behind the change?
- What is the specific gap or issue?
- What are the timelines?
- What are the budgets?
- What does success look like?
- What are the constraints?
- Who are the team and key stakeholders?
- Who will be impacted internally and externally?
  - o Who is responsible?
  - o Who is accountable?
  - o Who needs to be consulted?
  - o Who needs to be informed?
- What are the initial potential solutions?

Once these questions have been answered, an impact and effort exercise can be conducted.[3]

Step 3: Develop plans and strategies

From the work in Step 2, we can then create the vision and plan for the change, documenting clearly:

- vision: strategic goals and scope (what outcomes we are aiming to achieve)
- key performance indicators (KPIs) (how we are going to measure progress and success)
- how the vision will be achieved (detailed plan of how the change will happen and identifying as many potential roadblocks as possible and plan for mitigation, as well as post implementation support)
- communication strategy and plan
- engagement strategy and plan
- benchmark the 'before' state
- feedback loops are essential to effective change management, so we need to incorporate them into the plan[4]

In planning and communication of the plan, we need to be realistic and honest about the impact of change in terms of productivity, and there may be a lack of immediate benefits while getting familiar with the change.

We need to start thinking about communication early in the process. Change management always needs clear communications, communicating the right thing at the right time, to the right people.[5]

Figure 12.1 visualizes an internal communications strategy framework, to help us think about who needs to know what based on what we need them to do.

Individuals need to hear things five times on different channels that change is happening to really absorb it, and we need to create a sense of urgency, otherwise people will be apathetic, so planning our communications is key as it's communicating with authenticity.[6] We need to speak plainly about what is happening and why it is happening in order for people to trust us in making the change and to reduce the amount of resistance there is to the change.

The engagement strategy and plan may be different to the communication plan or they could be combined into one. It really depends on the scale and type of changes that are being made. If we have people who just need to be aware that a change is happening, and others that need to be trained to use a new tool for the change, we need to engage these groups in different ways. So with an engagement strategy we are targeting those we need to learn from and those who need training and in-depth knowledge to enable successful change. This engagement strategy may be led by ReOps, or we may be a part of or creating a Change Champions network to scale the capacity to support and enable change. This could be leveraging early adopters.[7] Not everyone is comfortable with raising concerns in a public forum, so we need to provide multiple channels for people to share their feedback in a way that makes them feel safe.[8]

Step 4: Implement/deploy change

Now that we are implementing the plan (whether it's a phased approach or happening all at once), there are many things to be done.

We will have been communicating and engaging with people already, but it will ramp up at this point. As we have been proactive in sharing details about the changes, we may already have met some resistance that will need to be managed and resolved, and this will continue throughout the process.

In complicated change processes, the answers aren't always clear during the process. When people have questions that are potentially difficult to answer immediately, we need to be upfront and transparent about this with

FIGURE 12.1 Internal communication strategy

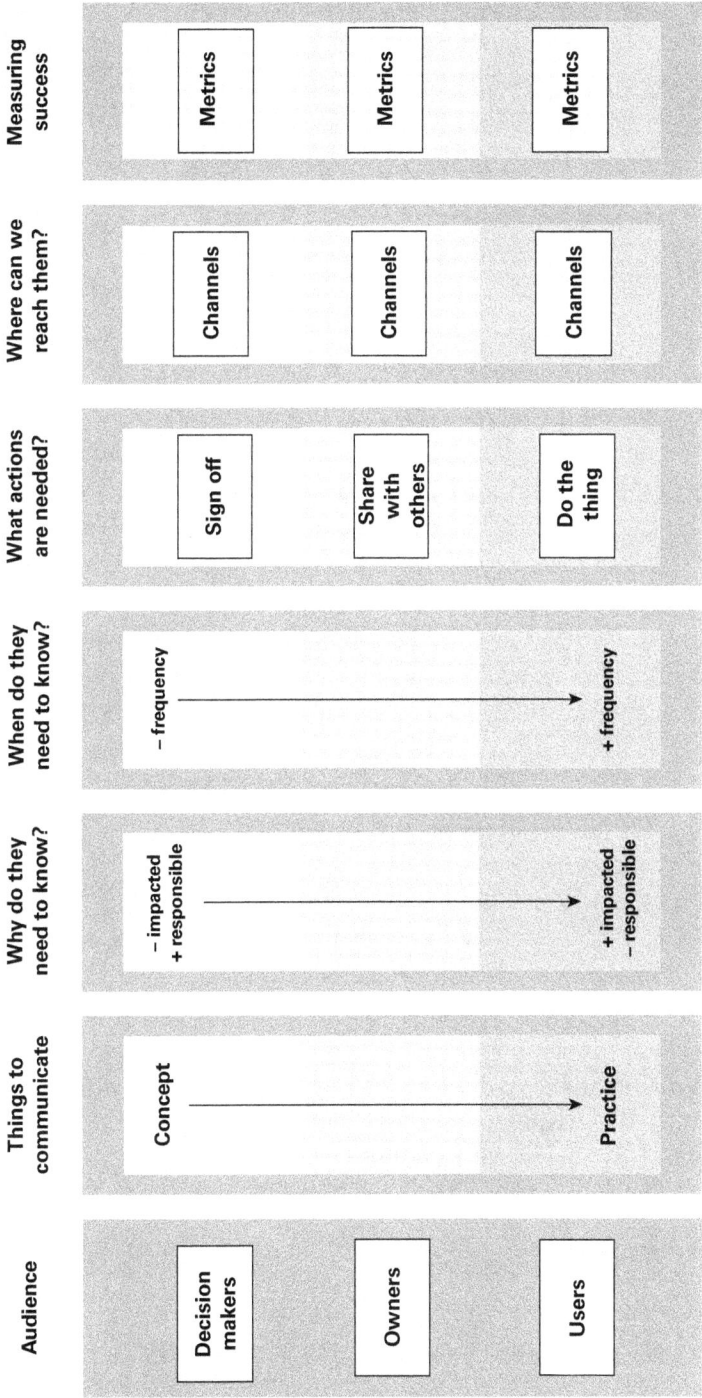

Audience	Things to communicate	Why do they need to know?	When do they need to know?	What actions are needed?	Where can we reach them?	Measuring success
Decision makers	Concept	− impacted + responsible	− frequency	Sign off	Channels	Metrics
Owners				Share with others	Channels	Metrics
Users	Practice	+ impacted − responsible	+ frequency	Do the thing	Channels	Metrics

SOURCE Inspired by work done with Tiago Pinto

everyone. This is when full group communication forms such as Town Halls are useful, and Town Halls (supported by other feedback channels) should be held before and after incremental changes to support implementation.[9]

If it is a large-scale change with a phased approach it will be useful to make use of a readiness checklist and a readiness status tracker; this will help us benchmark progress through the project.[10]

Step 5: Normalize the change

We need to continue to engage with and support people to help them successfully adapt to and sustain the changes. This is also a period for us to review and analyse the work that has been done, and iterate if needed.[11]

Part of normalizing the change is giving people time to adjust to change – continued support – the job isn't done when the change is implemented, there is always an adjustment period and teething problems.[12] Change management doesn't stop when the change is implemented; there is a period of time after the implementation (which can be long or short depending on the scale and type of change that is happening) when support is needed for those adjusting to the changes. This includes reminding ourselves and planning for adaptations to the change being needed. One size doesn't fit all; in major changes, teams/individuals will have to make adaptations to make it work for them so need to support that, without people circumventing the changes.

Step 6: Benchmark the changed status

It may be that we are handing something over to someone else once the change is made. If this is the case, we need to make sure everything is documented, people can access the documentation and everyone is aware who the points of contact now are. If we aren't handing over to others, then we will need to continue to measure and observe the impact of the change over time. We can also run retrospectives on the change implementation to learn how it can be done better in the future.

Process summary

- Start with the end in mind (and work backwards).
- Know when, where and who to ask for help.
- Documentation, documentation, documentation.[13]

How to mitigate some of the risks in organizational change

When documented in a step-by-step guide, it might seem relatively simple, if a lot of work, but when people and multiple moving parts are involved, complexity always appears. For example, people's reactions to change and understanding how that can impact the process is a critical part of managing the change. Whether we approach or avoid new situations depends on the threats and rewards we perceive across five dimensions:

- status
- certainty
- autonomy
- relatedness
- fairness[14]

We will need to have strategies in place for managing stress during change. And we will also need to manage and mitigate or resolve resistance to change(s). If people are emotional and stressed then they will stop absorbing the information. Stress comes because people's jobs can become more difficult for a period of time, as they need to develop new skills, undertaking training to be effective and productive again. And if you are stressed you have less capacity to think in the usual way.[15]

So we need to make space for acknowledging the endings that are happening as well as the beginnings (beginnings of change and its after state). There will be a mourning period, a venting period, that we need to make space for when change is upon us. However, we may need to timebox this period for public venting within a group for solidarity, moving to a more 1:1 space if individuals need to continue to vent, otherwise we risk a degradation of the mood and productivity of the whole group as it becomes a platform for stewing in negativity. Vent first, and then get down to the business of changing and managing the change, but we can't cut people off. Authenticity is important to help people out of it; don't dismiss the concerns of people but listen to and address them, be honest about the pros and cons of change and of not changing.[16] Lack of transparency and lack of clear communication will cause resistance and resentment.

When a major change is happening everyone has to wear multiple hats, continuing with business as usual while implementing the change and adapting. When change in tools or the research process is happening we need to ensure whatever research is in progress can keep happening with as little disruption as possible. Many are threatened by change, often for good reasons, and it also depends on people's attitude towards change:

- If you are an expert in one tool which is being replaced by another, it can be seen as something as scary as a demotion, because you won't be the expert any more. Or it can be seen as an opportunity to learn and expand one's skillset.

- If you already have a heavy workload, it can be scary to contemplate change, which will add to the workload for a period of time before things settle into a new routine.

Change is often associated with a fear of loss, particularly loss of power, and especially if you were an expert in whatever is being changed. This in turn will increase people's sense of imposter syndrome, which can lead to people resisting the change.[17]

However, we can identify common patterns for resistance to help manage and mitigate people's resistance, using Kotter's Leading Change model:[18]

- Stage 1: Create a climate for change (a sense of urgency).

- Stage 2: Engaging and enabling.

- Stage 3: Implementing and sustaining.[19]

As we are working through the change management process we need to look out for and identify the types of people we are dealing with in terms of their approach to change:

- **Innovators:** Can collaborate to pilot change before roll out.

- **Early adopters:** Change champions and social proof.

- **Early majority:** Typically need to see evidence that the innovation works before they are willing to adopt it, and need the psychological safety of the early adopters to join in the movement.

- **Late majority:** These people are sceptical of change, and will only adopt an innovation after it has been tried by the majority.

- **Laggards** are very sceptical of change and are the hardest group to bring on board.[20]

If it's an exciting change then you can create the fear of missing out (the sense of urgency), otherwise people will need to hear success stories from someone they trust (social proof as a change enabler). We need to think about what the incentives for change are, and what different types of people are incentivized by. For example, some people are incentivized by recognition (e.g. being recognized as innovative and rewarded for it), others want to be able to shape and influence the changes happening. Considering what is at stake will help us to predict how people are going to react.[21]

Be intentional about when and how to share the benefits; allow space for people to first vent, and be angry, frustrated and worried about the change before we start talking about the cons and then the benefits of the change (i.e. using framing in our communications).[22]

Framing communication in this context means providing people with information on:

- change pros and cons
- status quo pros and cons
- choices available[23]

Managing detractors and resistors

People will find ways around the change, and part of the post-implementation process is to cut off workarounds from being possible,[24] especially if it's detrimental to ways of working.

Some people will be detractors and resist throughout the whole change process. But we need to keep in mind that other people's thoughts and feelings will change over time, multiple times and in multiple ways. So we need to take both kinds of reactions into account when planning and managing change. The Satir change model shows us that resistance is a normal part of change, because stability is removed. So change makers and managers need to make changes as approachable as possible. We can plan for as smooth a change as possible but there will be chaos in change, and we need to be prepared for it to potentially last for a long time. This means when we are planning and prioritizing the business-as-usual work, we must account for a drop in productivity during and after the change has been implemented.

There are a wide range of reasons we haven't yet looked at, as to why people might be resistant to change:

- Learning anxiety can create resistance to change – people would think that it's too hard to learn new things without lowering self-esteem or losing group membership.
- Some may feel that their values are being compromised.

The key is to understand why people are reacting and behaving the way they are, before we can understand how to support or manage them through change. For example, if people aren't doing the things we're asking them to do for the new processes, they are either settled in the old process and silently resisting or they may genuinely not have the capacity to work on new things. Each root cause of resistance behaviour will need to be addressed in a different way.

If people are asking probing questions and pointing out possible obstacles, we should work with them to identify things that need to be mitigated, rather than shutting them down. Many people will ask no questions at all, as most will go along with the changes passively. But promoters and detractors will feel the need to take action. We want to harness the resistors who are thinking deeply and critically about the change; they may have identified potential roadblocks that others haven't seen. People may be proactive about getting onboard and spreading change. These are early adopters; they are a useful part of pilot groups and we can leverage social proof of early success.[25] We need to encourage feedback, whether it's positive or negative, so we can see what the perception of change is.

You may want to create an empathy map to identify who's who – adopters, detractors, passive majority. Empathy mapping is useful to help change instigators see the situation from other people's perspective and to understand their motivations, and the context for their motivations. Motivation for change depends on confidence levels and perceived importance.[26] Supporting people through change isn't necessarily about changing their mind, but creating the circumstance for the change to happen, whether we and they agree with it or not. This may seem rather oblique, so let's think about an example. Sometimes we need to instigate a change to save money; moving the organization from Google Workspace to Microsoft365, as an imaginary example. No one is necessarily happy about the change, but in order to keep the company solvent it's just something we need to do. And we need to create safety for all, whether they are adopters, detractors or the passive majority.[27] Leaders need to be willing to be vulnerable and be an early adopter to create safety for others.

Organizations also need to be aware of change fatigue. Too many large changes in quick succession is exhausting and can be demoralizing. Changes need to be staggered if possible, with appropriate sequencing, time frames and time periods in between changes, within the team/department/organization. As a ReOps team or person, we also have to be prepared to pause a team or departmental change to accommodate an organizational change first, as organizational level changes will always take precedence (speaking from experience). This is why, ideally, we would have transparency at all levels of the organization so change implementation can be planned and coordinated appropriately.

Notes

1 K Miller. 5 critical steps in the change management process, Harvard Business School Online, Business Insight, 2020. online.hbs.edu/blog/post/change-management-process (archived at https://perma.cc/ZBD3-UTAZ)

2 K Miller. 5 critical steps in the change management process, Harvard Business School Online, Business Insight, 2020. online.hbs.edu/blog/post/change-management-process (archived at https://perma.cc/ZBD3-UTAZ)

3 K Miller. 5 critical steps in the change management process, Harvard Business School Online, Business Insight, 2020. online.hbs.edu/blog/post/change-management-process (archived at https://perma.cc/ZBD3-UTAZ); OCM Solution. Best guide to change management project risk analysis and assessment to increase project successes, OCM Solution, 2024. www.ocmsolution.com/project-assessment/ (archived at https://perma.cc/J8PE-26XA)

4 K Miller. 5 critical steps in the change management process, Harvard Business School Online, Business Insight, 2020. online.hbs.edu/blog/post/change-management-process (archived at https://perma.cc/ZBD3-UTAZ); This is Alchemist. Supporting others through change and understanding theory of change, training run for Springer Nature, 2024. thisisalchemist.com/ (archived at https://perma.cc/2NUR-URA2)

5 OCM Solution. Change made easy: Applying practical change management process and phases, OCM Solution, 2024. www.ocmsolution.com/organizational-change-management-process/ (archived at https://perma.cc/6LML-DS7Z)

6 This is Alchemist. Supporting others through change and understanding theory of change, training run for Springer Nature, 2024. thisisalchemist.com/ (archived at https://perma.cc/2NUR-URA2)

7 OCM Solution. Change made easy: Applying practical change management process and phases, OCM Solution, 2024. www.ocmsolution.com/organizational-change-management-process/ (archived at https://perma.cc/6LML-DS7Z)

8 This is Alchemist. Supporting others through change and understanding theory of change, training run for Springer Nature, 2024. thisisalchemist.com/ (archived at https://perma.cc/2NUR-URA2)

9 This is Alchemist. Supporting others through change and understanding theory of change, training run for Springer Nature, 2024. thisisalchemist.com/ (archived at https://perma.cc/2NUR-URA2)

10 A Carracher. 6 components of change management to set you up for success, Alchemy London Market, 2024. alchemylondonmarket.com/blog/6-components-of-change-management-to-set-you-up-for-success (archived at https://perma.cc/AB3X-H2TX)

11 K Miller. 5 critical steps in the change management process, Harvard Business School Online, Business Insight, 2020. online.hbs.edu/blog/post/change-management-process (archived at https://perma.cc/ZBD3-UTAZ); OCM

Solution. Best guide to change management project risk analysis and assessment to increase project successes, OCM Solution, 2024. www.ocmsolution.com/project-assessment/ (archived at https://perma.cc/J8PE-26XA)

12 This is Alchemist. Supporting others through change and understanding theory of change, training run for Springer Nature, 2024. thisisalchemist.com/ (archived at https://perma.cc/2NUR-URA2)

13 J Forney. What migrating our research repository taught me about knowledge management, ResearchOps Community, 2023. medium.com/researchops-community/what-migrating-our-research-repository-taught-me-about-knowledge-management-38b26995402f (archived at https://perma.cc/E6NF-R95Y)

14 From: This is Alchemist. Supporting others through change and understanding theory of change, training run for Springer Nature, 2024. thisisalchemist.com/ (archived at https://perma.cc/2NUR-URA2) Source: D Rock. SCARF: a brain-based model for collaborating with and influencing others. NeuroLeadership Journal, 2008. neuroleadership.com/ (archived at https://perma.cc/P99D-YJZE) NeuroLeadership Institute Inc, the NLI Brain Logo and SCARF® are trademarks or registered trademarks of NeuroLeadership Institute, Inc. or its affiliates in the US

15 This is Alchemist. Supporting others through change and understanding theory of change, training run for Springer Nature, 2024. thisisalchemist.com/ (archived at https://perma.cc/2NUR-URA2)

16 This is Alchemist. Supporting others through change and understanding theory of change, training run for Springer Nature, 2024. thisisalchemist.com/ (archived at https://perma.cc/2NUR-URA2)

17 M Pauk. Managing resistance to change, O'Reilly training webinar, October 2023

18 M Pauk. Managing resistance to change, O'Reilly training webinar, October 2023

19 This is Alchemist. Supporting others through change and understanding theory of change, training run for Springer Nature, 2024. thisisalchemist.com/ (archived at https://perma.cc/2NUR-URA2)

20 This is Alchemist. Supporting others through change and understanding theory of change, training run for Springer Nature, 2024. thisisalchemist.com/ (archived at https://perma.cc/2NUR-URA2); W W LaMorte (2019) *Diffusion of Innovation Theory*, Boston University School of Public Health, Boston

21 This is Alchemist. Supporting others through change and understanding theory of change, training run for Springer Nature, 2024. thisisalchemist.com/ (archived at https://perma.cc/2NUR-URA2)

22 This is Alchemist. Supporting others through change and understanding theory of change, training run for Springer Nature, 2024. thisisalchemist.com/ (archived at https://perma.cc/2NUR-URA2)

23 M Pauk. Managing resistance to change, O'Reilly training webinar, October 2023

24 This is Alchemist. Supporting others through change and understanding theory of change, training run for Springer Nature, 2024. thisisalchemist.com/ (archived at https://perma.cc/2NUR-URA2)

25 M Pauk. Managing resistance to change, O'Reilly training webinar, October 2023

26 M Pauk. Managing resistance to change, O'Reilly training webinar, October 2023

27 M Pauk. Managing resistance to change, O'Reilly training webinar, October 2023

Concluding thoughts

Research operations uncovers tensions, bridges communication gaps and helps teams be more effective.[1] ReOps meets the needs of those doing research, especially when they find themselves in complex situations as they work across the organization with different team dynamics, hierarchies and budget constraints, as we all strive to improve outcomes.[2] ReOps challenges the status quo, identifying difficulties, at the same time creating and requiring accountability and that is a difficult and exciting space to work in. In the same way that researchers require resilience,[3] so do research operations people. Because we are disruptors (for good) it's important to develop a great personal perspective about whether we're not doing things well. Or is it that the organization isn't keen to use operations, process and documentation to mature and grow?[4]

It requires commitment from the organization to be a success, to resource research Ops properly. I think research operations are vulnerable to lay-offs in economically turbulent times because we aren't the shiny new thing that makes the organization look innovative, like using the latest AI tools. We are the infrastructure that many consider boring but essential. And we are essential – the trouble is, no one gets promoted or gets a bonus by fixing the infrastructure. People get promotions and bonuses for implementing or experimenting with the shiny new thing. And therein lies the rub – an organization can't effectively and sustainably innovate without a well-functioning infrastructure (how very boring!). As research operations as a discipline continues to grow and mature, I hope this viewpoint will also change. I think it needs to, for organizations to be run responsibly, so there is still some way to go. I think we will be fighting for the cause for some time, but it's a cause worth investing in.

We must be visible, and we must be pragmatic. We can't do it all without a very large team, but the more we do, the greater the demand, so we need to be very clear about what we do and what we don't do.[5] Currently the most common ReOps ratio is 1 Ops person to 10 researchers in large organ-izations.[6] Many will have a smaller ratio; however, much bigger ratios are more common, like 1 to 50. The ReOps people may be part-time or there may be none at all. Having no ReOps function has multiple consequences:

- A lot of the Ops work was done by the individual during the process of doing the research, which increases an already heavy workload.
- Some Ops work was done by one or two researchers focusing on things that require coordination and compliance in one part of the organization.
- Some is done collectively by the group of people doing the research, such as learning about new methods or discussing the pros and cons of a particular tool.
- Some is led by an individual for the benefit of everyone – e.g. iterating consent forms, coordinating recruitment of new researchers. This indi-vidual has made a choice to increase their own workload to make things better.

There is no getting around the fact that it's extremely hard work doing operations tasks in this way and that it leads to burnout. So ReOps is defi-nitely the way to go. If you are new to ReOps or thinking of moving into ReOps, there are a few things to consider. It is best to go in with eyes wide open:

- Changing the way things are done in the process of doing research, even if it is for the better, causes disruption and you need to change people's behaviour. You need to be prepared to give people time to learn and adjust, and each time there will be some sort of grief cycle. So there will be resistance and grumpiness, for example, before acceptance and improvement.
- Socializing the changes when you have co-ownership is different from when the changes are coming from a central team. You will need to take a different approach.
- How research Ops is done day-to-day and how it evolves over time depends on the experience, skills, interest and capacity of those doing it, whether it's the day job or in addition to the day job.
- There will never be enough time to do everything that needs to be done, whether you have to do the research Ops for yourself or you are a small team doing it for many. How to most effectively use your time is the

challenge – whether it's delivering the research and doing the Ops or balancing day-to-day work with tactical and strategic ReOps work.

- You can achieve a lot if you have groups of people working together with a shared goal, if they all have the time to do the extracurricular work, but this is easily disrupted and it is entirely understandable when you need to deliver research for a team or more than one team. With a dedicated team, even a small team, deep thought and hard work is put into Ops every (work) day, which means we can dig much deeper into the areas that will benefit those researching the most, consistently making incremental progress and ensuring those practices that are already established run as smoothly as possible.

- How ReOps gets done will also depend on budgeting – is it a central budget? Siloed budgets? A combination of central and siloed? No budget at all? This affects what you can get done, how it gets done and how much admin there will be.

But I want to finish on a positive note, as, despite and because of the challenges, I do love working in research operations. We make connections and, perhaps without intention, find ourselves in an amazing strategic place, because we have an overview of all the research that has happened, is happening right now and what's being planned. And knowledge is power that we can harness, not only to improve and support research being done, but enable the insights gained from all the data to be used purposefully in making user-centric, data driven decisions, reducing the risk of those decisions, ultimately improving things for the users, for people. Through research operations this can be done more efficiently, effectively (faster and saving money) and ethically. But, in the end it really is all about people.

Notes

1 E Ali and M Hack. How research operations impacts organizational culture, ResearchOps Community Blog, 2023. medium.com/researchops-community/ how-research-operations-impacts-organizational-culture-a09b4e8b2990 (archived at https://perma.cc/FC7W-V58G)

2 E Ali and M Hack. How research operations impacts organizational culture, ResearchOps Community Blog, 2023. medium.com/researchops-community/ how-research-operations-impacts-organizational-culture-a09b4e8b2990 (archived at https://perma.cc/FC7W-V58G)

3 J Waterworth. User researchers need to be resilient, but we're not made of stone, User Research in Government Blog, 2017. userresearch.blog.gov.uk/2017/10/13/user-researchers-need-to-be-resilient-but-were-not-made-of-stone/ (archived at https://perma.cc/DW44-WSYD)

4 E Ali and M Hack. How research operations impacts organizational culture, ResearchOps Community Blog, 2023. medium.com/researchops-community/how-research-operations-impacts-organizational-culture-a09b4e8b2990 (archived at https://perma.cc/FC7W-V58G)

5 C Hyland. Lessons from setting up a user research operations function, User Research in Government Blog, 2023. userresearch.blog.gov.uk/2023/11/02/lessons-from-setting-up-a-user-research-operations-function/ (archived at https://perma.cc/7VER-D8KA)

6 User Interviews. The state of user research: 2024 report, User Interviews, 2024. www.userinterviews.com/state-of-user-research-report (archived at https://perma.cc/S8NF-SJ9H)

INDEX

The index is filed in alphabetical, word-by-word order. Acronyms are filed as presented and page locators in italics denote information within a figure or table.

Looking for another book?

Explore our award-winning
books from global business
experts in Marketing and Sales

Scan the code to browse

www.koganpage.com/marketing

More from Kogan Page

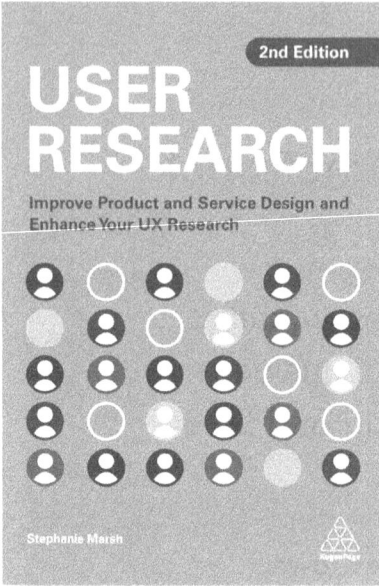

2nd Edition

USER RESEARCH

Improve Product and Service Design and Enhance Your UX Research

Stephanie Marsh

ISBN: 9781398603578

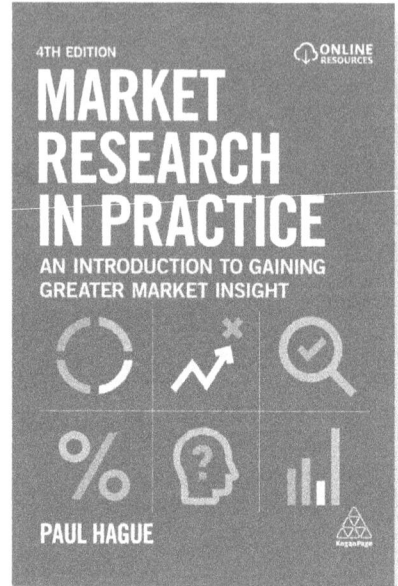

4TH EDITION

ONLINE RESOURCES

MARKET RESEARCH IN PRACTICE

AN INTRODUCTION TO GAINING GREATER MARKET INSIGHT

PAUL HAGUE

ISBN: 9781398602823

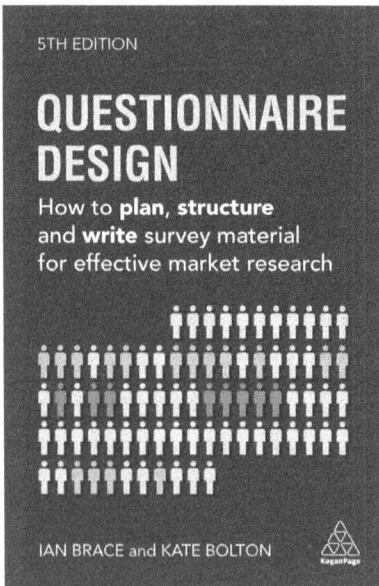

5TH EDITION

QUESTIONNAIRE DESIGN

How to **plan, structure** and **write** survey material for effective market research

IAN BRACE and KATE BOLTON

ISBN: 9781398604124

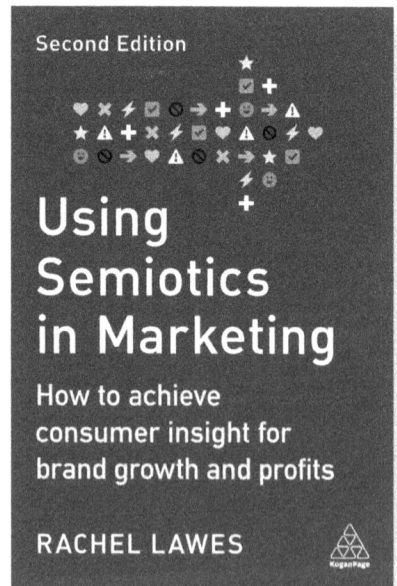

Second Edition

Using Semiotics in Marketing

How to achieve consumer insight for brand growth and profits

RACHEL LAWES

ISBN: 9781398607644

www.koganpage.com

KoganPage

From 4 December 2025 the EU Responsible Person (GPSR) is:
eucomply oÜ, Pärnu mnt. 139b – 14, 11317 Tallinn, Estonia
www.eucompliancepartner.com

www.ingramcontent.com/pod-product-compliance
Lightning Source LLC
Chambersburg PA
CBHW071543210326
41597CB00019B/3106

9 781398 620506